CAT ISLAND

CAT ISLAND

The History of a Mississippi Gulf Coast Barrier Island

John Cuevas

McFarland & Company, Inc., Publishers
Jefferson, North Carolina, and London

All photographs and illustrations are from the
author's collection unless otherwise noted.

LIBRARY OF CONGRESS CATALOGUING-IN-PUBLICATION DATA

Cuevas, John, 1942–
 Cat Island : the history of a Mississippi
Gulf Coast barrier island / John Cuevas.
     p.   cm
 Includes bibliographical references and index.

ISBN 978-0-7864-6328-2
softcover : 50# alkaline paper ∞

 1. Cat Island (Miss.)—History.
 2. Cat Island (Miss.)—Biography
   3. Cuevas family.
     I. Title.
F347.H3C84   2011   976.2'13—dc22   2011010652

BRITISH LIBRARY CATALOGUING DATA ARE AVAILABLE

© 2011 John Cuevas. All rights reserved

*No part of this book may be reproduced or transmitted in any form
or by any means, electronic or mechanical, including photocopying
or recording, or by any information storage and retrieval system,
without permission in writing from the publisher.*

On the cover: raccoon © 2011 Shutterstock;
Cat Island, view of South Bayou from dunes, 2005
(photograph by Bruce Richards and Tom Warner)

Manufactured in the United States of America

*McFarland & Company, Inc., Publishers
Box 611, Jefferson, North Carolina 28640
www.mcfarlandpub.com*

Acknowledgments

After so many years it would be impossible to list everyone who has contributed to this book, but there are those who deserve my special recognition. First I should acknowledge my grandmother, Catherine Garriga Cuevas, who planted the seeds that grew into a lifelong passion. This book might have never been a reality without her early stories. I also credit my father, Oliver John Cuevas, for making the most valuable contribution of all. He introduced me to a generation of relatives and friends, most who, like himself, had been born in the 1800s. For me he was like a bridge between two centuries. Even at my young age I recognized how fortunate I was to have known those warm and wonderful old families. I cherish the memories of our visits with them, many who were still living in the backwoods of the coast in the 1940s and early 1950s in much the same way my ancestors had lived for generations. We spent many evenings sitting on their porches and listening to their stories of the past.

My uncle Franklin J. Cuevas was also a great inspiration. At the age of 88, he wrote his own book about Cat Island, and with tireless enthusiasm marketed what became a great success for him. Even today there are requests for copies of his self-published work. I was fortunate to have inherited his copious notes and research materials.

I would especially like to acknowledge my cousin, Judy McFerren, for her entertaining interpretation of the Juan de Cuevas legend and pirates' capture. Her talent as a published writer enriched these pages.

Mia D. Burke, a newly discovered cousin, became my first editor after our meeting at the jazz funeral in New Orleans for our relative Jean Baptiste Baudrau II. When I learned of Mia's talent as a writer and editor, I felt as though destiny had brought us together. She was also working on a book about the family, and while she was extremely busy, she always found time for me. I appreciated her excellent suggestions and quick responses as I worked my way through my initial manuscript.

I am particularly humbled and thrilled by the contribution of my son, Dr. Bryan J. Cuevas, a respected academic whose books and articles are recognized throughout the world. Bryan's wise comments and suggestions added the final touches to my manuscript.

Finally, I give big hugs and kisses to my wife, Janice, of 46 years, who patiently listened to my tales of Cat Island for most of those years.

Thanks to all.

Contents

Acknowledgments	v
Preface	ix
1. About Cat Island	1
2. The French Discover Cat Island and Settle Biloxi	8
3. The Fort on Cat Island	13
4. The First Mutiny on American Soil	15
5. Jean Lafitte, the Pirates, and Buried Treasure	22
6. The Hero of Cat Island	33
7. Juan de Cuevas Captures the Pirates	42
8. A British Soldier Visits Cat Island After the War	45
9. The Cuevas House on Cat Island	50
10. Pioneer Life on Cat Island and the Developing Coast	58
11. The Seminole Indians on Cat Island	79
12. The Last Great Party on Cat Island	85
13. The Funeral of Juan de Cuevas	90
14. How the Truth Became a Legend	97
15. The Lighthouses on Cat Island	106
16. Turpentining and the Lumber Industry on Cat Island	115
17. Al Capone and the Rumrunners	120
18. The Goose Point Tarpon Club	124
19. The Secret War Dogs of Cat Island	129
20. Cat Island Owners from the Past to the Present	138
21. A Visit to the Cuevas Homestead in Spain	157
Notes	163
Bibliography	179
Index	185

Preface

Cat Island is unique in coast history. It was the site of the first mutiny on American soil. Jean Lafitte and his pirates stashed their stolen treasure there. The largest foreign military force to ever attack the United States mainland used it as a staging area. Juan de Cuevas reportedly fired the first shots against the invading British in the Battle of New Orleans there. It had one of the first lighthouses on the Mississippi Gulf Coast. It served as an encampment site for Seminole Indians being moved to the reservation in Oklahoma as part of the Trail of Tears. Rumrunners and bootleggers hid their illegal booze there in the 1920s. It was a secret military site of the U.S. government during World War II to train a special canine force to sniff out and attack the Japanese enemy. It served as rich grazing land for hundreds of cattle for several generations. And it provided a natural forest for a very successful business in turpentine and heart pine lumber.

While any one of these events would have been enough to assure Cat Island a place in the history books, there is one additional fact that makes the island even more distinctive. Cat Island is the only one of the barrier islands that was owned from the beginning by one family, the Cuevas family, not as an investment or a weekend retreat, but as their permanent home for over three generations. Juan de Cuevas, who was referred to as "The King of Cat Island," received the island by way of a Spanish grant, and was the only island owner in history to call Cat Island his home and to actually raise his family there — my family.

I was very young when I first visited the Cuevas family home site on Cat Island. I have never seen the water so emerald green as it was that day. I remember there was a warm summer breeze dancing across the waves welcoming me ashore as their foamy caps rolled onto the powder-white sand. The golden sun languished in a sky of perfect blue. Seagulls squawked and circled, then dove for the fish that glided just beneath the surface of the Gulf. As I ran barefoot along the shore I felt as though I had been there before. I was struck with a feeling of déjà vu, one of those sudden flashes of remembered present, normally only a fleeting sensation, but this time a feeling that has lasted forever. I could actually sense the weight of history as I stood where my great-great-great-grandfather's house once stood. Over the years I have seen the island's many moods, from stormy to serene, but it is the beauty of the island on my first visit that I still carry with me today.

Like the original Cuevas children, I played on the beaches, explored the lagoons, and fished in the warm waters of the Gulf. I also played in the old Cat Island lighthouse, or rather what remained of it. In the 1950s it was nothing more than a wooden shell perched on top of rusted pilings, looking much like a birdhouse on steroids. The lighthouse was an important part of Cuevas family history, and I felt a connection to it although it was not the original lighthouse built on Cat Island. I've always had a romantic image of the island and particularly of my great uncle Ramon Cuevas, the son of Juan de Cuevas and the light keeper until it closed in 1861. I picture Ramon as hardworking, manning his tower in the darkest night, lighting the oil lamp even in the fiercest storms to ensure the safety of the passing ships at sea. But there was nothing romantic about the dilapidated old frame building I played on. I was very moved when I heard the news that the old lighthouse had burned down. "A charred pile of wood and twisted metal braces" was all that was left.[1] The last remaining connection to the Cuevas era on Cat Island was now gone, and I was surprised at how much the news affected me.

It is hard to explain the deep connection the Cuevas family seems to have with Cat Island. Although most of the current generation has never walked its sun-drenched beaches or heard the sound of summer breezes rustling through its pines, they speak passionately of it as if they knew every grain of sand. It is as if an archetype was implanted in their souls, formulated over years of stories told and retold by parents and grandparents. There has always been an underlying awareness that Cat Island and the Cuevas family are inextricably connected, and will be so as long as the island continues to lie beckoning in the Gulf. The older folks are particularly passionate about the subject. They have never been able to accept the fact that there is a stranger in their home. They are convinced that like a thief in the night someone stole the island from them. They don't know how this happened, but they continue to believe Cat Island rightfully belongs to the Cuevas family.

I was a believer. Even at the age of eleven I would argue with my friends, "My family owns Cat Island!" From the time I first learned about it, I was completely captivated by the idea. As a young boy the thought of living on the island conjured up the most fantastic images of swashbuckling adventures set against the orange-red glow of romantic island sunsets. I fantasized about being there when Jean Lafitte and his pirates landed on the shore, with their wooden treasure chest, scouring the island for the ideal hiding place. I could imagine their victims made to walk the plank, and could hear the bloodthirsty pirates shouting, "Avast ye mateys!" as they swung from the yardarms of their ships. My family owned Cat Island! It was like something out of a fairy tale. How many people would ever know someone who owned an island? That's the stuff of billionaires like Bill Gates and Donald Trump.

For sure, none of my adolescent peers would concede that I had any claim to an island. In my favor, there was an attorney in Gulfport who, according to my father, also believed that the island legally belonged to the Cuevas heirs. This argument was important enough for me to take drastic measures. After school one day and without an appointment, I dragged a doubting friend into the man's office. I was confident this defense attorney would make my case. He graciously agreed to see us and came straight to the point: "In my opinion, Cat Island rightfully belongs to the Cuevas family."

I left the office with a glow of self-righteousness, believing I had won the argument. Unfortunately as dramatic as my action had been, my doubting friend was still not convinced the island was mine. It was apparent I needed solid proof. At that moment my mission was set. If I wanted everyone to know the facts about what I believed to be true, I would have to find the evidence myself. I would show the skeptics that Cat Island has always belonged to the Cuevas family.

This experience started me on a lifelong quest for information. I wanted to know everything about Cat Island. I spoke to anyone who had knowledge of the subject. I diligently searched the early history of Spain, Florida, and the Louisiana territory. I strongly believe that I am the only Cuevas to have returned to the home of Juan de Cuevas in Algámitas, Spain, to visit with his relatives — my relatives.

Although I was able to find documents about the island, my research about the early Cuevas family proved more difficult. Personal diaries and letters were unheard of in the wilderness, so there are no written accounts of life on Cat Island. Most of the early settlers could not read or write, skills unnecessary for survival in a primitive environment. As a result, the adults did not bother educating their children. Without any written materials, I have only my immediate family and Juan's family in Spain as sources of information. My grandmother, Catherine Cuevas, and her brother, Casimir Garriga, born in the mid 1800s, knew several of the Cuevas children who had been raised on the island. Since daily life did not change much in rural America until the beginning of the 1900s, they were able to share valuable details of the Cuevas era on Cat Island. I was fortunate to have benefited from their knowledge before they passed on. I have also come to realize how valuable to Coast history my comprehensive library of documents, articles, and interviews might be. There may not be anyone else currently who has done as much research and is more qualified to tell the history of Cat Island and the Cuevas era.

The more I learned of the Cat Island legacy, the more frustrated I became. There have been generally more articles written about Juan de Cuevas than any other of his peers, yet almost all of them are inaccurate on many of the details. Respected authors, journalists and historians have unknowingly made these mistakes. In seeking to uncover the facts, I was faced with so many unanswered questions. Who was Juan de Cuevas? Did he come from Spain, or was he a French Canadian as some have suggested? Did he come from a noble family as has been reported, even though he could not read or write? Was Juan de Cuevas a hero in the War of 1812, and was he granted the island as a reward from a grateful nation for his actions against the British? Did Juan de Cuevas receive a grant for all of Cat Island, or only half, as even his obituary stated?

Today, it would be impossible for most of us to be isolated on an island without running water, without electricity, without a gro-

Catherine Garriga Cuevas knew some of the Cuevas children who were born and raised on Cat Island, and was a major source about their life in the 1800s.

Casimir "Coco" Garriga shared stories about life on Cat Island.

cery store, without radio or television, without contact with others except those in our immediate families, and without any means of travel other than a rowboat. This is hardly the portrait of an island paradise. Considering these harsh conditions, what was it really like living on Cat Island in the early 1800s? What language did the family speak? What kind of clothing did the people wear? What food did they eat? How were meals prepared? What music did they listen to? And finally the question that started it all — does the Cuevas family still rightfully own Cat Island?

This is a book about Cat Island, one of the most historically significant landmarks on the Mississippi Gulf Coast. It is not only a celebration of the major events that have occurred on its sandy shores, but it is also a tribute to the legacy of one of the Gulf Coast's original pioneer families that now numbers in the thousands. Over the many years of research I have been able to answer most of the lingering questions about Juan de Cuevas and his island home. I believe this book will be a valuable source of information, not only to the Cuevas family, but also to historians interested in the early years of the Mississippi Gulf Coast. I invite you to join me in an exciting trip through history.

1

About Cat Island

Cat Island is part of a chain of barrier islands that were created by the ceaseless action of waves and underlying currents in the shallow waters of the Gulf. This group of islands includes Dauphin, Petit Bois (split from the western tip of Dauphin Island by a hurricane in 1717), Horn, and Ship. Located approximately nine miles from the mainland, Cat Island lies due south of a point about halfway between Long Beach and Pass Christian at latitude 30 degrees 13 minutes north and longitude 89 degrees 6 seconds west. The size of Cat Island has remained approximately 2,500 acres, relatively unchanged compared to the other barrier islands since the time of the first explorers.[1]

Cat Island is the most fascinating of the islands in the chain. There are some days when it is completely invisible from the mainland, as if it doesn't actually exist, while on other days it may appear so close that the individual trees can almost be counted. The mass of pines that stretch across its coastline seem to be sitting on top of the water, waving in the heat of the sun like a mirage in the desert. At those special times, Cat Island can seem so peaceful, so haunting ... so near and yet so far away.[2]

The island is "T"-shaped with each arm of the T approximately six miles long and one mile wide. The irregularly shaped island consists of four spits, each having its own distinct character. The spit pointing north is the location of the Great Sand Hills and is nothing more than large elevated sand bars, while the spit to the south called Goose Point is sandy and flat. The east-west portion is the main body of the island and is densely wooded with live oak, pine and other trees and shrubs. At the center of the island toward the south is Middle Spit with a single grove of squatty pines behind which are the marshes and lagoons that offer sanctuary to the alligators and other unseemly reptiles that inhabit the swampy areas. On the long beach facing the open Gulf, the waves break with a roar like voices from the deep that seem to be whispering tales from the many vessels that were wrecked over time and ultimately washed ashore. Pieces of these hapless boats can be found at times scattered about, half buried in the sands. The sand itself is hard and smooth on that stretch of beach, just right for those barefoot beachcombers who search for pastel-tinted shells and other treasures of the sea that have churned up from the ocean floor. As sea gulls and pelican circle overhead, the playful sand crabs scurry about on stilt-like legs as if they were the only things on the island with a job to do.

The Great Sand Hill is a legendary landmark that could be seen for great distances in the Gulf. In years past it reached a height of as much as seventy feet. The great mound of sand is constantly shifting from the actions of prevailing eastern winds. According to reports

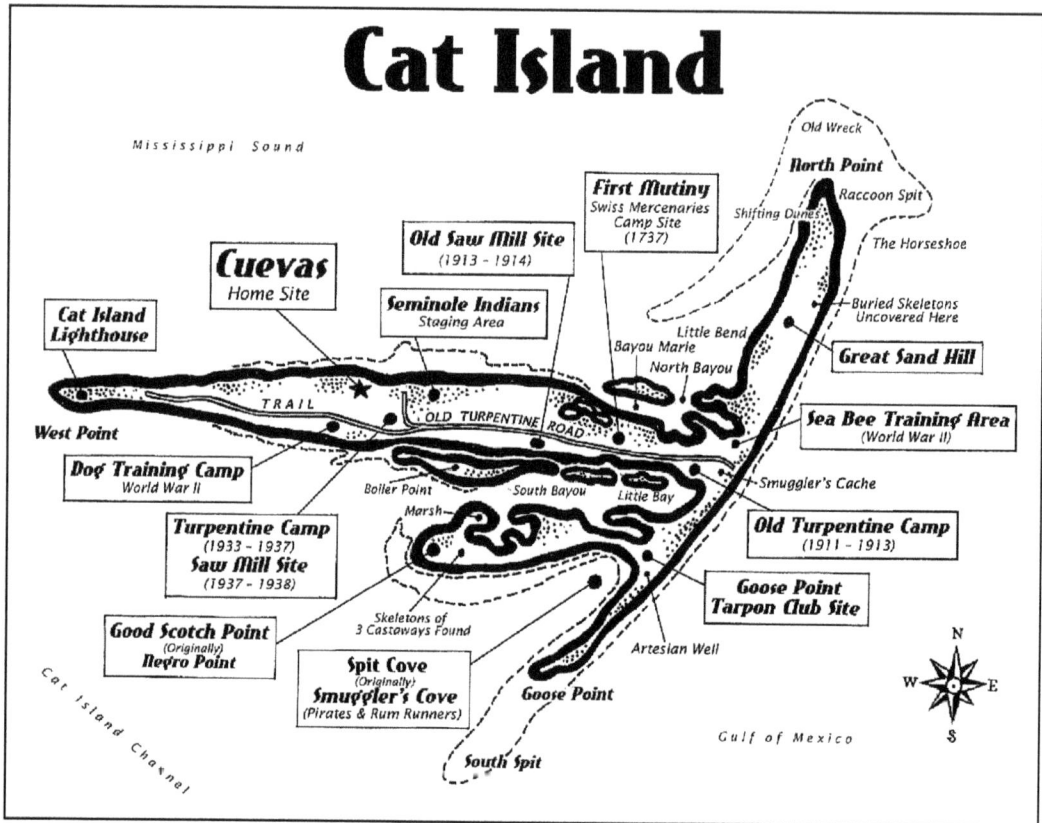

Map of Cat Island with important locations noted.

from 1847 to 1855 it actually shifted as much as fifty yards westward.³ It was used at that time as an observation point for the celestial bodies, but proved to be unsuccessful because the soft sand was not stable enough for the instruments. Ella A. Giles, a special correspondent with the *Wisconsin State Journal,* wrote this about the Great Sand Hill:

> I saw the trees on Cat Island, and the hemispherical summit of a snow-white mound near its eastern extremity. Its form, color and vast size, towering high above the pine trees on the island, astonished me. I had never seen or heard of it before. An old resident on the coast informed me that it was a huge sand hill; that it was about one hundred feet high when he first visited it sixty years before; but that the winds had removed it, until it is not now more than sixty feet perpendicular, and nearly half of it has been scattered over the island. I engaged a group of "old salts" into an animated discussion in regard to its formation. One argued that it was spewed up by an earthquake; others contended that the storm waves rolling in from Ship Island and the Chandeleurs have made it. One old seaman concluded that it had "made itself." I give no opinion about it, and will not until I can visit it; but it is a very remarkable pile of sand and there is enough of it, snow white, to make a beautiful cement for all the plaster that a hundred such cities as New Orleans will ever need."⁴

In the past a thousand tiny tracks could be seen in the sands around the great hills, made by the many raccoons for which the island was named. Unfortunately over the years a combination of natural forces and indiscriminate hunters decimated the island's natural population. Not only were the raccoons disappearing from Cat Island, but they were also

Marshes and lagoons offer sanctuary to the alligators and other unseemly reptiles that inhabit the swampy areas of Cat Island (courtesy of Randy Randazzo).

The Great Sand Hill is a legendary landmark that could be seen for great distances in the Gulf (courtesy of Randy Randazzo).

decreasing throughout the state. The Mississippi Conservation Commission that had just been formed in 1933 under the direction of Mr. Hunter Kimball was hoping to reverse this deplorable situation. Arrangements were made with the Game and Fish Commission and the owners of the island to use Cat Island as a giant breeding ground for the furry animals. Sixty raccoons, thirty males and thirty females, were released to breed with the island's natural population.[5] The raccoons that the French encountered were a brownish red in color, but these new animals had an exceptionally black coat. Since trappers found the darker raccoon more valuable, the group hoped to produce a better breed that would later be trapped and moved to the mainland. This program, which began in 1933, lasted until 1935.

Ramon Cuevas, the former lighthouse keeper, started accumulating a number of deer and rabbits at Bay St. Louis with the intent to populate the island with these animals. His plan was interrupted by the start of the Civil War.

Besides these animals, the fishing around Cat Island is superb. The waters virtually teem with oysters and crabs, and large schools of mullet in season can be found in all directions around the island. Redfish, porpoise and sharks are natural enemies of the mullet and can be seen circling the island during the months of September through June and feasting on these tasty fish.

Vegetation is lush on Cat Island. Although the soil is 90 percent sand, many places are covered in thick foliage; even the sandy beaches are covered with Bermuda grass. Drinking water can be found almost anywhere on the island by simply digging a few feet down. It bubbles up sweet and clear, especially at the foot of the Great Sand Hills, although one would expect it to be rank and brackish. Apparently the sand serves as the perfect filtration system, rendering the water as fresh as any found on the mainland.[6]

Pines are still found throughout the island, but not those majestic sixty-foot trees that once stood by the Cuevas home, now gone as a result of the extensive turpentine and logging operations of the past. Live oaks that are rarely found more than twenty-five miles from salt water grow abundantly on the Gulf Coast and on Cat Island. At times some of the old oaks had branches that spread almost twice the trees' height. Also abundant is the grey Spanish moss that drapes like cobwebs on nearly all of the island's oaks. A short evergreen holly bush called the yaupon forms a tangled, almost impenetrable growth in many places on the island. The holly bush with its red berries and smooth green leaves once formed a thicket around the Cuevas home like a wall that separated the family from the island wilderness. The leaves were made into a tea to serve as a laxative before there was medicine for irregularity. Large palmettos compete with the yaupon as the island's most common shrub. The large fan-like palmetto leaves give the island a tropical ambiance vividly contrasting with the pine and oak.

The U.S. National Park Service has described Cat Island as the "centerpiece" of the Gulf Islands National Seashore because of its natural amenities.[7] The island's unique "T" shape is the result of the merging of two islands, and is strikingly different from the cigar shape of the others in the chain. Dr. Ed Cake, a scientist with the Gulf Coast Research Laboratory, explains that the main east-west portion of Cat Island is a beach ridge system formed from an old Mississippi River delta, while the north-south portion is bar-built, similar to Horn and Ship islands. Bar-built islands begin underwater and eventually rise above the surface through the action of waves and high wind. These islands are considered very fragile because the sands and land mass are constantly shifting and moving toward shore.[8] At some point in time there is a chance that they could eventually disappear beneath the water. The constant threat of erosion renders them unsuited for any permanent or substantial development. Cat Island, on the other hand, is relatively stable and is, therefore, the only one of the barrier islands suitable for commercial development.[9] The island is further protected by the location of the Chandeleur Islands, a north-south oriented chain off the coast of Louisiana approximately 100 kilometers east of the city of New Orleans. The Chandeleurs, which are not part of the Gulf Coast barrier island chain, shield Cat Island by altering and diffusing the Gulf currents. The other islands are vulnerable to the direct forces of the Gulf and thus are subject to erosion.

The once popular Isle of Caprice is an example of the precarious nature of bar-built islands. It was at one time located fourteen miles off the coast of Biloxi between Ship and Horn islands. The name was originally Dog Key, so called when a dog was supposedly found on the island following an unnamed hurricane.[10] According to local folklore, the tremendous force of the winds seemed to have somehow blown the canine there from some unknown location.

The story of the Isle of Caprice is quite interesting. In 1923 Biloxi was experiencing a tourism boom, with many visitors flocking to the Coast for relief from the colder climates.[11] One of the grandest hotels of the day was the Buena Vista located on the current site of the Beau Rivage Casino parking decks north of Highway 90. Colonel J.W. "Jack" Apperson, the owner and builder of the Buena Vista Hotel, together with W.H. "Skeet" Hunt and Arbeau Caillavet, decided that a resort on one of the barrier islands would be just the thing to attract major national attention to the coast.[12]

Dog Key, positioned directly south of the Buena Vista, was perfect for their needs. With windswept dunes and white sandy beaches, it was the ideal location to create a gambling paradise in the Gulf, a "Monte Carlo of the South." Since it was beyond the twelve-mile

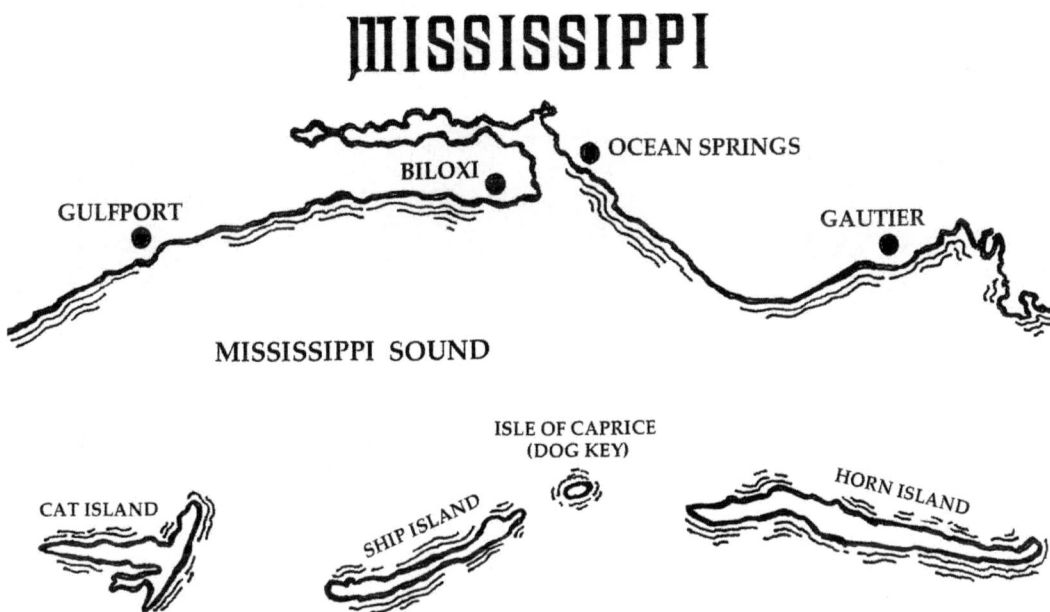

Dog Key, twelve miles off the coast of Biloxi, was so called when a dog was supposedly found on the island following an unnamed hurricane.

limit allowed by international law, the state would have no authority to impose any kinds of restrictions on gambling or alcohol.[13] Dog Key was romantically renamed "The Isle of Caprice" to signify its carefree character. The current Biloxi casino, Isle of Capri, derived its name from this once popular resort.[14]

The 487-acre island was approximately three miles long and one-quarter mile wide. Colonel Jack built two large buildings for the resort. One housed the gambling facilities and a dance floor, while the other housed a dressing room for swimmers. In addition, he built ten rental cabins that were nestled among the sand dunes and a boardwalk connecting all of the buildings. A 150-foot pier was constructed on the north side of the island opposite the Coast with an artesian well that had been dug at the pier's entrance to provide fresh water to the guests. An old boat named *Hercules* was purchased and renamed the *Non-Pareil*, "None Like It." The vessel made four trips daily from the Coast to the island landing.[15]

Dog Key's unique feature was its brilliant mountains of snow-white sand, created by the wind and reaching nearly twenty feet high. These dunes were always shifting, being swept from one location to another almost overnight. Originally they were anchored in place by a heavy growth of sea oats reaching a height of four feet. Oleanders and sycamores were also common, as were sea turtles and terrapins found nesting along the sloping sand beaches. The sea oats were so lush that the departing tourists would take armloads back for souvenirs. A large department store, realizing the commercial potential for these sea oats, signed a contract to harvest them to sell. With the removal of the sea oats, the sand was free to blow unrestrained across the island.

In 1926 a hurricane packing 90-mph winds struck a deadly blow to the Isle of Caprice. Without the sea oats for protection the winds whipped away at the Island until it was even-

The Isle of Caprice, a gambling paradise in the Gulf, was designed to be a "Monte Carlo of the South."

tually a flat sand bar. Over a period of eight years the island eroded down to nothingness. Vandals added to the destruction, burning the buildings to their foundations. What at one time had been a popular and thriving resort was eventually destroyed. By 1931, all that was left of the Isle of Caprice was the solitary pipe from the artesian well still visible above the water.[16] The island had simply disappeared, settling three to four feet below the surface of the Mississippi Sound. The wind and storms eventually swept the island away. This could easily be the fate of the other bar-built islands on the Coast, but was an almost impossible scenario for Cat Island, "The Gem of the Gulf."

The French first landed on the Mississippi Gulf Coast in 1699 and shortly after discovered Cat Island.

2

The French Discover Cat Island and Settle Biloxi

French explorer René-Robert Cavelier, Sieur de la Salle (1643–1687) discovered the mouth of the Mississippi River on April 9, 1682. Upon reaching the Gulf he planted a cross and claimed the entire basin for France, naming the territory La Louisiane in honor of the king, Louis XIV (1638–1715).[1] Fearing encroachment by England and Spain, which were already near the area, he returned home in 1683 to convince the French that the only way to retain control of Louisiana was to colonize the vast region. Backed by the king, La Salle left France again in 1684 with the orders to start a settlement at the mouth of the Mississippi. The journey proved to be disastrous. Nearing the Gulf he mistakenly went off course and landed near Houston, Texas. Having already experienced death and disease on their voyage, and now lost, his men implored La Salle to turn back. Refusing to give up his mission in the face of these tremendous hardships, he was ultimately murdered by his mutinous crew.

Louis XIV had become the most powerful monarch in Europe as a result of the Franco-Dutch War of 1678, but not satisfied with his new strength he launched an aggressive action to expand his control.[2] This resulted in the Nine Year War (1688–1697), which temporarily diverted his attention from the Gulf Coast, however it was not forgotten. At the end of the war the king commissioned a thirty-seven-year-old Canadian, Pierre Le Moyne Sieur d'Iberville (1661–1706) of Quebec, to return to the mouth of the Mississippi River and to colonize Louisiana.[3]

On an October day in 1698, d'Iberville, along with his nineteen-year-old brother, Jean Baptiste Le Moyne de Bienville (1680–1767), a group of about 200 colonists, two armed ships, and two smaller vessels, departed from LaRochelle, France.[4] Upon their initial arrival in the Gulf, the French missed the entrance to Mobile Bay but continued on, searching the shallow waters along the coast for a deep-water harbor. On February 10, 1699, they eventually dropped anchor at Ship Island, the only water they found deep enough to accommodate their large vessels.[5] After the ships were safely anchored, and a camp safely secured on the island, two smaller boats were sent out to explore Biloxi and the Bay of St. Louis. On Friday, February 27, 1699, as the boats rounded the tip of Ship Island, the men spotted another island in the west, now known as Cat Island.[6]

Captain Chateau, who was in command of one of the boats, reported in his journal that the other boat was manned by d'Iberville, his brother, Jean Baptiste Sieur de Bienville, the commandant, M. Jean de Sauvole, and a priest, Father Anastasias.[7] There was a total of 51

The French found a great number of raccoons on Cat Island, several of which they killed as the furry animals invaded the camp at night to scavenge leftovers from the evening meal. The men had never seen a raccoon before, since raccoons are native only to North America and were not known in France until their introduction in the mid 1900s.

men on the excursion, part of them Canadians and part "filibusters" (irregular army men who had joined the crew in San Domingo looking for adventure). The two boats had set out with provisions for twenty days and enough arms to defend against any Indian attacks. Having started late in the day, they chose to stay overnight on the newly discovered Cat Island.[8]

André-Joseph Pénigault, the ship's carpenter, also kept a diary. He reported a great number of raccoons were found on the island, several of which they killed as the furry animals invaded the camp at night to scavenge leftovers from the evening meal. The men had never seen a raccoon before, since raccoons are native only to North America and were not known in France until their introduction in the mid 1900s. Thought to be large cats, the men jokingly called the island Isle aux Chats aux Huitres, or Island of the Oyster Cats, because some of the raccoons were seen laboriously pulling apart oysters and devouring them with great relish.[9] Although never officially called by that name, or even Isle aux Chats Savage, the proper French name for raccoon, the shortened version of Isle aux Chats or Cat Island eventually became the accepted name.

After three days the expedition landed on the coast at Biloxi. The group determining that the mouth of the Mississippi was not a suitable location to establish a fort spent most of March searching the coastal area before finally returning to the Biloxi site on March 30, 1699.[10] Here d'Iberville ordered the construction of Fort Maurepas, named after the French minister of the Navy, Jean-Frédéric Phélypeaux, comte de Maurepas (1701–1781).[11]

The young colony at Fort Maurepas in Old Biloxi (now Ocean Springs) suffered greatly in its first long, hot summer of 1700.[12] The food crops were destroyed by the blistering sun and drought of that year. Even more dangerous than the heat was the resulting lack of drinking water. As if the weather wasn't enough to contend with, the men were attacked by hordes of mosquitoes and other biting insects. Fever, dysentery, and just plain boredom drove the troops' morale to a depressing low. Alligators and snakes posed a threat, while the dwindling food supplies were further reduced by a steady stream of Canadians who continued to arrive on the coast.

On Dec. 5, 1701, d'Iberville returned from a visit to France with orders to move the exposed Biloxi colony to a site on the Mobile River to be closer to their new Spanish allies for support.[13] This order was out of fear of the expected outbreak of colonial hostilities resulting from the War of Spanish Succession (1701–1713). Through marriage-diplomacy, Philip, duke of Anjou (1683–1746) and grandson of Louis XIV of France, became Philip V of Spain with the inevitable event forming a practical union of Spain and France.[14] The English, who objected to this blatant upset of the balance of power in Europe, declared war on both countries. Iberville complied, ordering the immediate transport of munitions and supplies from Fort Maurepas to warehouses on Dauphin Island. Throughout the war, the French government almost completely abandoned the Gulf Coast colonies.[15]

In August 1717, the first hurricane ever recorded put an end to the capital in Mobile.[16] The severity of the storm split Dauphin Island in two, forming what became known as Petit Bois Island. The devastation in the Mobile area forced Bienville to seek yet another new capital for Louisiana. He selected a site in a bend of the Mississippi River on the old portage route from Lake Pontchartrain. Construction began in March 1718 on the new settlement he called New Orleans.[17] Bienville's choice for the capital received little support from the superior council of the colony, citing the importance of the proximity to the port on Ship Island.[18] New Orleans was vetoed and the capital in Mobile was relocated in November 1719 back to Biloxi near the vicinity of the old Fort Maurepas. A year later the capital was moved across the bay to what was then called New Biloxi, our present-day Biloxi, and construction of Fort Louis, facing the Mississippi Sound, began.[19]

In less than a year, the struggling colony was dealt an almost terminal blow when the colonial council reversed its decision, ordering the capital to again be moved, this time to the fledgling city of New Orleans.[20] Fort Louis was abandoned when its construction had scarcely begun. A second blow came in that same year when another powerful hurricane swept across the coast, destroying the Biloxi area and raising questions as to whether the village would survive.[21]

In 1712, France was facing a financial collapse and no longer able to support the Louisiana territory. As a way of relief, Louis XIV awarded a grant to Antoine Crozat, marquis du Châtel (1650–1738), the wealthiest man in France, giving him a fifteen-year trade monopoly in the Louisiana territory.[22] This contract gave Crozat absolute control of and full responsibility for the Louisiana territory. Crozat saw this as a way to increase his wealth. Crozat's plans to make the new colony profitable were unsuccessful and, realizing the effort was fruitless, he surrendered his monopoly, reverting it back to France.

With the failure of Crozat, France found itself in even more financial trouble. It was deeper in debt, with the entire economy of the country on the verge of bankruptcy as a result of the expenditures of the throne.[23] Louis XIV, although considered one of France's greatest kings, was the archetype of an absolute monarch with total power over his people and the land. Without any laws or controls, Louis was free to do whatever he pleased.

Unfortunately for France, he proved to be an extravagant spender. His greatest expenditure was the palace of Versailles, which he spent $100 million building, and by some estimates, half of the French treasury maintaining.[24] Louis also spent heavily supporting the arts, improving the Louvre Museum, and supporting such cultural and literary figures as Charles Le Brun, Jean-Baptiste Lully and Molière.

In addition to his lavish lifestyle, Louis XIV attempted to dominate Europe by fighting three major wars: the War of the League of Augsburg, the Franco-Dutch War and the War of Spanish Succession, along with two other minor conflicts, all of which were costly. During his reign there were three main targets of taxation: trade through custom duties, the usage of salt, and land. The nobility and the clergy were exempt from these taxes, placing the burden on the peasants and the middle class.[25] The outrage over this unfair taxation would eventually fuel the French Revolution (1789–1799).

The French-controlled colony of Louisiana continued to cause a desperate strain on the country's meager resources. The situation was complicated by the government's lack of knowledge about the territory and its needs. The land in America was much larger than France itself, and the French did not even really know where it was.[26] The sorry state of the French economy made the government vulnerable to the economic ideas of John Law (1671–1729), a Scottish financier. Law convinced the king and the country that he could succeed where Crozat had failed.[27] He was sure he could turn France into an economic powerhouse. Upon the death of Louis XIV, the duc d'Orleans (under Louis XV) awarded the territory to John Law.

John Law and his associates took control of the Louisiana territory by a royal grant in 1717. They were collectively called John Law's Company of the West, but popularly known as the Mississippi Company, and the terms of the royal grant were essentially the same as those issued a few years earlier to Crozat. Law's company, however, was given the exclusive trade rights in the territory for a period of twenty-five years, ten years longer than Crozat. Other terms included the right to appoint their own governor and officers in the colony, and the right to make land grants to potential developers.[28]

Law set up the Mississippi Company as a way to sell stock. People were quick to invest what little they had, in hopes of turning their small investment into big profits. To legitimize the plan, a board of directors was created to manage the business.[29] The board in turn elected John Law as the CEO. A frenzy of speculation gripped France based on the unsupported stock offered by the Mississippi Company.[30] In order to set his plan in motion, Law created deceptive brochures and promotional materials presenting the territory as a Garden of Eden.[31] Even with his slick marketing, however, very few people volunteered to move to Louisiana. In desperation, and in order to promote the illusion of prosperity, Law agreed to import six thousand whites and three thousand Negro slaves.[32] Charles Etienne Gayarré (1805–1895), known as the "historian of Louisiana" because of his comprehensive books on the early history of the territory, described how Law accomplished this goal. According to Gayarré, the jails and hospitals of France were ransacked. Disorderly soldiers, black sheep of distinguished families, paupers, prostitutes, and any unsuspecting peasants straying into Paris were taken and transported by force to the Gulf Coast. Those who voluntarily came were offered free land, free provisions, and free transportation to the new territory.[33]

This swarm of new immigrants landed on Dauphin Island, where they were crowded, unsheltered, and unfed.[34] All were disheartened, some grew sick, and many died. The group was eventually dispersed in small boats throughout the area to Pascagoula, Biloxi, Ship Island, and other places along the coast. Food was so scarce that the provincial government was hardly able to feed the soldiers who were necessary for the defense of the colony. To make matters even worse, those respectable émigrés who had chosen to come to the coast had found themselves thrown in with the hardened criminals and derelicts that comprised most of the group.[35] Because of the squalid conditions, the good and the bad alike must certainly have been more than anxious to leave Biloxi at the first opportunity.[36] The elite Europeans who had initially arrived from France to create and shape the Louisiana colony shifted their attention from Biloxi to the new capitol of New Orleans.[37]

The promise of a bright future for the coast was dashed when the money and resources moved east. The city of New Orleans benefited and prospered from this onslaught of disgruntled immigrants and wealthy elite to become, at one time, the third-largest city in the United States.[38] The settlers who remained on the Mississippi coast were determined to forge a life in their recently adopted home despite the desperate situation. No longer protected by the French soldiers who had once made up the majority of the colony, these families were vulnerable to vengeful Indians that were roving around carrying out violent attacks and stealing cattle. By 1767, the few families living along the coast had been driven out to the barrier islands for safety.[39] Cat Island, approximately nine miles from the mainland, was close enough for access, yet far enough away from the coast for the occupants to ensure their security.

Security was a priority from the beginning of the colony. There is evidence that shortly after d'Iberville and his men began work on Fort Maurepas a smaller fort was constructed on Cat Island.

3

The Fort on Cat Island

Frank Heiderhoff, a journalist with the *New Orleans Times*, visited Cat Island in 1871, only ten years after the last member of the Cuevas family left the island. He reported seeing the outline of a fort, which, at the time of his visit, was plainly visible.[1] A number of bricks were reportedly scattered about and Heiderhoff claims to have personally collected a few of them. The bricks certainly appeared to him to have been used in the fort's construction. He described them in his article as seven inches long, four inches wide, and only one and a half inches thick. He observed that they were the same kind of bricks used throughout France for construction.[2]

Heiderhoff described the Cat Island fort as being situated on a little cove at the foot of the Great Sand Hill. Unlike Fort Maurepas, which was made of lumber indigenous to the Coast, the Cat Island fort was constructed of bricks made in France and brought to the Biloxi area on some of the frigates as ballast.[3]

The small fort, supposedly built shortly after the discovery of the island, would have been the second fortress built by the French after arriving on the Gulf Coast. On April 8, 1699, Pierre Le Moyne d'Iberville had ordered the construction of Fort Maurepas, the first French fortress in the Louisiana territory. The fort was built according to the plan created by Marshal Sébastien Le Prestre de Vauban (1633–1707), Louis XIV's chief military engineer.[4]

Remy Reno,[5] d'Iberville's architect, would have been the man who designed the fort on Cat Island, using the same plan he employed in the construction of Fort Maurepas.[6] He had utilized Vauban's innovative star-shaped design, which was by then being used on most French fortifications.[7] Heiderhoff reported seeing concrete flooring within the walls, which he concluded must have been made on the spot due to the evidence of badly burned oyster lime.[8] He further observed from the existing ruins that a dozen light caliber guns were probably used to defend the fort.[9]

Most of the old medieval forts were made of bricks and stones, but by the 1600s they were mostly useless against the modern weapons and tactics that were being employed by the well-organized, modern armies of the day.[10] The new cannons with their unprecedented power could simply crumble the stone walls of the old fortifications after repeated bombardment. To provide adequate defense, the design of the forts had to be changed.

King Louis XIV called upon Marshal Vauban to study the weaknesses of the forts and to make improvements.[11] Vauban had joined the king's army in 1658, and proved to be brilliant in warfare. After many successful campaigns he developed a keen eye for detecting weak spots in a town's defenses. His impact on the military was tremendous. By the late 1600s, his reputation as a military strategist was world-renowned.[12]

Vauban was a genius at planning attacks against strongholds, and then designing a defense against such attacks. One of his revolutionary solutions was a pentagonal or star-shaped fort design that left no blind spots in which an attacker could hide.[13] In conjunction with the new shape, Vauban added raised areas of ground around the walls of the fort. These artificial piles of dirt, called glacis, were created with sloped sides.[14] The angle of the dirt piles caused cannonballs to ricochet and to miss their target. The glacis also eliminated the zone of safety that is inherent with the straight walls of a fort. There was a natural blind spot at the foot of the perpendicular walls, which made it impossible to see the enemy once he got near the fort. The slant of the glacis kept the attacker in the direct line of fire, making it impossible for anyone to hide or avoid detection.[15] To further enhance the fort's defenses, a ditch was dug around the circumference and filled with dangerous pointy obstacles, or what the French variously called pallisades, fraises, or abatis.[16] These were nothing more than logs and branches that had been sharpened. Vauban also added slits in the thick walls through which handguns could be fired.

One of the reasons for Vauban's success was his meticulous planning and detail of construction. He would go so far as to create scale models of the forts before he began building, which was unheard of in his day.[17] Great consideration was given to the site, its location and the materials to be used. Vauban employed the skills and knowledge of the local workers, and built the walls of the forts using local materials.[18] To promote the health, well-being and the discipline of the soldiers, Vauban was one of the first since the Roman Empire to include proper and permanent barracks and accommodations for the men.[19] His defensive systems were so superb that many of his forts still survive today, even after withstanding centuries of assaults. Fort McHenry in Baltimore, La Citadelle in Quebec City, and Fort Ticonderoga in New York are a few examples.

Despite the bricks that Frank Heiderhoff found, there is some question as to whether the fort on Cat Island ever existed. There doesn't seem to be any other historical reference to a fort on the island, although it is difficult to refute the first-hand observation and the physical evidence collected by a reporter of that day.

At various times during Coast history there have been several military groups that have occupied Cat Island. While there are many stories to be told, the first and perhaps the most dramatic occurred in 1757 when several soldiers rebelled against their commanding officer.

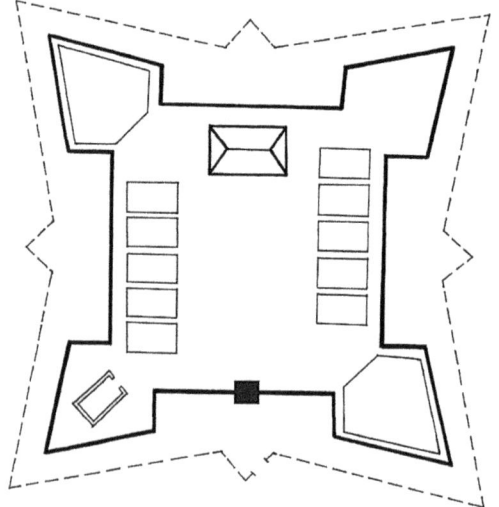

One of Vauban's revolutionary solutions for defense against attack was a pentagonal or star-shaped fort design that left no blind spots in which an attacker could hide.

4

The First Mutiny on American Soil

There was blood on the beach that day when Cat Island became the site of the first mutiny on American soil. A French officer was assassinated by a firing squad of four of his men on April 22, 1757. It was the first officially documented, dramatic event in Cat Island's history.[1]

The seeds of rebellion were planted during the rule of Pierre François de Rigaud, marquis de Vaudreuil-Cavagnal (1698–1778), who had succeeded Bienville as governor of Louisiana in 1743.[2] Vaudreuil's administration was marked by vice and corruption, with an immoral military engaged in a system of plunder authorized by the governor himself. The thieves, prostitutes, and other assorted misfits that had been sent to the Louisiana territory by John Law's Mississippi Company still constituted a near majority of the population. Life in the colony was unbearable for decent people, who were threatened by the drunkenness, brawls, and so many duels that nearly half of the population of New Orleans was destroyed.[3] Under his lax regime, the vicious and criminal elements from all over the territory flocked into New Orleans. This atmosphere of crime and corruption was in full swing when Vaudreuil was promoted to the governorship of Canada and sent north.

Louis Billouart, chevalier de Kerlerec (1704–1770), a distinguished captain in the French Navy, succeeded Vaudreuil as the new governor of Louisiana. He arrived in New Orleans on February 9, 1753, naïve to the situation he would face. Kerlerec, sincere about his duties, was appalled at the conditions he found.[4] Public money was being recklessly spent and the officials in charge were totally corrupt. This lawless culture presented a daunting challenge for the new governor, who sources say was an honest man with the interest of his country at heart.[5] He was hampered at every turn in his efforts to clean up the situation. Vincente de Rochemore (1713–1769), the intendant-commissary, was an enemy from the start, as well as the followers of Vaudreuil whom Kerlerec had dismissed when he took office.[6]

This was the beginning of the period known as the Seven Years' War, in which the French fought the British for possession of Canada. Most of the French troops had been sent north with Vaudreuil and replacements had not been forthcoming.[7] Kerlerec made many appeals to the government for men and money, but the French, preoccupied with their European interests, basically abandoned Louisiana when Vaudreuil left for Canada.

Without money, Kerlerec was unable to continue furnishing gifts and trade goods as yearly tributes to the Choctaws and other important Indian allies of the French.⁸ Without these promised payments, the Indians were gradually being won over by the English, who were beginning to encroach on the Louisiana territory. Alarmed by the growing British threat to the French colonies, Kerlerec began to organize a defense of the territory, particularly New Orleans.⁹ Since the treasury had been depleted, he had no funds with which to operate. Ever loyal to his country, Kerlerec pledged not only his salary, but also his personal credit. With these limited resources he was able to dig a trench and erect a palisade around the city. Unfortunately, there was not enough money left after the work was completed to put an adequate army together to man the posts.

The few troops that had remained after the departure of Vaudreuil were of the same rowdy bunch that had been the source of much of the city's problems in the past. Not only that, but the officers who commanded them were of questionable character, treating their men with little respect.¹⁰ Without the means to pay the troops, Kerlerec's disgruntled soldiers, living without money, food or clothing, began to desert to the British. It was Swiss mercenaries that ultimately held firm, while defection of the demoralized French soldiers was a sorry show of military discipline.

The English fleet patrolled the Atlantic and the Gulf of Mexico, allowing English privateers to intercept and capture any supplies arriving from France. As the fear of war continued to grow, Kerlerec stationed a guard post on Cat Island to monitor the enemy's activities and to warn of any impending attack on the city.¹¹ The force of twelve men included three Swiss soldiers and a Swiss corporal from the regiment of Halwyl, six French soldiers, a French sergeant, and their French commanding officer, Captain Duroux.

After the end of the Burgundy Wars in 1477, Swiss soldiers were hired to fight with other European countries.¹² These were not renegade individuals, but entire regular Swiss regiments. These soldiers were contracted by their respective cantonal governments to serve a particular monarch, which they did faithfully. Large sums of money were paid and were a substantial part of the income of the canton. This practice was halted after 1874 when the Swiss constitution prohibited it.¹³

For the first few months this small garrison appeared to be working well, but things were not what they seemed. Isolated from his superiors, Captain Duroux began to abuse his authority. He forced the soldiers to work both night and day, for his own personal gain, at jobs completely outside of their roles in the military.¹⁴ They were made to cut trees and burn the logs in large kilns to produce valuable charcoal. They were also forced to make lime from the abundant oyster shells that were on the island. These products were shipped regularly to New Orleans and sold, with Duroux keeping all of the profits for himself. Duroux also confiscated and sold what little provisions were issued to the soldiers, leaving the men with no food except the few fish they managed to catch.¹⁵

The harsh treatment that most of the soldiers received at the hands of their commanding officer was unbearable. Duroux would have the soldiers beaten, mutilated, and thrown into a makeshift prison to starve. When the soldiers complained, they were stripped naked and tied to stakes, exposing their unprotected skin to the scorching hot sun and the ravenous swarms of thirsty mosquitoes. This torture went on for months, until almost all of the men were covered with bloody welts. Duroux was able to control these wretched soldiers with the help of a chosen few of his men who were treated well and given food in return for their loyalty. His special troops were the only ones allowed to have guns, while all other firearms were kept securely locked away.¹⁶

Eventually several of the soldiers managed to escape. They headed immediately to New

Orleans, where they reported the horrifying events on Cat Island to the governor.[17] But Kerlerec would hear none of it. Being a sailor with many years of service at sea, he took the side of the officer. With little remorse, he admonished the men and sent them back to the tyrant, Duroux, where they were severely punished.

Soon afterward, the men noticed crates weaving and bobbing in the grey waters on the southeast side of the island. They waded out into the sound and began dragging the boxes onto shore. A Spanish ship loaded with food and supplies heading to the presidio at Pensacola had sunk near Dauphin Island.[18] The wreckage was beginning to wash ashore along the barrier islands lining the Coast. With such valuable cargo practically handed to them, it was not long before some of the men began looting the goods and hiding the booty in the woods among the palmettos and pines.

Along with the troops, several settlers were also living on Cat Island. The most prominent was Nicholas Christian Ladner, who had been on the island for the past ten years.[19] Jean Baptiste Baudrau II, whose sister was married to Ladner, was probably staying at their home while on Cat Island. Born about 1716, Jean Baptiste and his sister, Magdelaine, were the bastard children of one of the first settlers in the territory, a wealthy and influential Canadian Jean Baptiste Baudrau called Graveline. Jean Baptiste Baudrau II's mother was an Indian slave named Susanne who raised her biracial son between both cultures, French and Indian. He learned to read and write his father's language, but he also mastered every Indian dialect in the colony.[20]

Described as a very strong man, almost a giant in size, Baudrau was respected by the Indians for his bravery and grasp of their languages.[21] Even so, he remained an outcast, never fully accepted by the French nor by his mother's people. Even his father eventually disowned him. His sister, Magdelaine, married Nicholas Ladner the following year.[22] Their daughter, Marie Hellene Ladner, would later become the wife of Cat Island owner Juan de Cuevas.

Baudrau was a misfit constantly at odds with the law. He was always challenging Governor Vaudreuil's right to control the goods flowing into the colonies. Caught in the act of smuggling with the Spanish at Pensacola, and engaging in an early form of bootlegging, he was jailed on more than one occasion. King Louis XV finally granted him a pardon in 1747, in part because of Baudrau's influence with the Indians.[23] He was not heard from after the pardon until that infamous day on Cat Island when the mutiny occurred.

One of the passengers on the ill-fated ship was Don Arturo O'Neill de Tyrone (1736–1814), the new Spanish governor of Pensacola.[24] The governor survived the accident, and sent word to Kerlerec informing him about what had occurred. He thanked Kerlerec for all of the help that he had received at the French post in Mobile, but also requested the prompt return of any of the cargo that had been recovered. As soon as Kerlerec got word of the shipwreck, he immediately instructed Duroux to personally see that none of the cargo was looted, and to be sure that all of the goods were returned to the Spanish.

Duroux's soldiers, who had plundered the wreckage, blamed Jean Baptiste Baudrau II for the missing cargo. Baudrau's questionable past made him a perfect scapegoat. The Spanish governor informed Kerlerec of the men's accusations and asked that Baudrau be arrested. Several days after Duroux received the alert, Jean Baptiste was captured and placed in chains to await extradition to New Orleans.[25]

In the early morning of Tuesday, April 22, Duroux boarded a small boat for a daylong hunting trip to nearby Ship Island.[26] He took one of his men, Francois Vidou, and one of the settlers along with him, probably a Ladner kin. This was the opportunity the soldiers

Self portrait of Jean Baptist Baudrau II hammered out on a copper fireplace implement called a "salamander." It was believed to have been a gift to his sweetheart, Marie Henriette Huet.

were waiting for. As soon as Duroux's boat was out of sight, they acted quickly on a plan to kill their commander and escape from their horrid conditions on Cat Island. First they commandeered the weapons, and then overthrew the few soldiers loyal to Duroux. A self-appointed firing squad consisting of a Swiss corporal and two privates, one Swiss and one French, positioned themselves on the beach to wait for Duroux's return.[27]

At sundown they saw Duroux's skiff making its way back to the island. As he pulled his boat ashore, the men stepped out of the shadows. Drummers beat a salute, while a soldier raised the French flag as if in respect to their superior. The captain stepped out onto the sand, as the corporal gave his command to fire. A bullet from each of the muskets ripped through Duroux's chest as his blood-drenched body was thrown back into the dark murky water. The men then dragged his lifeless body into the Gulf and left him to be eaten by the fish and crabs.[28]

The assassins quickly released the remaining of Duroux's prisoners, including Jean Baptiste Baudrau II. In return for his freedom, Baudrau agreed to guide the group of fugitives into the English-controlled territory. They loaded all of the equipment, including Duroux's personal belongings, into two rowboats, and headed off toward Mobile.[29]

The group arrived on the mainland and retreated through the woods. The soldiers directed Baudrau to take them to Georgia. Jean Baptiste led them up the Tombigbee River in canoes he had borrowed from the Indians, finally reaching the Chattahoochee River. The men released Baudrau after reaching Coweta in Georgia. The soldiers gave him a written paper stating that he had nothing to do with the murder of Duroux, and that they had forced Baudrau to act as their guide. Confident that the document would clear him of any wrongdoing, Jean Baptiste left the men and made his way back to Mobile, where he quietly blended into the city. Some of the soldiers continued their escape into safe English territory in Georgia, while others remained in Coweta and Cusseta, enjoying the Indians' hospitality.[30]

Word of the mutiny finally reached Governor Kerlerec. Taking immediate action, he selected a few of his most trusted officers to deliver a sealed package of orders to Montberaut, the commandant of Fort Toulouse at Mobile.[31] He directed him to capture the fugitive soldiers, and gave him the authority to make any promises necessary to ensure that the Indians would assist in their capture. The governor still believed that Jean Baptiste was the instigator of the mutiny and emphasized the importance of his arrest as well.[32]

Jean Baptiste Baudrau II was taken by surprise in Mobile nearly six weeks later, having been betrayed by Indians he thought he could trust.[33] His two sons were unknowing accomplices in his arrest. The boys had been living with their mother in New Orleans, and came to Mobile to visit their father. Kerlerec had them followed. A group of Alibamons led by Mr. Rossever, the king's interpreter, along with some carefully chosen settlers, captured the unsuspecting Baudrau.[34]

Montberaut received word from his scouts that some of the fugitive soldiers had remained with the Indians on the Chattahoochee River. He quickly dispatched a small detachment to arrest them. A party of Tallapoosa Indians and some Alibamons led by Mr. Baudin, an ensign attached to the Alibamons, conducted a raid on the English cabins where the soldiers had been hiding. The Swiss corporal who was the leader of the mutiny, seeing that he would be captured, pulled out a knife and plunged it into his own chest, committing suicide to avoid the inevitable punishment by the French.[35]

The remaining soldiers, one Frenchman and two Swiss, were captured by Baudin and carried to New Orleans. They were placed in irons and thrown into separate prison cells to await their trials. Mr. de Belle-Isle, a major in the French army, questioned the prisoners at length. The Council of War assembled, and on June 7 the officers of the Swiss regiment held a court-martial. Two of the three soldiers, one French and one Swiss, were found guilty and condemned to die.

The third soldier, Francois Vidou, was cleared of all charges.[36] The other two soldiers that had just been convicted verified he was only a passenger in Duroux's boat at the time of the assassination, and had not participated in either the planning of the murder or the desertion. According to Jean Bernard Bossu (1720–1792), the French agreed that Vidou had acted out of fear for his life, and had been forced to desert so there would be no living witness to the crime. He was, therefore, acquitted and allowed to return to his company and to continue his service.[37]

Following the men's conviction, Jean Baptiste faced the court. In his defense, Baudrau presented the document signed by the mutineers proclaiming his innocence of any participation in the assassination of Duroux, and stating that he was forced to act as a guide to Georgia. Even with this compelling defense, Jean Baptiste Baudrau II was found guilty.[38]

Three hours after their trial ended, the men were summarily executed. The French soldier, Joseph Francois Bazille, and the Frenchman, Jean Baptiste Baudrau II, each died on

Jean Baptiste Baudrau II suffered a horrific death by execution on the French wheel.

the French wheel, the bones of their bodies broken and their bodies cut into four pieces.[39] To avoid the possibility of an Indian uprising over Baudrau's death, Kerlerec had the pieces of his body thrown into the river so there would be no grave to visit.[40]

The second man convicted suffered an even more horrific death. The commander of his regiment, Mr. Volant, had the terrified Swiss soldier placed in a coffin-shaped box. After the lid was nailed shut, two soldiers, using a crosscut saw, sawed the box in half. After his horrible death the criminal's head and one hand were amputated and displayed on a post for eight days thereafter.[41]

The death of these men did not go unnoticed. There were many protests from important French citizens about the horrible way these executions were handled. Kerlerec was strongly condemned, and in 1769 he was recalled to France, where he died in exile a year later.[42]

Jean Baptiste Baudrau II, who died such an ignominious death, was finally given a proper funeral exactly 250 years after his execution. On Sunday, June 10, 2007, I and a group of his descendents attended a Mass for the Deceased in his honor at St. Louis Cathedral in New Orleans, and then paraded through the French Quarter in a traditional Jazz procession replete with band and umbrellas. The mourners paused briefly at the site of his imprisonment and ended at the banks of the Mississippi River. After a ceremony that included oral tributes and written thoughts and prayers, we threw a commemorative wreath into the rushing waters accompanied by sendoff cheers of "Vive Jean Baptiste Baudrau!"[43]

Captain Duroux may have been the first tyrant to inhabit Cat Island, but the pirate Jean Lafitte was the most romantic scoundrel to grace its shores. Not only was he well liked in New Orleans, and even admired, but he was also ultimately a hero.

5

Jean Lafitte, the Pirates, and Buried Treasure

Cat Island is located just on the edge of Christian's Pass, the deep-water channel that leads from the Gulf of Mexico through Lake Borgne down Bayou St. John into the city of New Orleans. In the early history of the Coast, Cat Island's position in the Gulf was the equivalent of sitting on the fifty-yard line of history as the drama of life played out on the open waters. Passing in front of the Cuevas family home were boats of all sizes from the most powerful countries in the world.

In the early 1800s the Gulf of Mexico was also teeming with pirates, although not the ones that most of us remember from our history books.[1] By the middle of the eighteenth century the golden age of piracy was over. England, France, and Spain, the three major European powers, had joined forces to clean up the western seas.[2] The systematic violence that terrorized the shipping lanes and involved such notable buccaneers as Sir Henry Morgan, Captain Kidd, and the infamous Blackbeard had come to an end. This did nothing, however, to eliminate piracy, but rather only created a new breed. These new pirates operated as usual, only now they worked within a system that offered a questionable degree of legality to their activities.

Private ship captains were pressed into service by nations at war that issued papers called letters of marque[3] that gave the captains the authority to seize, search and even destroy enemy ships. To add an air of legitimacy, the men who carried out these attacks were no longer called pirates, but rather were referred to as privateers. But regardless of the slightly veiled attempt to cover up their true nature, these ruffians were still pirates.

In reality this was a way of doing battle with the enemy just short of a full declaration of war. These new-age pirates could attack an enemy ship, keeping not only the shipment, but also the ship so long as they satisfied only two requirements. The captured ship had to be brought back to the country that issued the marque and the captain had to appear before a maritime court for an approval of the action.[4] The privateers found an easy way to scam the system. They made an arrangement with the city of Cartagena, Colombia, to fly the Cartagenian flag. Cartagena had declared its independence from Spain and had issued the letter of marque to the privateers with the understanding they would only attack Spanish ships.[5] The pirates, of course, attacked every ship they thought they could overpower regardless of the country.

Trade with the Europeans increased dramatically after the United States purchased

Louisiana in 1803. With the increased traffic in the Gulf, New Orleans became a much more convenient base of operations. It was not long before the pirates were bringing their captured cargo to New Orleans rather than making the long journey to Cartagena. Since the goods confiscated under the letters of marque had to be cleared by an admiralty court, it was necessary for the pirates to find locations near New Orleans where they could stash their booty until the necessary arrangements were made to clear the goods through U.S. Customs. Cat Island was among the several ideal locations the pirates found to hide their goods. It was small, the inland cove was secluded, and it was uninhabited except for the one small family of Juan de Cuevas.

In addition to temporary holding sites like Cat Island, the pirates needed a permanent base of operation where they could warehouse their stolen cargo. The Bay of Barataria was the perfect location. It was only about two hours from New Orleans and, with its tricky maze of bayous and swamps, had been a favorite hiding spot for dangerous criminals since the French controlled Louisiana.[6] The bay was literally a fortress. The early Frenchmen found the area so inaccessible that they named it "The Island of Barataria" after the unattainable island kingdom of Sancho Panza in Cervantes' *Don Quixote*.[7]

The island of Grande Terre in the bay was finally chosen for the pirates' headquarters partially because of the heavy growth of trees surrounding the perimeter that provided additional cover from the prying eyes of the authorities.[8] Grand Terre was also one of three islands including Grand Isle and Cheniere Caminada that protected the Bay of Barataria from the open waters of the Gulf. Any vessels traveling in or out of the Mississippi River had to pass by these three islands, allowing the pirates to monitor all shipping activity in and out of New Orleans.

Pirates and privateers overran the new colony, setting up a business that provided New Orleans merchants with valuable goods well below market prices. Legitimate importers in the city found it impossible to compete with this black market merchandise. Total chaos developed when the hardened criminals that had begun to infiltrate the island fought over the distribution of loot. The situation grew more dangerous as bloody and senseless killings became commonplace. With the wild reports of these murders, the merchants who would often visit the island for their goods were no longer willing to take the risk. Like a ship without a captain tossing about in a sea of turmoil, the reckless band of criminals was without leadership or direction.[9]

Jean Lafitte and his brother, Pierre, arrived in New Orleans about 1804 just as the chaos within the pirates' enclave was at its worst.[10] Lafitte's history before this date remains a mystery. There are several contradictory documents signed by Jean Lafitte himself giving his place of birth at different locations. He stated at various times that he was born in Bayonne, Brest, Marseilles, and sometimes St. Malo in France. In one document his birthplace was said to be the most unlikely Westchester, New York.[11] There are some who say he may have even been born in or around French Louisiana because he seemed to have an immediate and uncanny knowledge of all of the inlets and bayous in the New Orleans area.[12] People who had spent their whole lives on the fringes of the swampy maze of cypress and moss would not venture too far into the swamps for fear of never finding their way out, and yet Lafitte could navigate the waters as if he had a second sense. According to Lafitte's biographer Jack C. Ramsay, Lafitte had a more accurate knowledge of every inlet on the Gulf than any other man.[13] There are also conflicting reports about his physical appearance, although most agree he was a muscular six feet two inches tall, with black hair and a characteristic moustache.

Jean Lafitte could speak fluently and correctly in English, French, Spanish, and Italian. According to Lyle Saxon, he possessed a warm personality and a natural ability to charm all that he met. He was well educated and could converse on almost any topic, including the New Orleans political scene. He seemed to know and understand the intricacies of Louisiana law better than the veteran politicians. These are outstanding qualities for anyone, but even more so for the young Lafitte, who was only twenty-four years old when he came to New Orleans.[14]

Jean Lafitte blended well with the Creole and Cajun cultures of the city. His accent and obvious French heritage facilitated his acceptance in the social and business communities.[15] Backed by the wealthy banker, Jean Baptiste Sauvinet, the Lafitte brothers opened a blacksmith shop on the Rue de St. Philips.[16] Shortly afterward they opened a second store, this one on Royal Street, that featured fine European goods. Although these were thriving businesses, they were only fronts to hide their real profession as pirates. The brothers had become very wealthy attacking Spanish ships in the Gulf and lived like aristocrats in a lavishly furnished mansion on the corner of Bourbon and St. Philip Streets.[17] Even with the façade of respectability, however, they were not deceiving anyone. The locals reportedly knew how the Lafittes came by their wealth, but chose to look the other way, so long as they continued to benefit from this popular charade.[18]

As Jean became more active in the Gulf, the chaotic way the pirates and privateers were haphazardly attacking ships was beginning to interfere with his own profits. After studying the pirates' operations, he realized the fortune that could be made if these renegades could be organized. If piracy was to survive in the Gulf, someone had to confront these vicious cutthroats. Only a man like Jean Lafitte would ever consider such a foolhardy thing.

While Pierre remained in the city, Jean Lafitte headed for Grand Terre.[19] Jean made his way into the lion's den. Upon arrival he was confronted by some of the most notorious ruffians in the Gulf. These included men like René Béluche and the infamous Dominique You, known as Captain Dominique, and the hot-tempered Italian, Vincent Gambi, a vicious killer who had slain many men with his broad-ax.[20] There was also Chighizola, one of the most feared pirates in the Gulf.[21] Chighizola was commonly called Nez Coupé (Cut Nose) after a fight in which a pirate's blade made a nasty gash across his face. In addition to these leaders there were between four and five hundred men and nearly two hundred women who were as ruthless and hardened as their male companions.

According to an embellished account taken from Herbert Asbury, Jean Lafitte, who had a natural ability to command attention whenever he entered a room, looked the bloody tyrants in the eyes and calmly listed his grievances. In effect he called them idiots to their faces, complaining how their thoughtless behavior not only was hurting his operations, but was costing themselves as well. He pointed out

Jean Lafitte the pirate blended well with the Creole and Cajun cultures of the city.

how their mindless forays into the Gulf were almost childish. The room was silent and the atmosphere so laced with tension that Jean could hear his heart pounding in his ears. He proceeded to call their actions stupid, but without receiving the angry retaliation one would expect from a group of ruffians. The pirates were beginning to fall under the spell of the great Jean Lafitte. The dull-headed thugs were easily persuaded by the logical plan Lafitte presented. It was hard to argue with common sense. Like organizing unruly teenagers who are looking for an authority figure to give them direction, Jean used his charm and ability to unify the various renegade bands of pirates into one combined force under his command.[22]

His organizational skills were such that within a short while he was running the pirate operations like a well-oiled machine. Over time, more and more of the pirates came to trust Lafitte and looked to him to tell them who to attack and when. After they saw their profits soar as a result of his proven leadership, they readily turned over all of their loot to him to distribute as he saw fit. Jean Lafitte had become the undisputed leader of the Baratarian pirates, and throughout his long reign, he never faced any meaningful opposition from his men.[23]

After his historic meeting with the pirates, Jean Lafitte moved to Grand Terre, where he built a brick mansion overlooking the water. It was the largest house on the island and was furnished with the finest European furniture, carpets and linens that the pirates could steal. In only a year he had a thousand men and fifty ships under his command, all flying the Cartagena flag.[24]

Pierre Lafitte remained in New Orleans and continued to operate the store and blacksmith shop, while Jean supplied him with a luxurious line of goods. As Lafitte's reputation continued to grow, the merchants would take the two-hour ride to Barataria to shop directly from Lafitte's stock. In the city, Pierre would take special orders using the Grand Terre warehouses like a catalogue operation. By 1813, Lafitte was supplying virtually all of the merchants in New Orleans with his hijacked goods.[25] With such control of the marketplace, it was almost impossible for any legitimate merchant to operate. After many complaints the United States government finally made some weak attempts to shut down the Lafitte operation, but the failure only served to increase Lafitte's reputation.

Back in Barataria, the governor of Louisiana, William C.C. Claiborne (1775–1817), was strongly against Lafitte and his operation and lobbied Washington to send help in closing him down.[26] The United States, which had suffered heavy losses as a result of the War of 1812, was not eager to participate in a distracting skirmish. Claiborne made a meager effort to break up Lafitte's operation, but with little success. While continuing to defy the governor, the Lafitte brothers became involved in a conspiracy to take over smuggling operations in Texas. A group from New Orleans — led by none other than Father Antonio de Sedella, Pierre Lafitte, and Don Juan Mariano Picornell, president of the Provisional Government of the Free Men of the Internal Province of Mexico — devised a plan to seize control of Galveston from the pirates operating there.[27]

With the onset of the British invasion of New Orleans, the plot was temporarily put on hold. After the war the scheme was revived, with the additional plan of opening a port on the Texas coast, not only as a base from which to attack other points in Texas but also as a safe haven for pirates and smugglers.[28] Louis-Michel Aury (1788–1821) was the leader of the Galveston pirates who were the targets of the Lafitte/Sedella plan.[29]

By 1816 Aury had established a settlement on the Galveston coast that served as a base of operations for his privateers who cruised the Gulf looking for prizes.[30] Described as "a terror to the Spanish at sea," he was born about 1788, and joined the French Navy at the age of fifteen, during which time he also served with French smugglers targeting Spain.[31] By 1810 he had accumulated enough bounty to own his own ships. While Aury was away on a raid in New Spain (Mexico), the group of New Orleans plotters refined the plan and Jean Lafitte went to Galveston to organize a government for the city. Two weeks later Lafitte returned to New Orleans to report to Father Antonio and to confer with Felipé Fatio, who had been called from Cuba to direct the capture of Aury and his pirates.[32]

Aury returned to Galveston while Lafitte was in New Orleans. Working behind the scenes, Pierre Lafitte had already convinced so many of Aury's men to desert that Aury no longer had any power. Realizing the futility of trying to regain control of Galveston from the colorful Lafitte, Aury abandoned his operations there. Lafitte returned to Galveston in 1817 after his pardon in the Battle of New Orleans and remained in control of the city, making it his new center for smuggling and privateering.[33]

While operating in Barataria, Jean Lafitte owned a home for several years on the beach in Waveland, Mississippi, at 649 North Beach Boulevard. The two-story, white-frame house that was situated across the sound from Cat Island later became known as "the Pirate House" because of Lafitte.[34] The house was supposedly owned by Jean Lafitte and used for his operations on the Coast. Although no one can confirm he ever actually lived there, it is believed he visited the house and Cat Island quite often.[35]

I had the personal pleasure of touring the Pirate House in 1962 before hurricane Camille demolished it completely in 1969. I was working as a consultant to the owners Mr. and Mrs. Borjn Lister, and knowing of my interest in Coast history, Mr. Lister invited me to visit the house. As we made our way through each of the rooms, I could feel the spirit of those old buccaneers in every nook and cranny. The secret closets in the house and the tunnel that supposedly at one time ran from the basement to the open waters of the Mississippi Sound had long been dismantled, but I was assured that those architectural secrets did at one time exist. The owner pointed out to me all of the existing evidence of the house's notorious past. The walls of what would have been the windowless dungeon were black and obviously quite old and worn. They were constructed of heavy cypress timbers. Although the room now had the appearance more of a sub-cellar than a torture chamber, there were iron spikes driven approximately two feet apart in the cypress walls at a height suggesting that shackles were once attached. The ceiling of the room was less than seven feet tall, accentuated by heavy crossbeams. Behind the brick wall at the front of the house, Mr. Lister opened a small door that looked more like the opening to a closet than a normal room. Inside was a darkened hallway that I was told was the remnant of the once fabled tunnel leading to the Gulf. As there were no lights in the structure I was cautioned not to enter. Mr. Lister explained that this passageway no longer went to the Gulf, but rather ended not far past the front of the house.

Finally in September 1814, after constant pleading, the United States agreed to help Louisiana clear up the piracy just before the impending Battle of New Orleans.[36] Under the command of commodore Daniel Todd Patterson (1786–1839) of the U.S. Navy, six large boats equipped with heavy artillery and several smaller armed vessels headed towards the Bay of Barataria. Lafitte and the pirates were aware of the Navy's presence, but gave it little notice, believing that the fleet's mission was to further engage the British.[37]

The pirates were totally taken by surprise when the first guns were fired. Scrambling to regroup, they found themselves in the midst of a heated battle. In the end the buccaneers were no match for the U.S. Navy. Ultimately the colony on Grand Terre was destroyed, with many of the pirates taken captive, including René Béluche and Dominique You. Although many were captured or killed, a large number of pirates were able to escape into the swamps, including Jean and Pierre Lafitte.

Just days before the attack, a British ship had anchored in the Barataria Bay off the island of Grand Terre. The commander had been sent as an emissary of the British government to meet with Jean Lafitte.[38] They knew of Lafitte's reputation and knowledge of the water routes into the city of New Orleans and had come to persuade Lafitte to join with the British in the impending battle. Lafitte was offered thirty thousand dollars in gold, an

What appears to be an old pirate's chest can be seen in the lower right corner of this interior view of the Pirate House (courtesy of the Hancock Historical Society with special thanks to Russell Guerin for his extensive research into the history of the Pirate House).

unbelievably large amount of money for the times, if he would agree to lead the British through the intricate marshes and shallow spots of the Rigolettes into Lake Borgne.[39] In addition, he was also promised a commission as an officer in the British Navy. Lafitte questioned the commander about the details of the attack on New Orleans, and after garnering as many of the details as possible, he asked for a few days to consider the offer.

Once the British ship had left the bay, Lafitte immediately sent word to Governor Claiborne requesting a meeting. When the two men were face to face, Lafitte laid out the British plans to attack New Orleans. Claiborne believed the pirate and sent an urgent message to Washington. Not only did Jean Lafitte disclose the details of the attack, but he also offered to fight on the side of the United States. Washington was not as convinced about Lafitte's warning and ordered Patterson to continue with the planned attack on Grand Terre without even answering Lafitte's offer to help.[40]

After the destruction of the pirates' compound, the Lafitte brothers fled to New Orleans, where Jean again contacted Governor Claiborne, making him the same offer to fight with the Americans. This time General Andrew Jackson, who was still in Mobile, personally rejected the offer, considering the pirates to be untrustworthy. Jackson's response took on a different tone when he finally arrived in New Orleans and saw what a ragtag group of

The dining room in the Pirate House was filled with antiques reminiscent of the 1800s (courtesy of the Hancock Historical Society with special thanks to Russell Guerin for his extensive research into the history of the Pirate House).

semi-trained civilians he had to fend off the powerful British. Jackson contacted Lafitte and accepted his offer. All of the pirates that had been captured were released into Jackson's army, including Lafitte's lieutenants Dominique You and René Béluche.[41]

Without the Baratarians the U.S. would have had little chance for success in the Battle of New Orleans. After the British were defeated, both Governor Claiborne and General Jackson informed President James Madison (1751–1836) of the heroic service of Lafitte and his men. On January 21, 1815, Andrew Jackson sent the following summary to the president describing the pirates' service to America:

> Captains Dominique and Béluche, lately commanding privateers at Barataria, with part of their former crews and many brave citizens of New Orleans, were stationed at Batteries Three and Four. The general cannot avoid giving his warm approbation of the manner in which these gentlemen have uniformly conducted themselves while under his command, and of the gallantry with which they redeemed the pledge they gave at the opening of the campaign to defend the country. The brothers Lafitte have exhibited the same courage and fidelity, and the general promises that the government shall be duly apprised of their conduct.[42]

President Madison agreed with the assessment of the men's service and in recognition of their heroic involvement in the Battle of New Orleans, issued a complete pardon on February 6, 1815, to Lafitte, his brother, and all of the Baratarian pirates who had patriotically defended America.[43] After years of piracy in the Gulf of Mexico these dangerous privateers had not only earned their freedom, but became duly authorized citizens of the United States. The once-feared Jean Lafitte, "the terror of the Gulf," along with his associates, Dominique You, René Béluche, Cut Nose Chighizola, and even the ferocious Gambi were no longer enemies of the state.

Unfortunately, once a pirate always a pirate, so Jean and Pierre continued with the only profession they knew. Lafitte first tried to set up a new operation at Port-au-Prince, Haiti, but was unsuccessful.[44] The governor of that city would have nothing to do with a group of cutthroats and thugs and forced Lafitte and his crew to move on. After a few more years of wandering throughout the Gulf in search of a new base, Lafitte landed on an island off the coast of Texas that was already the base of several pirates. He had already been involved with the leader of the pirates on the island, Louis Aury. In fact, it was Lafitte who named the island after the once Spanish governor of Louisiana, Bernardo de Gálvez.[45] Over time the name Galvez-town was commonly known as Galveston and quickly became even more popular with pirates, privateers and hardened criminals than the infamous Grand Terre.

The United States was no longer willing to overlook the pirates' activities, having already given Lafitte and his men a more than grateful opportunity to reform. Washington again shut down the pirates' colony, forcing Lafitte to leave the island of Galveston.[46] The once heroic Jean Lafitte ended up in a seedy shack on a small island off the coast of Yucatan. At the relatively young age of forty-seven he contracted a fever and within days the great pirate was dead, alone and forgotten.

There have always been stories circulating about the Lafitte treasure that may still be hidden somewhere on Cat Island. Speculation was strengthened in the late 1800s when a party of four men from New Orleans arrived on the island with the expressed intention of locating the loot.[47] Catherine Garriga Cuevas related the following episode, which was also reported by Frank Heiderhoff in the *New Orleans Sunday Times*.[48] The men anchored their small boat at the entrance to South Bayou and went inland about thirty feet from the shoreline. The area was a clearly defined circle of tall pine trees that appeared to have been notched. After a long period of digging, one of the men struck something solid in the soft sand. On all fours, they dug with their hands, as the sand would flow back into the hole almost faster than they could dig. Finally an old box was recovered. Breaking the rusted lock, they discovered a jumble of loose silverware. After rummaging through the pile they uncovered bars of silver hidden underneath the forks and spoons. The estimated worth at that time based on the description was approximately $20,000. According to Catherine Cuevas, there was a lighthouse inspector on the island who had been meeting with Ramon Cuevas, the lighthouse keeper at that time. Cuevas and the inspector happened upon the men just as they were loading the stash into their boat. Ramon stopped the men and asked for an explanation. The men described what they had been doing. After realizing the Cuevas family owned the island, they showed only a single item of the silver before immediately casting off. Ramon and the inspector returned to the lighthouse after seeing the broken pieces of the box that were lying near the hole. The Cuevas children had passed that spot on many occasion, but never thought to dig for treasure.[49]

Another person who was convinced there was pirates' gold on Cat Island was a Mister Andrew J. Newell. Newell's body was found in Lake Pontchartrain near Fort Pike, apparently the victim of foul play. An article that appeared in the *Bay St. Louis Gazette* shortly after the corpse was found describes the man's attempted trip to Cat Island.

> We had the pleasure of a visit from Andrew J. Newell, a New Orleans typo from the Picayune office, who, longing for a week's recreation from the ceaseless toil of the printing office, concluded to indulge in a sailing excursion to Cat Island opposite Bay St. Louis. He started in a trim little craft that has often figured with credit in seacoast regattas. Sailing leisurely through Lake Pontchartrain, Chef Menteur and Lake Borgne, he came in due time to Bay St. Louis, where he anchored his boat near Martin's wharf, and hunted up like a true type — the Gazette offices, where he made such a pleasing impression by his entertaining and intelligent conversation that we insisted on his remaining over night at our house, which he did. But, alas! For the treachery of wind and wave! That night a sudden and furious flaw from the west stirred up the water along the beach into angry fury, tore his boat from her cable, threw her against the wharf, and washed out all the contents — provisions, bedding, cooking utensils, etc. Mr. Newell saw himself reluctantly compelled to forego his pleasant trip, and return home on the mail boat.[50]

Although no treasure was found at that time, Andrew Newell made a statement to the *Gazette* that his intention for visiting the island was not only for fishing and hunting, but also for seeking the buried treasure.[51] Mr. Newell was convinced it existed. Why and how he was killed and the body dumped in Lake Ponchartrain was not reported.

With these and other stories continually surfacing in the local newspapers in the past, it has only been in recent history that the actual search for the treasure has pretty much subsided. The idea, however, continues to be a dull possibility in the back of the minds of some visitors to Cat Island who have heard the story of Jean Lafitte and his pirates.

The James Copeland Gang

Jean Lafitte was not the only pirate thought to have buried treasure on Cat Island. It is believed that James Copeland, south Mississippi's notorious outlaw, also hid some of his loot in the marshes of the island.[52] Although he was not a pirate in the true sense of the word, he was often called a land pirate for committing the same heinous crimes on shore that the infamous pirates of history committed on the open seas. Some of the Cuevas family witnessed suspicious activity on Cat Island, and later others recalled seeing mysterious signs scratched in some of the trees that could indicate members of the Copeland clan were regular visitors to their island home.

Born in Jackson County near the Pascagoula River on January 18, 1823, James Copeland began associating with the wrong crowd even before his teens. As a teenager he became quite an accomplished thief and would always succeed in one way or another in stealing what he wanted. He was a master at manipulation and delighted in telling lies about his classmates just to see them punished. He would often set up an innocent victim to cover for the crimes of one of his friends.[53]

After his first major arrest, he became involved with Gale H. Wages, an infamous criminal in Mobile.[54] The young James joined Wages, who was the head of a band of sixty rogues, many who were wealthy businessmen, and who were never suspected by the community because of their cloak of respectability.

The Wages clan was able to avoid the law by a number of methods, but the most valuable was a secret language using a new alphabet designed by James Murrell (1806–1845), another petty thief who was somewhat notorious in the Mississippi territory.[55] Over time Copeland learned every water hideout and slip along the coast as well as he knew the land, including the area of Cat Island known as Smugglers Cove. One day while gathering their crab traps in the inlet, Ramon Cuevas and his sister Pauline, each about thirty years old at the time, heard voices coming from a clump of pines. Later they recalled seeing four white men on a boat that had anchored in the shallow waters, and tied to the mast were two black men, who were struggling to free themselves.[56] Realizing this was not a matter they could handle, Ramon and Pauline quickly retreated to the center of the island. When they were able to return with other members of the family for support, the boat was no longer in sight.

After learning about the Copeland gang, they believed the men were more than likely the two brothers, Jim and Wash Bilbo, along with two other brothers, Jim and Jack McArthur.[57] The four had recently joined the outlaws, and had been assigned by Copeland to work the area between the Pearl River and Pascagoula. With these men in charge of this location, the gang could pass horses, or Negroes, from Georgia through Florida and along the Gulf Coast on to Louisiana and back again without being discovered. Ramon and Pauline had apparently witnessed two hapless Negroes suffering at the hands of the Copeland thugs. After witnessing this incident, the Cuevas family began calling this part of Cat Island, Negro Point. The name was eventually changed to Good Scotch Point, partially out of political correctness, but mostly after the rumrunners began using the island as a hiding place for their booze.[58]

In the mid 1840s Gale Wages was killed by James Harvey, an angry victim of one of the gang's swindles.[59] To avenge his fallen mentor, James Copeland, along with some of the gang, tracked Harvey down, and after a local version of the gunfight at the O.K. Corral, Harvey was killed. James Copeland was eventually captured, convicted of Harvey's murder and hanged.[60]

Copeland made it clear that he and his gang had hidden the spoils of their crimes in barrels or brass pots in various places between New Orleans and Mobile. Since his death, people have mostly searched in vain for some of his loot. In the 1980s, however, a barrel was discovered by one of the treasure hunters in a swamp near Pascagoula. The barrel contained $22,000, and sparked a new interest in the search for the Copeland gang's hidden cash.[61]

Sometime during the 1840s while Juan de Cuevas was still alive, some of the family

James Copeland, the notorious outlaw, went to the gallows on October 30, 1857, after a lifetime of crime.

told of seeing strange markings that had been carved on some of the trees in the Middle Bay area in the center of the island.[62] Those who saw them speculated at the time that they appeared to be more than just random etchings. When it was learned that the Copeland gang had a secret alphabet, it was believed that these strange carvings could very well be part of their special code. It was never known whether these marks were meant as direction signs to the buried treasure, since they were never deciphered. From that time on, however, many of the old people on the Coast have believed that one day part of the Copeland treasure would be unearthed on Cat Island.

The story of Jean Lafitte continues, as he becomes even more involved with the Cuevas family on Cat Island. We shall see how the legend of Juan de Cuevas and the actions of Lafitte become intertwined.

6

The Hero of Cat Island

The story of Juan de Cuevas and his confrontation with the British just before the Battle of New Orleans is the most significant event in the colorful history of Cat Island. The story was well known to the early families on the Coast, but many today may be unfamiliar with the tale of how this lone Spaniard faced the largest foreign invasion force to ever attack the mainland of the United States.

The following is a narrative retelling of the Juan de Cuevas saga. As with any legend, much of it is folklore. Later, in Chapter 15, I will separate the fact from fiction, and explain how the truth became a legend. But for now, this is the story of the hero of Cat Island that has been passed down for generations.[1]

His thrilling story begins in Spain a short distance north of the Costa del Sol, in the town of Algámitas, where the white stucco buildings reflect the sun and dazzle the eye. Only on the cool shaded balconies is there respite from the heat. Here Juan José de Cuevas was born to Don Pedro Martin Lopez de Cuevas and Isavel Bautista—both from titled and wealthy families with political influence and recognition from the king of Spain. Members of the families had been great Spanish poets and writers whose works are found in libraries throughout Europe. Juan received his education from specially selected tutors in the expectation that he would bring further honor and privilege to his family through his own literary accomplishments. A man's birth sets expectations for his life, but life is unpredictable.

Spanish colonies in the New World began growing independently from Spain, partly because they could obtain much-needed goods from other countries, causing King Charles III, who ruled at that time, to fear losing control of the colonies. In response he placed restrictions on commerce, resulting in prohibitively high prices of imported goods from other European countries, in Spain as well as in the colonies. An illicit trade with English, French, and Dutch smugglers developed to solve the problem.[2] It was these circumstances and his meeting of Friar Antonio de Sedella (1748–1829) which changed young Juan's life.

Father Antonio was a close friend of Juan's parents and the favorite priest of King Charles. Although loyal to his king, Father Antonio opposed the government's policy on foreign goods, believing the increase in prices harmed the Spanish people. The king would not listen to his ideas about the necessity of purchasing from other countries, which led Sedella to begin working with the smugglers to provide the much needed goods to the people of Andalucía. Otherwise he was a strong supporter of the king and later delivered a magnificent eulogy at his funeral rites. In recognition of this great tribute, King Charles IV (1788–1808), the successor to the throne, bestowed upon Father Antonio the title of "His Majesty's Honorary Preacher" (Orator).[3]

Born at Sedella, a small Spanish community located in the diocese of Málaga not far from Juan's home, Father Antonio was baptized Francisco Ildefonse Mareno in the same parish as the Cuevas family. After joining the priesthood, Mareno was given the name of Reverend Father Antonio de Sedella. He became attracted to the work of preaching and spiritual ministrations among the poor and joined the Capuchin Order.[4] The Capuchins are the only permanent offshoot of the Franciscans. They became one of the chief factors in the Catholic Counter-Reformation. Working tirelessly, they won the hearts and minds of the common people by the great poverty and austerity of their lives. As a result they were extraordinarily successful in converting Protestants to Catholicism all over Europe and in America.[5]

When Juan became old enough to be trusted with such dangerous information, he learned that his parents were also supportive of the smugglers. They met with Father Antonio and the smugglers' leaders in the Cuevas home, coordinating the details of their clandestine activities. In evenings by the hearth, Juan listened to Father Antonio share thrilling tales of their adventures. Feeding Juan's imagination were images of storms at sea, crossing mountains in darkness, and eluding soldiers.

One evening after the adventurous tales had been told, the conversation turned to the suffering of the people of Andalucía before the smugglers began bringing in goods. Listening, almost unnoticed in the shadows of the fire, Juan was enthralled by Father Antonio's passionate speech about the need to put humanity above government. Juan knew he would never be a poet. He would never fulfill the dreams of his parents and tutors. Standing up for what is right, living an adventurous life—this was the course Juan set for himself. He resolved to join the smugglers for the good of Spain and the well-being of its people!

The next morning Juan confided in Father Antonio, who took the eighteen-year-old's ambition seriously. The priest introduced Juan to Michel, the smugglers' leader. Impressed with the young Spanish noble's ability to speak and read Spanish, French, and English, as well as his knowledge of sailing and his proficiency in math, Michel knew Juan would be a beneficial addition to his crew. Knowing his parents would never agree, Juan stole away in the predawn hours, following Michel through the mountains to his ship hidden away at the western end of the Strait of Gibraltar in the Gulf of Cádiz. Winding through the villages of Ubrique, Alcalá de los Gazules and Medina Sidona, the men followed the route known as La Ruta del Toro (Route of the Bull), passing many of the ranches that bred the mean, black toros bravos (fighting bulls).

Juan found his place in the world: sailing to the French coast, loading cargo, sailing back to Spain to unload at midnight, moving goods through the mountains, hiding in caves when soldiers approached, living always in an exciting and dangerous male milieu. His intelligence and enthusiasm earned him the place of a trusted aide, whose ideas and innovations were invaluable.

Unfortunately, a few months later, Juan's adventures ended abruptly in a cove below Las Alpujarras. Betrayed by a villager, the smugglers were captured by soldiers and transported to a prison in Granada. Juan remained there for several months, in a grimy cell with no outside windows, until Father Antonio heard of his capture and sent word to Juan's family in Algámitas.

Charles III, a passionate hunter, was in residence at Coto Doñana, a hunting estate in

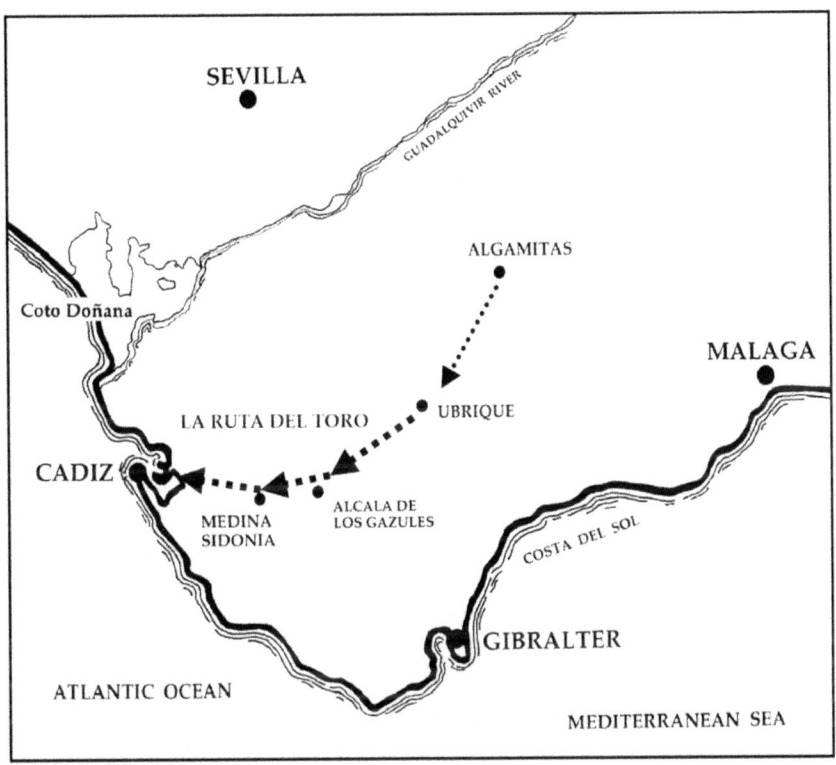

This is the route reportedly taken by Juan de Cuevas and the smugglers to the port of Cadiz.

the delta of the Guadalquivir. As members of the nobility, the Cuevas family had influence that would gain Don Pedro an immediate audience, so he rushed to Coto Doñana, hoping the king's mood would be generous after a day spent hunting in the marshes. Charles was known for his cynical view of mankind and his caustic tongue, making Don Pedro fearful of the king's reaction. Would Charles be lenient with this poor boy that had openly defied the king? Fortunately, due to his great regard for Don Pedro, whose olive groves had provided the monarch with a great deal of cash, King Charles softened his hard stance. Young Juan was offered a choice. Not ideal, but at least it was a choice. Spain needed men to continue the exploration and settlement of her new territories across the Atlantic. Juan could choose to go to prison or to join the military and be stationed at the fort in Florida. Both choices were life sentences. If he chose prison, he would spend the rest of his life behind bars, and if he chose the military, he would never be allowed to return home to Spain. Wishing to cause no further embarrassment for his respected family, Juan chose the life of a soldier knowing he would never see his family again.

After his release from prison, Juan was escorted directly to the port in Málaga where a ship was waiting to carry him and his fellow soldiers across the Atlantic Ocean to the Florida territory. Juan learned he would be part of the troops sent to help the Spanish governor Bernardo de Galvez defeat the British and recapture Fort St. Miguel in Pensacola. A worthy and exciting goal! Juan looked forward to his encounters with adventure in the New World.

Over a month later, Juan had his first glimpses of Florida as the ship sailed down and around the peninsula. Surf broke on the beaches, reminding him of the southern coast of Spain. But beyond the water, the tropical wilderness was like nothing seen in Andalucía. He heard tales about the fierceness of the alligators sunning at the edges of the swamps. He learned about the annoyance of mosquitoes. He was eager to reach Pensacola and explore this exotic land. Yet, he was most eager for the thrill of his first battle!

At the start of the Revolutionary War (1776–1881), Spain joined its European ally, France, in a declaration of war against the British, although for no particular reason relating to the British-American conflict. Spain never really got involved in the American war of independence, although it was always looking for ways to antagonize the British. After successful naval victories at Baton Rouge and Mobile Bay, Spanish Governor-General Galvez saw an opportunity to retake the Spanish fort at Pensacola, which had come under control of the British. King Charles sent a ship of new recruits from Spain to help with the attack.

The ship carrying Juan de Cuevas landed on Santa Rosa Island at the entrance to Pensacola Bay. As new recruits, Juan and his unit were to protect the rear of the Spanish forces from the British as the Spanish Armada made its way into the bay. There was concern that once the Spanish ships began their attack of the fort, British warships might try to come in from behind and surround the attacking forces. When the battle began, the noise was disorienting and the thick smoke from the gunpowder made it hard to see. The fighting enveloped the recently arrived soldiers, who found themselves involved in the main battle to capture the fort. When it was over, the Fort called San Miguel de Panzacola had been retaken and the British military presence in Florida was finished. Spanish prisoners and soldiers then staffed the presidio, which was the last of three military posts built there since the first Spanish occupation in 1668. This post developed into current-day Pensacola. As a part of the Treaty of Paris (1783) England formally ceded the rest of its Florida territory to Spain.

During the intense fighting, Juan had accounted for more than his share of enemy troops without ever coming close to being wounded. Perhaps Juan's months as a smuggler had given him a special awareness. Whatever the reason, he had easily followed the chaotic action of the battle. After completing his first successful military confrontation, the young soldier knew he was destined for a life of adventure.

In the early summer of 1781, Governor Galvez moved a small number of troops, including Juan, from Pensacola to Cat Island in order to scout the territory along the coast and report on the conditions of Spain's newly acquired land. Juan found a French family had been living on Cat Island for thirty-five years, the family of Nicholas Ladner dit (called) Christian. Juan, the only French-speaking soldier in his unit, developed a friendship with Ladner.

From the moment Juan arrived on the coast he fell in love with Cat Island. He explored the island's lagoons and canals, while enjoying the hospitality of the Ladner family. At the time of his first visit, Marie Helene, the second-youngest daughter of Nicholas Ladner, was only six years old. Marie was a charming and affectionate child who spent most of her time in her father's company. Juan and Nicholas often included her in their conversations.

After several months on Cat Island, the Spanish troops returned to Pensacola with their report. Action was never taken by the Spanish government to use the island as an outpost, but Juan often returned whenever on leave. By 1790, Juan realized he visited the Ladner family as much to see the beautiful young Marie Helene as to visit with Nicholas. Marie, who was growing into a very mature young lady, always arranged to spend most of her time with Juan whenever he was on the island, and the young Spaniard dared to hope she felt the same ardor for him that he felt for her.

Juan loved soldiering, but now he had a greater passion. He sent a request to Charles III for release from the military, asking his father to intervene with the king. It took several years, but Juan was finally a civilian again, although forbidden to return to Spain. The thought of never seeing his family again was distressing, but Juan had a new home, a new dream. In 1794, Juan José de Cuevas and Marie Helene Ladner were married. Juan was thirty-two and Marie was nineteen. Shortly after their marriage, Nicholas Ladner moved his family to their new home site on the mainland, leaving Cat Island to Juan and Marie.

The new couple took over the old Ladner home and stocked the island with cattle. The cattle thrived on the rich marsh grass and soon Cuevas beef was in demand from Mobile to New Orleans. With the island's heavily wooded areas Juan built charcoal kilns, furnishing fuel to the city markets. Their prosperity allowed Juan to buy slaves to help him work the land. Over the next thirty-five years, he became one of the wealthiest men on the Coast.

The Cuevas family developed many friendships along the Coast, including Jean Lafitte, the infamous leader of the Baratarian pirates. Juan was well aware that Lafitte often anchored his ships on the south side of Cat Island in what we now call Pirate's Cove. While Juan did not approve of Lafitte's nefarious activities, he admired the pirate's bravery and envied Lafitte's adventures. An affection and trust developed between the two men, as Juan turned a blind eye to the illegal booty that the pirates stashed on Cat Island. Part of his attraction to Lafitte was Juan's own desire for an adventurous life. Realizing that his dreams of the open seas would never again be a reality for him, he reveled in Lafitte's stories. Juan and Marie were living a dream-life on their island paradise. Events on the rest of the continent had little effect on them, not even the War of 1812.

Early on the morning of December 8, 1814, Juan left the house to begin the day's activities. As he approached the southern side of his island, he realized something unusual was happening. An eighty-gun war ship had dropped anchor in the dark gray water off nearby Ship Island and Juan could see the outline of other ships stretching out into the Mississippi Sound. A British expeditionary force arrived, hoping to strike a surprise blow to New Orleans. The fleet had landed to seek information since British maps weren't sufficient to guide them through the tricky shallows, passes, and marshes inherent in the Lake Borgne route to New Orleans.

The Cuevas family also observed five small warships moving east along their coastline. They recognized the flag with fifteen stars and fifteen stripes as American. They did not know the commander of this small fleet was Lieutenant Thomas Catesby Jones, but they knew he and his men were patrolling the coast in anticipation of the British arrival. The family knew British ships were already anchored to the south, in the channel between Cat and Ship Islands.

The American ships rowed past the Cuevas family home and headed toward the southeastern peninsula, now known as Goose Point. It was apparent that the fleet planned to circle around and continue its patrol on the south side of Cat Island. Just three days earlier, there had been only a handful of British ships in total. Now there were fifty war ships along with hundreds of transport and supply ships. Neither the Cuevas family nor Lieutenant Jones knew the personnel count (10,000 sailors, 1,500 British marines, and 9,000 battle-proven soldiers who had recently defeated Napoleon), but neither one of them had ever seen such an awesome array before. So many enormous enemy ships silhouetted against a grey sky presented an unearthly appearance, almost as if hundreds of UFOs had suddenly landed in the Gulf.

The American gunboats immediately began to row away, hoping to avoid a confrontation. The Americans would try to reach Fort Petite Coquilles in the Rigolets to warn New

Orleans about the vast British armada. Once the American boats were spotted, the British lowered forty-five boats, manned by twelve hundred sailors and marines. The hard-rowing British must have seemed to fly toward the American gunboats, whose crews had already been rowing for hours. If the Americans had sails on board, they would have been no help since the day was unusually calm. The boats were surely still in sight of Cat Island when the British came within range of the American gunboats.

The Americans opened fire. The British responded. The noise thundered over Cat island like the world was about to end. Juan and Marie and their children watched the battle rage for three hours. When it was over, the British brought their prisoners, including Lieutenant Jones, and the gunboats to Cat Island. British scouting expeditions had been sent out to find fresh vegetables and meats. Instructions to the men were to pay for everything they took and noted that they were not to molest the residents. Juan was willing to sell beef to the British since he owed no allegiance to the United States. He assumed the British would negotiate for his cattle.

Three days later, while hunting, Juan heard shots from the south side of the island. He discovered three British soldiers and a Chinese cook shooting his cattle. Ordering them to stop and explain themselves, Juan aimed his weapon. Instead of explanations, the men turned and fired. In retaliation, Juan wounded one of the soldiers and killed the cook before being brought down by a shot to the leg.

Helene and Brigitte, Juan's eldest daughters, had also heard the shots and came running to assist just as their father fell. Juan insisted the girls not fire at the British. These soldiers were clearly not obeying orders and Juan would not risk his daughters' lives. He ordered the girls to return home and warn the family not to resist, sending word to Marie to keep the children indoors until the commanding officers heard of the situation and took control.

The soldiers, taking Juan prisoner, transported him to the flagship, where he was imprisoned in the hold. The admiral was informed that a prominent citizen had been taken prisoner and ordered Juan's wound to be tended. Aware that Juan could probably guide them to New Orleans, the admiral and his senior officers received Juan in the admiral's quarters and offered a formal apology. They spoke of giving Juan his freedom, and of compensation for his losses — all of which Juan expected. What he hadn't expected were the conditions attached. The admiral wanted Juan to guide the fleet through the shallow marshes of Lake Borgne to the Rigolets, then into the heart of the city of New Orleans via Lake Pontchartrain. Hints of retribution against Juan's family as well as confiscation of his property were intended to be further incentives. To the surprise of the British officers, Juan de Cuevas refused.

Being neither American nor British, Juan had no intention of becoming involved in the current war until he saw his cattle being slaughtered. Now, having been personally attacked by British soldiers and threatened by British officers, Juan felt a new kinship with the Americans resisting British invasion. As in his youth, Juan chose the course he believed to be right.

Juan lied to the British officers, denying that he knew the route through Lake Borgne. Not believing him, the soldiers tore the shirt from his back and lashed him repeatedly with leather straps. The strong-willed Spaniard continued to insist he was ignorant of a passage through the marshes. Convinced Juan could help them if he wanted to, the British poured vinegar and salt on his back where the whips had lacerated his skin. Still Juan insisted he did not know the route! He was then returned to the hold, where he languished for several days. Finally a junior officer came to tell Juan that British soldiers had surrounded his family and home. Knowing Marie's fiery temper and realizing his children would be anxious to fight the British, Juan devised a new plan. Pretending to give in, he again told the British he couldn't guide them through Lake Borgne. However, he could lead them to the Mississippi River, navigating the marshes at the mouth of the river, and from there, on to New Orleans. The fleet set sail with Juan in the bow of the flagship pointing the way.

With every movement, Juan felt his resolve reinforced by pain from the lacerations. So, with no intention of taking the fleet to the Mississippi River, which was some distance south of them, he instead led them west, straight into Lake Borgne — an area he knew well, in spite of his assertions to the contrary. Juan led the ships through the misty marshes of Lake Borgne to the mouth of the Pearl River. The Pearl is a wide river, leading the British to believe they had reached the Mississippi. As the huge flagship ventured through the mists into the shallow waters, Juan waited nervously for the inevitable.

The ship moved slowly upstream, followed closely by the rest of the fleet. As they left the marshes of Lake Borgne behind, the mists began to clear and Juan began to worry — if the British could see the Pearl clearly, they would know they had been tricked. But the mist held long enough. The ship sailed into the top of a wide sandbar, her forward speed driving her starboard side deeply into the sand. Before the sailors understood what was happening, the ship lurched and tilted. Sailors and soldiers flew around the deck, some thrown overboard and many injured.

While attention was focused away from him, Juan slipped over the port side rail. The splash of his hitting the water was unnoticed over the noise of shouting sailors. He swam quickly to the western shore and moved into the pine woods lining the bank. Once hidden from the sight of anyone on the ships, Juan began to run. He knew where a group of friendly Indians were camping and he thought he could reach their site before the British realized he was missing.

At the camp, the Indians wanted to treat Juan's wounds but he insisted he could not take the time. He asked only to borrow a pirogue. The Indians, who were resentful of the British for inciting the Chicasaw against them, were more than willing to help. They guided Juan to a stretch of shoreline where he could not be seen from the Pearl River and placed the pirogue into Lake Borgne. Juan, now between the ships and New Orleans, knew the route through the Rigolets.

Juan began to row, the effort causing his back to begin bleeding again. His shirt stuck to his bloody wounds and pulled away with each stroke. In great pain, Juan paddled. He was determined the British would be defeated. Once he reached the Rigolets, he found Americans stationed as lookouts to watch the Gulf for the approach of the British fleet. Juan was able to tell them the exact location of the fleet, its approximate strength, and the number and types of warships. This message was immediately relayed to officials in New Orleans.

General Andrew Jackson, arriving only days before the British fleet anchored at Ship Island, needed as much time as possible to prepare the people of south Louisiana for the coming battle. Lacking an army large enough to face the mighty British attackers, Jackson was forced to press into action every able-bodied male in the city. This ragtag army consisted of free Negroes, a band of Choctaw Indians, and the Baratarian pirates led by Jean Lafitte. Once he knew the approximate strength of the British fleet, Jackson was able to plan an effective defense.

The personal courage of Juan de Cuevas stopped the enemy from successfully attacking New Orleans before Jackson was ready to defend the city, saving the United States from

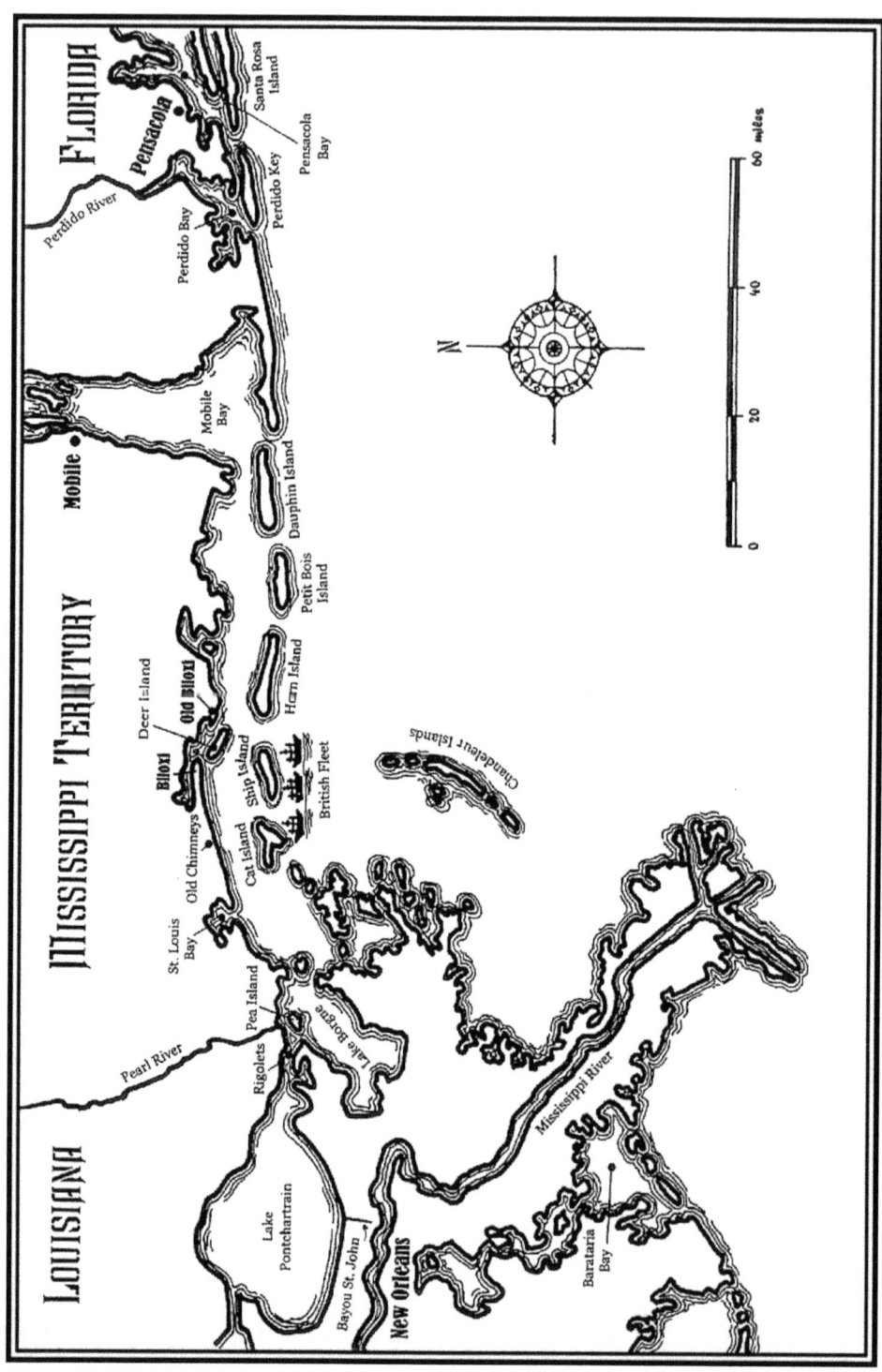

losing half a continent to Great Britain. After the Battle of New Orleans, the British — shattered and beaten — limped back to their base at Ship Island and released Juan's family before sailing away.

For Juan's act of moral and physical courage, a grateful United States government presented Juan de Cuevas and his descendants the whole of Cat Island tax-free forever. Thus ends the tale of Juan de Cuevas. Spaniard by birth and American by choice, this man exemplified the rugged individualism that made our country great. And although Andrew Jackson and Jean Lafitte have rightfully been hailed as heroes in the Battle of New Orleans, the legend tells how Juan de Cuevas actually fired the first shots against the British invaders.

Over the years, not all of the pirates that came ashore on Cat Island, however, were as exemplary as Jean Lafitte. In a lesser-known incident, Juan de Cuevas took action against two notorious brigands, proving once again that he was the true hero of Cat Island.

Opposite: Map of the Mississippi Gulf Coast c. 1812.

7

Juan de Cuevas Captures the Pirates

Juan de Cuevas is well known for his heroic stand against the British, but a second and lesser-known heroic event occurred one July day in 1820. The following is a narrative retelling of this brave man's capture of two pirates in the Gulf near his home on Cat Island.[1] Juan de Cuevas woke early and realized the world was silent. His family slept peacefully, the trees outside were still, and he could see on the floor a small sliver of light from the rising sun. The violent storm of the night before had ended. In an hour, his friend, Jacob Ferris, would arrive from the mainland to help harvest some oyster beds. Juan's island was once again peaceful, and life would be as usual.

Dressing quickly, he went outside and breathed in the smell of clean salt air. Juan would check on some of the storm damage before returning to have breakfast with his wife, Marie, and with Jacob, who took advantage of every opportunity to eat Marie's cooking.

The live oaks just outside the clearing did not seem to have any storm damage; the Spanish moss still hung daintily, unscathed. Juan walked through the plum orchard and noticed some small branches and fruit lying on the ground. Later he would send the children out to check all the orchards. They would rescue the fallen fruit that was still edible and pick up the debris.

He headed south, where the storm would have hit hardest. The beach proved him right. Mounds of driftwood lay tangled on the sand, a tattered piece of cloth waved from a patch of Bermuda grass, and a metallic object lay winking at him from further east. The shoreline had changed in places and Juan walked along it, noting each shift of water and sand. Soon he decided there was no significant damage. With his heart a little lighter, he stopped to watch the sun rising higher in the cloudless blue sky.

Then the wind shifted and he heard voices, ill-humored voices. Hurrying a bit, he climbed a sand dune for a better view. Amazingly, a schooner lay partway up on the sand. From her size, Juan judged she carried cargo and came from some distance. Probably headed for New Orleans. The only sign of life was two men desperately digging in the sand, trying to re-float the schooner.

Juan slid down the sand dune and hailed the men. They did not look up from their digging. As Juan got closer, he saw by their cuts and bruises that they had been battered by the storm, and their clothes were crusted with salt spray. But there was something besides the obvious results of fighting a storm, something about the men that made Juan look at them carefully. There were only two of them, yet they had not taken a dinghy to the mainland to get help. And when Juan showed up, they ignored him.

The schooner had come in at an angle, her stern toward Juan. As he walked past the ship toward the men, Juan passed near enough to the hull to hear strange sounds coming from inside. Thump ... and a scraping sound. Again, thump. He could hear a voice but it was muffled.

Juan squared his shoulders as he approached the digging men, stopping just short of them, suspicious that something was wrong. Introducing himself, he asked if he could be of help. The smaller man scowled and kept digging. The larger one turned his head slightly and then looked back at his work; he muttered something that sounded like "Mind your own business." Juan shrugged, hoping to give the impression of a man who did not care one way or the other, and turned back.

When he passed by the schooner again, he tapped twice on the hull. A loud muffled groan answered him. Nonchalantly Juan went back up the sand dune, but, on the other side, he headed straight into the pine woods that bordered the sand. Out of sight of the two men now, he began to run. The ground was slippery with wet pine needles, but still faster than walking on sand.

He arrived home to find Jacob Ferris already sitting at the breakfast table. Juan was glad his friend had arrived; Ferris had fought gallantly with General Jackson at the Battle of New Orleans and would be an able assistant in dealing with whatever was happening on the schooner. Juan told Jacob about the beached ship and the men digging her out. After hearing Juan's tale, Ferris agreed that someone was obviously on the ship. Regardless what else was going on, it sounded like someone might be hurt and in need of help.

Juan suggested they postpone breakfast until they had checked out the schooner. He gathered up rifles and rope, warning Marie to keep the children at home until the situation had been dealt with. Juan and Jacob ran around the vegetable garden, crossed the corner of the peach orchard, and skirted a thicket of yaupon holly. They ended up at the bottom of another sand dune directly behind the bow of the ship. Cautiously they crept up the dune and watched for a few moments. The two men were still digging. At Juan's signal, he and Ferris moved further down the beach and climbed aboard the stern of the schooner. They found a man chained hand and foot to the cabin floor, with a dirty cloth gag in his mouth. He looked as if he had been beaten before being chained. When they removed the gag and explained they were there to help, the man whispered, "Pirates," and lapsed into semi-consciousness.

Fearing the pirates might come back aboard at any moment, Juan led Ferris back to the beach. They quietly crept up behind the men and ordered them to surrender. The small man yelped in alarm, but the larger one took a swing at Juan. Juan swung his rifle butt and blocked the blow, then aimed his rifle at the two pirates and ordered them to lie on the sand. Ferris stepped to Juan's side and aimed his rifle at the pirates while Juan tied them hand and foot. They dragged the men toward the pines and tied the ropes around a tree.

Then they hurried back to the cabin, freed the prisoner, and carried him gently to the beach. After making sure the pirates were still secure, they carried the injured man to Juan's home and left him in Marie's care while they went back to get their prisoners. They marched the men through the woods and tied them, none too gently, to the trunk of the sturdy oak in front of the house. They found Marie had put the released prisoner to bed and was feeding him weak soup a tablespoon at a time. She had learned he was the captain of the schooner, but he had not been able to tell her what had happened aboard the ship.

After resting for a few hours, the captain was able to tell his story. The schooner had come from France with a load of silk for New Orleans. The two mutineers, John Baker and Martin Hogan, had overpowered him just before the storm and chained him in his cabin; he heard them talking about accomplices who would be waiting to help them transfer the silk to another ship. He did not know where that ship was waiting or what had happened to the other crewmembers. Juan and Ferris loaded the two pirates, John Baker and Martin Hogan, into a pirogue and rowed to the Bay of St. Louis, landing on the beach at Shieldsborough (now known as Bay St. Louis). They saw a group of men gathered at a nearby house and gestured for them to come help. Ferris offered to stay and help guard the pirates until the justice of the peace could be summoned; Ferris could then give evidence for holding the men until they could be tried.

Juan headed out to get help for the captain and the schooner. Once out of the bay, he headed west along the shoreline until he entered Lake Borgne. His intimate knowledge of the lake's shallow marshes enabled him to travel quickly and soon he was skirting Pea Island and entering the Rigolets and then Lake Pontchartrain. He found the offices of the insurance company for the shipping line and reported what had happened.

The insurance company came to Cat Island and took the captain and the silk back to New Orleans. John Baker and Martin Hogan were tried and convicted. One of the men, Martin Hogan, was executed, but John Baker escaped before his sentence was carried out.[2]

On November 24, 1821, the Senate and House of Representatives of the State of Mississippi approved an act recognizing the heroism of Juan de Cuevas and awarded him a reward of $200.[3] This is documented fact, not legend, and cannot be disputed. The state of Mississippi recognized Juan de Cuevas as a hero by an act of the State Legislature signed by Cowles Mead, speaker of the House of Representatives, and James Patton, lieutenant governor, president of the Senate.

The act said in part:

And whereas it is considered important to the interest of this Statethat persons should be encouraged in deeds of valor, humanity and patriotism such as this has been represented to have been specially in relation to the atrocious crimes committed on the high seas and sea coast.

Therefore, Be it enacted by the Senate and House of Representatives of the State of Mississippi in General Assembly convened that the sum of $200 (two hundred) be paid to Jean Quave (Juan Cuevas) for having detected and detained to justice John Baker and Martin Hogan for robbery committed in the Gulf of Mexico within this state out of any money in the state treasury not otherwise appropriated.

History has left us with only sketchy details of this and other events of the early Coast. Since few could write about themselves or their families, I was excited to learn of a British officer who returned to Cat Island only a day after the Battle of New Orleans had ended. He is the only person who ever met the Cuevas family living on the island, and the only person to have recorded his firsthand observations about Juan de Cuevas and his island home.

8

A British Officer Visits Cat Island After the War

I attended a cocktail party at work some years ago. Throughout the evening I moved about the guests engaging in mundane chatter and mindless conversations. Small talk is rarely meaningful at such social gatherings, but amidst the clinking glasses, phony jokes and contrived laughter, someone asked me a thought-provoking question. "If you could spend one hour with any person living or dead throughout history, who would you choose?" At first I dismissed the question, putting it in the same inane category as "What's your sign?" but throughout the evening the thought kept haunting me as I began to realize how exciting that would be. I could discuss with Thomas Edison his invention of the phonograph, while playing tunes for him on my iPod, or show Alexander Graham Bell the new cellular phones of today, and explain how to send a text message and receive an email. I could even question Juan de Cuevas about our family, Cat Island, and the early Mississippi Gulf Coast.

Sadly, meeting people from the past is impossible, but I was excited to discover the next best thing. I learned there was a man who had visited with Juan de Cuevas on Cat Island and wrote about the Cuevas family in a book about the War of 1812. British officer Lt. George Robert Gleig (1796–1888) made several trips to the Cuevas home only days following the Battle of New Orleans. Lieutenant Gleig's book is quite provocative since it is the only first-hand account by anyone who had a direct conversation with Juan de Cuevas during his lifetime, and more specifically during the timeframe of the historical controversy concerning the "Hero of Cat Island." I was hopeful that Gleig's book would answer some of the questions that have puzzled me over the years.

Lieutenant Gleig kept a detailed journal of his military experiences and also wrote extensive letters to his family. Drawing on those notes and letters, he became a frequent contributor to various reviews and magazines. One series of articles for *Edinburgh Magazine*[1] was later collected into a book titled *The Subaltern*.[2] The extent and depth of Lt. Gleig's writings have proven to be invaluable, but his works are not without controversy. *The Subaltern*, in particular, has been a source of dispute. It gives an overstated account of the war and includes events that Gleig could not have witnessed. He apparently colored the facts trying to present himself as a military strategist. But even with these acknowledged shortcomings, his diary and letters are considered mostly accurate and authentic. In his book, *The Campaigns of the British Army at Washington and New Orleans*,[3] Lt. George Robert Gleig wrote the following about his visits to the home of Juan de Cuevas:

> Nay, so great was the despondency which had taken possession of men's minds, that not even a rumor respecting the next point of attack, obtained circulation; while a sullen carelessness, assort of indifference as to what might happen, seemed to have succeeded all our wonted curiosity, and confidence of success, in every undertaking.
>
> In this state we remained wind-bound till the 4th of February [1815], when, at length, getting under weigh [sic], the fleet ran down as far as Cat Island. This is a spot of sandy soil at the mouth of the lake [Borgne] remarkable for nothing except a solitary Spanish family, which possesses it. Completely cut off from the rest of the world, an old man, his wife, two daughters and a son, dwell here in apparent happiness and contentment. Being at least one hundred and twenty miles from the main, it is seldom that their little kingdom is visited by strangers, and I believe that till our arrival, the daughters, though grown up to womanhood, had seen few faces besides those of their parents and brother. Their cottage, composed simply of a few boughs, thatched and in-woven with straw, is beautifully situated within a short distance of the water. Two cows, and a few sheep grazed beside it, while a small tract of ground covered with stubble, and a little garden well stocked with fruit trees and vegetables, at once gave proof of their industry, and showed the source from whence they supplied themselves with bread.
>
> It may appear childish, but I confess that the sight of domestic peace flourishing, as it were, in the midst of wars and tumults, extremely delighted me. While we continued at anchor, therefore, I paid frequent visits to this cottage, and forming a sort of acquaintance with the old man, soon possessed myself of his little history. He had emigrated from Spain many years ago, and married in America. Having been unsuccessful in business, he had saved from the wreck of his property only enough to hire laborers, by whose assistance his present cottage was erected, and his little farm cleared; when, with his wife and three children, then very young, he had withdrawn from society; and settled himself here, where he had remained ever since. Once a year, he or his son visited the main [sic] to sell their wool, and purchase such necessaries as their island could not produce; but excepting on these occasions, or when a fishing-boat arrived in his bay, which rarely occurred, he had had no intercourse with any human being, besides his own family, for a great lapse of time. As may be imagined, I found this tribe as simple in their ideas as in their mode of living. Of reading and writing all except the patriarch himself were ignorant, nor did they seem to waste a thought upon any subject not immediately connected with their bodily wants. They professed, indeed, to be Christians, and would have been probably shocked, had I questioned their claim to sound Catholicism, though I much doubt whether they in the slightest degree understood the meaning of either term.
>
> Having remained here till the 7th, we again took advantage of a fair wind, and stood to sea. As soon as we had cleared the lake, we directed our course towards the east, steering, as it was rumored, upon Mobile; nor was it long before we came in sight of the bay, which bears that name. This is formed by a projecting headland, called Point Bayo, in a large island called Isle de Dauphin. Upon the first is erected a small fort, possessing the same title with the promontory, which commands the entrance; for though the island is at least five miles from the main, there is no water for floating a ship of any burthen, except within a few hundred yards of the latter. The island is, like Cat Island, uninhabited, except by one family, and unprovided with any works of defense.[4]

After reading Lt. Gleig's description of the Cuevas family, I was disappointed because his observations were not consistent with the facts. The lieutenant's conspicuous mistakes raise some very intriguing questions. There is no doubt Lt. Gleig was writing about Juan de Cuevas although he was not mentioned by name, since Cat Island was the only barrier island owned by a Spanish family at the time. There are many questionable errors throughout the piece, but the most glaring is about the Cuevas children.

There were many more children living on the island than Gleig reported. In 1815, Juan and Marie had eleven children whose ages ranged from nineteen years to newly born. Where were all of these children? Marie's new baby, Henriette Pauline, born on February 2, 1815, just two days before Gleig's first visit to the Cuevas home, was not even mentioned. If Gleig had made frequent visits to the cottage, as he reported, how could he not know of a newborn baby? Some have said that the youngsters may have been staying on the mainland with their grandparents, the Ladners, while Marie gave birth to Henriette. This could well be true, since it was unheard of in the prudish society of the early 1800s for men to be present during the birth of a baby, even if the men were doctors. Young children were also removed during the birthing process to avoid the embarrassment of having to explain to inquiring minds where babies come from. But even if we accept this premise, it does not explain why the rest of the large family was not even mentioned, and it certainly does not explain why and how a new baby could be kept a complete secret.

Furthermore, there is no indication that the Cuevas family had intentionally isolated itself from society. Quite to the contrary, it is well known and reported that the Cuevas family gave large parties on the island that lasted for days. This is hardly what one would expect of someone who had withdrawn from the world. Gleig also got the impression that because of their seclusion the girls were socially naïve and had only seen a few other people. While it is true that the family probably did not have many visitors on a daily basis, to say that the children had seen only a few people is a stretch. There were other families living on the island at various times when the children were growing up, including the Greenbergs, J.B. Morin, Maturin Ladner and possibly others.[5] Furthermore, the Ladner family was quite large and certainly came in contact with the Cuevas children. There must have been a reason that Juan de Cuevas led Gleig to believe that he and Marie had only three children, and that this small group was so isolated from current events they had no knowledge of the British or the war.

Gleig was also told that Juan de Cuevas was a failure in business when all published accounts report that Juan was very successful in raising cattle for markets from Mobile to New Orleans. In fact, it is known that the Cuevas herd grazed on the rich marsh grass on the far end of the island, yet Gleig was only aware of two milk cows and a few sheep kept in a pen near the Cuevas house. Otherwise why were the cattle not mentioned?

It was no surprise that Lt. Gleig learned of the Cuevas family's strong religious faith. Juan grew up in Spain, a country that was, and is to this day, 90 percent Catholic. The Ladners were also staunch Catholics, as were the great majority of the early European settlers. Catholicism and Christianity were one and the same to these people, and for them to try to separate the two would have made no sense. Gleig was obviously unaware that their religion was not based on the understanding and acceptance of a certain religious precept or philosophy; Catholicism simply meant serving God in the only way they knew how. To them it was not just their religion — it was an integral part of their culture and their way of life.

Although it is widely reported that Lt. Gleig had a propensity for skewing the truth in his writings, he would have had nothing to gain by fabricating this story. But, if he was only reporting what he saw, is it possible he was deliberately misled? If he learned Juan's "little history" as the book reports, why did that not include the entire family, the existence of Juan's cattle, and the truth about the family's isolation?

It appears that Juan de Cuevas may have intentionally made up a story about his life to deceive the British officer. Juan could have pretended to be just a naïve old Spaniard who had cut himself off from the rest of the world and whose "small" family hardly ever saw another living soul. Juan may have played the part of a broken old man who had lost everything. But, if this were so, why would Juan go to such lengths to deceive this stranger?

The story of Juan de Cuevas and his participation in the Battle of New Orleans has always been controversial. There are those who have used Gleig's book as a prime source to refute the legend, believing that the Cuevas family, as described by the lieutenant, knew nothing about the war in progress and certainly never had a personal conflict with the British. But the soldier's written account may actually prove just the opposite. I believe this story shows that the Cuevas family may have had a confrontation with the British when the armada first landed on the Coast. Cat Island is west of Ship Island in the same direction as New Orleans, although Lt. Gleig is totally inaccurate about the island's location. The island is obviously not "at least one hundred and twenty miles from the main." I suspect the soldier was using that number to dramatically reinforce his assertion that the family was isolated. It is not realistic to think the foreign military would have totally ignored Cat Island, since it sat directly on the edge of the channel leading into Lake Borgne and the city of New Orleans. The British armada anchored nearby would have certainly sent a scouting party to determine if there was any possible threat on the island. While the soldiers explored Cat Island it is also probable that they discovered Juan's cattle and slaughtered some for food. It is also likely that Juan and the soldiers had a heated conflict over his cattle, just as the legend states.

The sight of a British officer returning to their home after the war would have certainly frightened Juan and Marie, who would have still been stinging from the earlier confrontation. When Juan saw Gleig's ship anchor in the Gulf, his first thoughts would have surely been to protect the family from a second clash with the enemy. It would be a reasonable reaction to try and hide the children. The two older children, John Joseph (19) and Helene (18), could have hurriedly taken their younger siblings, including the new baby, to another part of the island, possibly to the Moran's cottage, to hide. The next three oldest children stayed behind to support their parents and to serve as messengers to the others. The three who remained at the house, according to Gleig's description, would have been Francois (16), Bridget (15), and Celeste (12).

If Juan had caught the British slaughtering his livestock, he would have done anything to prevent a repeat of that incident. There is a possibility that Juan could have concocted the story of how he had lost his business and as a result had retired from society to hide the truth from Gleig about his herd.

It is impossible to think that Juan had no idea a major battle had recently ended, because we know Juan's good friend, Jacob Ferris, fought with Andrew Jackson during that conflict.[6] It is also impossible to believe that the large British fleet, which had only days before used the deep water channel nearby to prepare an attack on New Orleans, somehow slipped totally by Cat Island without anyone even noticing. Captain Jones' ships could not have circled the island scouting for the large contingency of British vessels without detection by someone on the island.

This theory does not attempt to prove that Juan de Cuevas was a hero in the Battle of New Orleans, but it does explain the contradictions that Gleig described. It is highly likely that the British had harassed the Cuevas family previously, otherwise Juan would have had no reason to go to such lengths to concoct such an elaborate hoax for a harmless stranger.

Lieutenant Gleig's book actually adds more questions than it answers. One of the revelations suggests that Juan de Cuevas may not have been an illiterate Spanish peasant after all. It is a fact that Juan signed all his known documents with an "X," leading to the assumption that he could not read or write. But Gleig seems to indicate otherwise. The British officer states, "Of reading and writing all except the patriarch himself were ignorant." How would Gleig know that Juan could read and write if he had not observed it? Juan would have had no reason to even discuss his literacy with a total stranger. So, could Juan read and write, or not? We will never know for sure.

The heroic deed of Juan de Cuevas in the Battle of New Orleans continues to be a controversial epic in Gulf Coast history. But, after all of these years of research and discovery, I believe I know the truth about the story, and in a subsequent chapter I will illustrate how the truth became a legend. But before that there is much more to learn about Cat Island during the Cuevas era, beginning with the old Cuevas homestead that survived the many storms in the Gulf for over a hundred years.

9

The Cuevas House on Cat Island

In the early 1900s Edward J. Younghans (1858–1934) boarded a boat with his camera and tripod for a photo shoot on Cat Island. From 1899 to 1931, Younghans operated a small photography shop in the rear of his novelty store on 13th Street in Gulfport. From his first day in business, picture postcards were his biggest selling items, and he found it increasingly difficult to keep the cards in stock.[1] The development of printing technology and the widespread use of photography combined with the growing acceptance of postcards to create a fad that was spreading like wildfire around the world. In the United States the Rural Free Delivery system played an important part in fanning the flames.[2] The telephone was still unavailable for the majority of people, but mail at that time was delivered twice a day. Spend a penny or two for the postcard, add a penny stamp, and you could communicate with family and friends with a speed rivaled only by the telephone. Postcards were a fast and convenient way to keep in touch. Postcard collecting grew to be the largest collectible hobby that the world has ever known. The U.S. Post Office reported the official number of postcards mailed in the fiscal year ending June 30, 1908, was 677,777,798 — at a time when the U.S. population only numbered 88,700,000. The golden age of postcards, which had begun about 1895, was in full swing.[3]

Photographers all over America began shooting postcard scenes. Some traveled from place to place, while others recorded notable locations around their hometowns. These local photographers distributed their work through large national publishing companies. Edward Younghans began snapping photos of downtown Gulfport, Biloxi and other significant places along the Coast. After contracting with the Detroit Publishing Company to produce and distribute his postcards, Younghans became one of the most prolific photographers of the genre, providing an historic record of the Mississippi Gulf Coast in the early 1900s.[4] The picture he took on Cat Island that day is the only professional photograph ever taken of the old Cuevas homestead, and it remains the definitive surviving image of the Cuevas era on Cat Island.

The old Cuevas house, which had been vacant for years, was destroyed by fire in 1931. Careless campers staying in the old building set a fire that destroyed one of the oldest landmarks of early Coast history.[5] Sadly, no one living today ever saw the house. I visited the site when I was young, but it was almost too overgrown to locate precisely. I contacted everyone who might have personal knowledge of the house, including the Archie Cameron family, but even the oldest remaining members were too young to have seen it.[6] Older members of the Cuevas family who had been to the house described what they remembered

This photograph of the Cuevas house on Cat Island taken by Edward J. Younghans was the only professional photograph ever taken of the old homestead, and remains the definitive surviving image of the Cuevas era on Cat Island (courtesy Mississippi Department of Archives and History).

about the structure. Unfortunately they are no longer living, but their accounts, along with old newspaper articles, existing photographs, and architectural studies of Creole vernacular homes, provide a most likely description of the building.[7]

Experts do not agree on the origin of traditional Creole architecture. Some believe that it grew out of Creole ingenuity and ability to adapt to Louisiana's hot, humid climate. Most agree that it was a likely combination of local needs and imported ideas. Creole architecture, which developed around New Orleans in the early eighteenth century and was dominant in the area for over a hundred years, is the only style that actually evolved in America. The Swedes, Dutch, Flemish, Spanish, and British imported their building types from their homelands and never developed their own native styles.[8]

The original buildings in New Orleans were French in design, but through a series of accidental fires, Spanish architecture came to dominate the look of the new French Quarter.[9] The Spanish-style buildings were made of brick and set directly at the sidewalk with common firewalls for protection. These were unlike the wide townhomes common during the French occupation of the city. Roofs of baked tile and quarried slate replaced the wooden short-hipped roofs of the past, while ornate wrought iron balconies, mezzanines, and walled courtyards used as gardens became the norm. All of these features were similar in style to the houses one finds in Spain even today. Considering the changes that were made, the old section of New Orleans should more appropriately be called "The Spanish Quarter."

The earliest Creole or Cracker style houses built on the Coast in the eighteenth and early nineteenth centuries were not as large as one would expect for the large families common at the time. Even today small houses are still referred to as cracker-box houses. Those houses utilized the British pen tradition of construction and incorporated most of the features common to that design.[10] Cracker houses usually began as a square one room log cabin, called a single pen, measuring approximately 20 feet by 20 feet.[11] As families grew, more space was needed. The easiest solution was to build two of these one-room log cabins next to each other to form a double-pen house. If the new room was added with the fireplace on the middle wall, they were called saddlebag houses. Often two pens were built with a passageway between. The second pen was a mirror image of the first with a fireplace on each gable end, and a common roof that joined the two rooms. These became known as dogtrot houses, because a dog could "trot" through the open breezeway.

A classic of the dogtrot style was the Nicholas Ladner house on the mainland in the Long Beach area.[12] The Ladner house became known as "The Chimneys" because of the characteristic smokestacks on each of the gable ends. When the house was finally

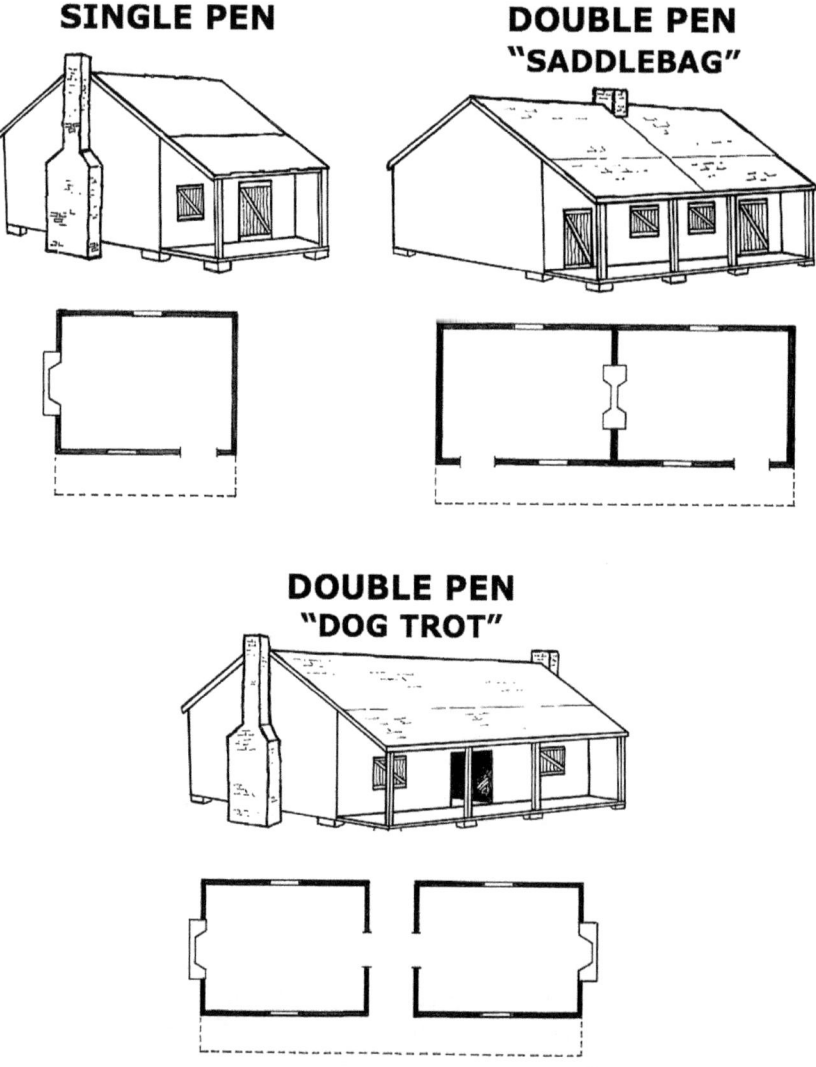

To increase the size of the house, one-room log cabins were built next to each other. These elevations and floor plans show the configuration of single pen and double pen houses.

destroyed, the two chimneys remained for many years, providing a landmark for sailors in the Gulf.[13]

The Cuevas house on Cat Island did not match any of the styles exactly. Although best described as a cross between a single pen and a dogtrot, the house had some unique characteristics. Notably there was only one chimney on the house instead of the two usually found in the dogtrot style. The interior was asymmetrical and lacked an interior dogtrot hallway. The inside doors were placed solely for convenience and for airflow, without regard to aesthetics.[14]

Like the traditional dogtrots it featured a built-in, broken-pitch roof that extended over two porches running the whole width of the front and back. The wide shade porches were not just architectural embellishments, but provided much-needed relief from the hot southern sun. The Cuevas house did not have a separate kitchen. The meals were cooked in the log-burning fireplace located on the east end and extending nearly across the whole wall of the main room. It was constructed of bricks made in kilns on Cat Island. These bricks were commonly used by the early Gulf Coast settlers and were fashioned from the readily available oyster shells and lime.[15] An outdoor bake oven was used during the summer months when the heat from the fireplace would have been almost unbearable. This oven was made of the same bricks as the fireplace.

The house originally had two rooms and measured approximately 40 feet wide by 20 feet deep. As the Cuevas family grew, the back porch was eventually enclosed to add an additional 10 feet of living space, and creating two more rooms.

The windows in the little house were very important, providing cross-ventilation in the hot sticky weather. The wooden shutters were attached to the windows by thick

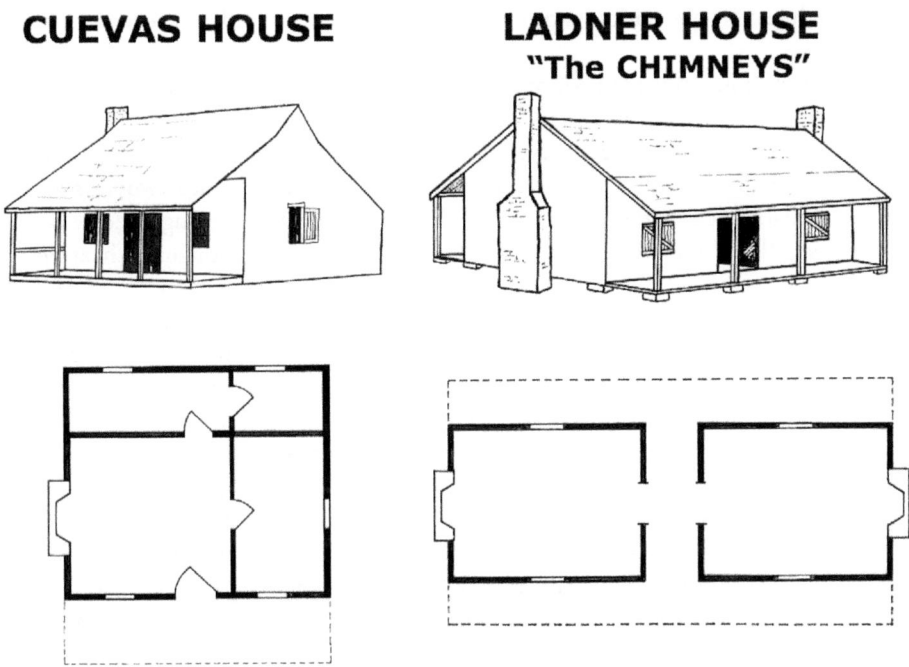

Elevations and floor plans of the Cuevas house on Cat Island and the Ladner house, known as "The Chimneys," on the mainland waterfront in what is now Long Beach.

rawhide hinges and provided protection from the wind, rain and direct sunlight, as well as.[16]

The old Cuevas house was located on the north shore of Cat Island facing the mainland, approximately two miles from the western tip where the lighthouse would later be constructed. That distance was a little over halfway from the Great Sand hill at the eastern leg of the T-shaped island. The site had been carefully chosen to be protected against storms that would come from the Gulf on the south. The land was high and not prone to flooding.

Much preparation would have been necessary when the house was originally constructed. The site was first cleared of all trees and underbrush. All leaves, pine needles and debris were raked clean, leaving an expanse of sparkling white sand. The Spanish settlers on the east coast of Florida built their homes directly on the ground with the sandy soil as their flooring. The families on the Mississippi Gulf Coast, however, began raising their houses above ground on low brick or wooden piers after experiencing rains, floods, and insect invasions.[17] The resulting crawl space provided air circulation, which kept the house cooler in the summer and provided shelter for the family's chickens and hunting dogs. In turn the dogs kept rats and snakes away from the house, while the chickens helped to control the roaches, fleas, and palmetto bugs. The floorboards themselves were loosely fitted, which helped the ventilation and also made cleaning the house much easier. The dirt on the floor could be swept between the cracks to the ground below. The Cuevas house was raised about two feet above ground with wood facing that covered the pilings for a more finished look.

The sandy yard around the house was swept clean with brooms made of sassafras branches tied together in a bundle. This was as much for safety as for looks. Trash or debris close to the house posed a potential threat of fire caused by the frequent lightening strikes to the tall pine trees nearby. No ivy or decorative vines were allowed to grow on the house, since they reduced air circulation and invited insects to nest or feed on the wood construction.

The Cuevas house was made of heart pine, the name given to the actual heartwood of the tree. After thirty-five or forty years, the wood in the center of the pine trees will harden and "die." The hardening process prevents nutrients from passing up the tree. Heart pine is harder than regular sapwood and resistant to warping and decay. Heartwood is generally no longer available due to the lumbering of the old trees. Our pressing need today for a continuous supply of wood does not allow the trees to age long enough for heartwood to develop.[18]

The Cuevas house was not hastily thrown together. Meticulous and lengthy planning was required. Tall straight trees were first cut down and sawed into logs during the spring when the sap was just beginning to flow. The ideal time to cut the trees was while the sap was lowest, since the presence of any sap could lead to warping during the drying process. The bark and spongy outer growth on the logs were stripped away to prevent bugs and worms from furrowing under them. The logs were then stacked in piles to dry for a period of two seasons. The natural moisture inside of the wood would cause warping, shrinking, and even termite infestation if the logs were not allowed to dry out completely.

Every piece of lumber used in the house's construction had to be handmade. The thick planks for floors and siding were cut with a platform saw. This saw allowed two men to cut together with the same long blade. The logs for the walls were hewn flat about 12 inches wide by 4 inches thick. A pole ax was used to chop scores in the surface of the round logs about a foot apart, then a broad ax was used to strip away flat sections between each score. The workers became quite skilled, producing thick timbers that were relatively flat and smooth.

The first row of logs for the outer walls was formed by laying flat boards over squared logs and then notching them into position. Each new row was placed on top of the last. It took at least four strong men to lift the heavy timbers high and into place. To facilitate the work, greased poles were leaned against the rising wall. By pushing and pulling the workers maneuvered each of the logs up the poles and into position. With some persistent hammering and tapping they were able to drop the logs snugly into place on the row below. Large wooden pins were used to hold the frame together.[19]

The notches that were made on the ends of each log locked the plank in place with a fairly sophisticated cut called a "half-dovetail." Full dovetail notching was first used in Europe and was the most elaborate form of construction. Over time in the colonies, the full dovetail evolved into the half-dovetail, which proved to be just as sound and required less labor.[20] All of the surfaces of the logs were cut to slope downward toward the outside of the walls so that the rain would be repelled, keeping the exposed joints dry.

Some of the early houses along the Coast followed the same basic principles as the medieval half-timber houses of Europe.[21] The logs would be cut longer so that the ends extended well beyond the notch. Since the open ends of the logs were susceptible to moisture the extra length allowed the homeowner to trim away any rot that might occur over time. The Cuevas house, however, was built with the ends of the logs cut flush at the notch. Corner boards were then used to cover the ends, protecting them from exposure to moisture and providing a more finished look.

The broad porches at the front and the back were each about a third of the width of the house, and provided not only shade in the summer, but also additional space for the Cuevas family to live and work. The porches were created by extending the top logs on the north and south walls to support the sloping log rafters that formed the gabled roof. Logs of smaller diameter were inserted between the perpendicular rafters. These purlins provided supports upon which the cypress shingles were attached. Short cypress logs were split to form the shingles.

The spaces between the log walls were "chinked" with *bousillage*, a natural insulation commonly used in traditional Cajun houses.[22] This was made by mixing water in a hole with ordinary soil and adding Spanish moss. It was trampled and then rolled out in sections approximately two feet in length. These rolls were squeezed between the cracks in the logs. Unlike the houses in Europe, where infill and timbers were often exposed, flat boards were attached to the outside walls of the Cuevas house to seal off these spaces and to shut out the weather. The interior walls themselves were plastered with a mixture of mud and lime. This wall covering was not very stable, so a never-ending cycle of maintenance and repair was a part of the house's upkeep.[23]

There was very little furniture in the house, because of the limited space. The living room featured the large fire-

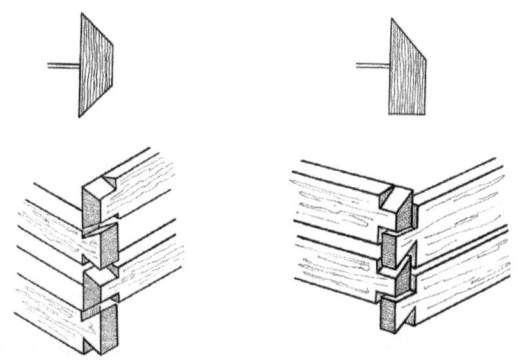

Full Dovetail Notch   **Half Dovetail Notch**

Full dovetail notching was first used in Europe and was the most elaborate form of construction. Over time in the colonies, the full dovetail evolved into the half-dovetail, which proved to be just as sound and required less labor.

place, and in the center of the room was a dining table. This was the largest piece of furniture, which consisted of a few long boards set across two barrels. A chair was at one end of the table for the head of the family. Two long benches on either side served as seating even when the family was not having their meals. There were a couple occasional chairs in the house and a rocking chair that was usually found on the front porch or by the fireplace inside. Shelves near the hearth held the eating and cooking utensils, although in later years a cupboard was added.[24]

The French settlers developed a recognizable style of chairs over the years based on the ones they could recall from their homeland.[25] They were handcrafted with simple edged tools like an axe or draw blade, and were held together by wooden pegs rather than nails or screws. The most popular kinds of wood for these chairs were birch, maple and pine. Occasionally they were painted red or green, but mostly they were left uncolored. The chairs in the Cuevas home were made from the pine trees that were so abundant on the island, and were never dyed.

In the master bedroom, the furniture consisted of a pole bed used by the parents, and a trunk for clothing. In the two bedrooms at the back of the house, the children slept on the floor on mats filled with Spanish moss for padding.[26] The babies and toddlers slept in the parents' room. In each bedroom there was a barrel used for storage as well as additional seating. There were no closets, so pegs were set on the walls to hang their garments. When privacy was needed, fabric was hung on a wire that was stretched across the room.

There were no screens or glass for windowpanes in the rural colonies. In the winter months the shutters of the Cuevas house remained closed both day and night to retain the heat. During the hot, muggy months of the year, the shutters were kept open throughout the day to take advantage of the cool breezes off the Gulf. Since electricity was not available in American homes before 1905, there were no fans to cool the homes. The only effective way to deal with the heat was to locate the windows and doors in such a way as to utilize the air currents. But even on the warmest nights the shutters had to be closed for protection. There was always a threat from curious creatures, particularly the numerous raccoons that came scavenging around for food. One could never know what may come crawling through an open window. The closed shutters also offered some, if only minimal, protection from the invading hoards of mosquitoes and other flying pests.

Insects were part of every household. There was virtually no protection against them other than the almost negligible effect of the smoke from the cabin fire. In New Orleans those who could afford such a luxury used mosquito netting, but the material was scarce in the wilderness. Any available fabric was used to cover the windows when mosquitoes were at their worst.

The Cuevas house, like the others in colonial America, had no running water, septic system, or bathroom. Cham-

There was a rocking chair by the fireplace, and shelves near the hearth held the eating and cooking utensils.

ber pots were used during the night, as it was too dangerous to leave the house in the total darkness. One of the most undesirable daily chores was the emptying and cleaning of these vessels. During the day the family used crude outdoor toilets, called privies, which were nothing more than holes dug in the sand. These waste pits were covered over when they became too unbearable.

The interior of the house was dark even during the summer months. With only one door and a few small windows, sunlight was restricted, particularly when the weather was cloudy or rainy. Candles were the only means of lighting through the mid to late 1800s. The familiar hurricane oil lamps with glass chimneys that are part of early Americana were not introduced until 1853.[27] Drilling for petroleum did not begin until 1859, so kerosene was not available for fuel until after that date. Candles made from wax myrtle were the sole source of lighting in the Louisiana territory. The wax myrtle, which is closely related to the northern bayberry, is native to the area along the coast between Texas and Florida and was abundant on Cat Island. Myrtle wax candles were much more suited to the climate on the coast. They were less greasy in warm weather and their aroma was much more pleasant than that of candles made from paraffin.[28]

With only candlelight available, the darkness of the nights on Cat Island is impossible to imagine. The moss-draped trees take on ominous shapes that seem to come alive in the Gulf breezes and then slowly fade into the inky darkness as the sun finally sets. Yet, when the moon is full, the night is as bright as daytime seen through a blue colored filter. On those clear glorious evenings the moonlight creates a road of shimmering white that leads almost to the heavens.

The Cuevas house was only a small part of life on Cat Island. It is true that living was much simpler then, but it was also very crude by our standards. To fully appreciate our lives today, we should look at the way things were on the Gulf Coast during the early 1800s.

10

Pioneer Life on Cat Island and the Developing Coast

The pioneer era in America (c.1790 to 1840) was a dichotomy. Although on the one hand still very primitive, it was also a time of rapid change. The effects of the Industrial Revolution, which began in the 1780s, were just beginning to be felt by the 1830s. The world's economy that had previously been based on manual labor was relying more on machines to accomplish many of the same jobs. Production capacity greatly increased with the introduction of steam-powered machinery.[1] Railroads began to expand during the 1860s and proved their importance during the Civil War.[2] New canals and improved roads fueled trade expansion. A second Industrial Revolution around 1850 grew out of the first as technological advancements increased dramatically. With the development of the internal combustion engine and the generation of electrical power, economic progress continued at a lightning pace.[3]

Even though there were dramatic technological and economic advances, daily life in America did not change all that much. In 1800, most Americans were farmers living in rural communities and by the close of the century the majority were still farmers, or at least still living in small rural areas. In 1800, women spent almost twenty hours a week doing laundry by hand, and by 1900 they were still doing the same. At the close of the century many Americans were no longer cooking their meals in an open fireplace, but the work required to haul fuel and to keep the fire going in a wood or coal stove was just as strenuous.[4]

It is true, that people's lives were very hard on the frontier, but while living conditions were crude by our standards, they were not so unusual for the times. There was virtually no difference between the standard of life in the colonies and that which the settlers had left behind in Europe. Even the monarchs in their castles lived without indoor plumbing in the same primitive way as the common people.[5]

Our modern lives have become so sanitized that we would be overwhelmed by the rudimentary environment that was common throughout the world at that time. Large families lived in small houses with no bathrooms and only the dim glow of candles for lighting. Even the smells that were part of everyday life in the 1800s would be difficult for us to endure. The air everywhere was filled with the odor of animals and manure. There was the stench of dirt from the gardens nearby and even from the dirt floors common in many houses. In an effort to control the dust, dishwater was often emptied on different parts of the floor around the one-room house. The grease from the grimy water would harden in the dirt, sometimes adding a slight rancid smell to the already pungent air.

It was during the pioneer period that many of the old families began to settle on the Gulf Coast. The British government had given land grants freely, although some of the settlers never applied for a grant because of the vastness of the territory.[6] Many believed they could choose a spot anywhere and simply start clearing the land for a homestead. It was not until later, when the legal owners received a grant, that an unsuspecting family would be forced to move. After taking control of the territory in 1781, Spain issued grants to those settlers who had already requested land from the British.[7] Nicholas Ladner requested Cat Island.

The barrier islands were a valuable part of life on the Coast. Not only did they protect the mainland from the ravages of storms, but they also served as natural defenses against marauding bands of hostile Indians and renegade bandits who would plunder, rob, and even threaten the lives of the settlers and their families.[8]

The Choctaws, who had been staunch allies of the French, despised the British for providing weapons to the Chickasaws and the Creeks to be used against the Choctaws. As a result the vengeful Choctaws struck the people along the Coast, targeting their large herds of cattle and stealing their possessions. By 1767, the few families living on the mainland had been driven out to the barrier islands for safety.[9] Cat Island, approximately eight miles from the mainland, was close enough for access, yet far enough away from the Coast for the occupants to feel secure.

In 1785, Estéban Rodríguez Miró (1740–1802) succeeded Bernardo de Galvez as governor of Louisiana, and as one of his first acts, issued orders for a census of the Gulf Coast area.[10] The report showed the people living on Cat Island were Nicholas (Ladner) Christian, his wife, Marianne, and ten children, José Morin and his wife, Marie Louise, the eldest daughter of Nicholas Christian, two free blacks named José Klucer and José Mirer, and a free mulatto name Diequir Duret.[11]

When Juan de Cuevas moved his family to Cat Island in 1803, the population along the Coast was sparse. Ephraim Kirby (1757–1804), the special commissioner on Spanish boundary under president Thomas Jefferson, reported, "From the town of Mobile to the Pascagoula there are about 18 families settled along the shores of the Bay and at the mouth of the river; and from thence to Pearl River, and upon the same are about 30 families."[12]

Six years later an unnamed traveler reported there were only eighteen families living on the lower Pascagoula River, with a few more living upstream.[13] In Biloxi there were twelve families, and at Bay St. Louis there were ten to fifteen French families and just under twenty families on the east bank of the Pearl River.[14] Four or five free Negroes and mulattoes were living in Pass Christian, along with a number of wealthy families from New Orleans who had built summer homes on the beach. In 1810 the population of New Orleans was 24,550 while the population of Mobile had dwindled to only 300.[15]

The tax rolls show that only eight families were living at "The Chimneys" (present day Long Beach) in 1814. Those families were Joseph Moran Jr. (José Morin II) married to Marquerite Panquinet, Jean Baptiste Carco married to Pegagia Moran, Claude Ladner married to Ann Maria Francoise LaFontaine, Lewis Couidot, Soinsint Peare, George B. Dameron, Joseph Clower, and Joseph Labatt married to Marie Theresa Krebs.[16]

At that time the United States was a weak union of colonies scattered along the East Coast. In the Louisiana territory and along the Gulf Coast, correspondence depended mostly on messages carried between friends, merchants, and helpful Indians. Good roads were necessary for successful mail delivery, which limited the expansion of mail service to the Coast. In 1804, roads were almost nonexistent, and the few that did exist were deplorable.[17] It would take an average of 25 days to travel from Mobile to New Orleans, including some unavoidable travel over water. Mostly transportation was over trails cut through the forests by the settlers and Indians, but even those were sparse.

Biloxi was described as being wild, uncleared and uncultivated. Before Lameuse Road in Biloxi was constructed in 1836 only two footpaths existed.[18] There had been very little growth in almost a century, since the capital of Louisiana had been moved from Biloxi to New Orleans. Roads had not been necessary because there were no horses, carts or wagons in Biloxi before 1836.[19] Furthermore, many of the Coast inhabitants were living on the barrier islands, or in Mobile or New Orleans, so the early French settlers traveled mainly by water rather than land.

There were two kinds of small boats that became the mainstay of early transportation in the territory. One of the first crafts used was called a *cajeu*.[20] It was very practical for the wilderness, since it was made of cane and could be constructed easily. It was more like a raft than a boat. The cajeu was not only suitable for the small streams and rivers, but it could also navigate rivers as large as the Pearl and the Mississippi.

The most important vessel for the area was a dugout canoe originally used by the local Indians called a pirogue (pronounced "pee-r-rogue").[21] The French and Spanish quickly recognized it as the perfect boat for navigating the winding shallow swamps and streams of Louisiana and the Gulf Coast. Using European boat-building techniques, the Indians' pirogue was transformed into a lighter, more stable craft. The name in both Spanish and French translates as piragua, meaning "dug-out" because of the way the boats were made.

Pirogues were made from cypress trees because of the wood's resistance to rot. A fire built at the base of a large cypress tree was allowed to burn until it caused the tree to fall. Once the tree was down, the log was split in half. Fire was then used to burn the trunk off at the desired length The inside of the log was alternately burned and scraped with crude tools or even shells until the boat was hollowed out. Pirogues have been used for centuries, and have become a part of the Cajun heritage. These sturdy boats could be as long as thirty feet and could carry heavy cargo.[22]

The Mississippi River was difficult to navigate before the government began a cleanup effort. It was well into the 1800s before the river was suitable for passage. Most people relied on flatboats until the steamboats became a regular means of transportation.[23] Flatboats were used to carry heavy loads over short distances. These boats were simply barges, many with a curved or flat roof to protect cargo and sailors from the weather. Flatboats were steered from the rear by a centrally located pole on which a flat board rudder was attached. Oars were sometimes used to increase speed, but were mainly used to push the heavy boat off sandbars. Flatboats were built with large flat beams that could support thirty or more tons. Since there was no means of power, the boats could only travel downstream. They were usually dismantled at the end of the trip and the lumber reused for other purposes such as firewood. The size of the boat could vary from twenty feet long and ten feet wide, to larger ones that were sixty feet long and twenty feet wide. Some were built with pens on board, which permitted the transporting of animals to markets in New Orleans.

The schooner was also popular on the Coast. This small vessel was fitted with two masts at first, but had as many as seven masts in some later designs. It required fewer men to operate, and could be used in shallow waters as well as in the open waters of the Gulf.[24]

Another favored vessel among the residents of the Coast was a goélette.[25] It was closely related to the schooner, and there probably was little real distinction between the two except for the position of the masts. The goélette, which translates as "seagull," was an elegant sailing ship that was even easier to maneuver along the coastal waterways. It was this French-style boat that was used by Juan de Cuevas and the family on Cat Island.[26] Ramon, the lighthouse keeper and son of Juan de Cuevas, had a goélette built that was about forty-five feet long. It cost $3,000 at the time, and was named the *Creole*; the cabin and deck of this boat were constructed of highly polished hardwood, and according to his son, James, the boat was very attractive.[27]

The era of steamboats in America began when John Fitch (1743–1798) made his first successful voyage on August 22, 1787, on the Delaware River.[28] In 1811, the SS *New Orleans*, designed by Robert Fulton and Robert Livingston, was built in Pittsburgh.[29] It was a shallow-bottomed side-wheeler that eventually became synonymous with the riverboats of New Orleans. By 1814, Fulton and Edward Livingston, brother of Robert Livingston, were operating a regular freight service between New Orleans and Natchez.[30] Slow by our standards, these early steamboats traveled eight miles per hour downstream and a sluggish three miles per hour upstream. By the time the *New Orleans* was operational, steamboat travel was already established on all the major river systems in America. On July 3, 1830, regular steamboat service began along the Coast between Mobile and New Orleans.[31] By 1834, steamboat traffic into the port of New Orleans increased from 20 to 1,200 per year. By 1853, the design had improved so much that the trip from Louisville took only four and a half days.[32] This new method of transportation contributed greatly to the U.S. economy.

Railroads developed separately from steamboats, but did not begin to flourish until trains switched from coal to steam. The first railroad to transport both people and freight began on February 28, 1827, and by the 1870s railroads were beginning to replace steamboats as the main method of transporting goods and passengers.[33]

Life on Cat Island

In 1815, the last of the twelve Cuevas children was born on Cat Island at a time when the Coast was finally beginning to show signs of growth. Mississippi became a state in 1817, and the town of Shieldsborough (now Bay St. Louis) was incorporated by the first state legislature a year later in 1818.[34] The total population of the Gulf Coast was 1,594 according to the first official United States census made of the area in 1820. That same census found only six families lived in Biloxi.[35] Although the population on the mainland was slowly increasing, the territory still consisted of only a few spotty settlements.

The first settlers who came to the Louisiana territory from other countries became known as Creoles (originally "Criolles"). These people arrived from France with Bienville in the 1700s followed by others from Spain, Africa, Germany, Italy, and England.[36] Although Frenchmen from Quebec were the first people on the Gulf Coast, it was the settlers from the French colony of Acadia that dominated the culture of the Louisiana territory. The Acadians had originally come to Nova Scotia in 1604 primarily from Brittany, Normandy, Picardy and Poitou.[37] While the Creoles settled mainly in what would become the city of New Orleans, the Acadians were settling the swamps and bayous to the west and south of the city. The cultures blended together while still retaining certain customs of their own countries.

Acadia, or "La Cadie," was one of the initial European colonies in the New World.[38] Its boundaries loosely included Nova Scotia, New Brunswick, Prince Edward Island, and parts of Maine. The Acadians called themselves "Acadiens" or "Cadiens," which eventually became Anglicized as "Cajuns." These Cadiens were forced to adjust to political changes as their colony repeatedly changed hands between the British and the French. Despite British attempts to convert the French-Catholic culture to a British-Protestant one, the French-speaking Acadians held fast to their own traditions.[39] The refusal by the fiercely French-Catholic Acadians to pledge their loyalty to George II, the king of England, ultimately led to their deportation in what is known as Le Grand Dèrangement, or the Expulsion of 1755.[40] About three-fourths of the Acadian population were forced from their homes and their lands confiscated. Gradually by 1756, the French-speaking Acadians who did not choose to return to France landed in the southern United States, mostly in areas of south Louisiana and east Texas.[41]

The Acadians arrived while the region was under Spanish control, but they continued to remain loyal to France while virtually ignoring the Spanish. The women had the greatest influence in preserving the Cajun culture, since most of the marriages during the time of Spanish control were between Spanish men and French or Cajun women, and the children of these marriages tended to speak the French language of their mother. Over time the Spanish became more assimilated in the French culture. The transformation was so great that common Spanish names like Ortega, Diaz, Romero, and even Cuevas became thought of as French names by the general population.[42]

There was one notable Spanish influence on the Cajun French language, aside from the many Spanish words that were absorbed. The Spanish naturally rolled their "r" on the tip of their tongues, while the "r" of Parisian French is guttural. As the Spaniards spoke French with their Spanish accents, this Spanish sound eventually became the Cajun "r."[43]

Anyone who has studied French in school and tried to relate it to Cajun French soon realizes that the French spoken on the Gulf Coast and the Louisiana territory differs from the modern French language. There are several reasons for this disparity. Language is a living thing that changes with the ever-developing and advancing culture. The Cajun French language did not evolve with the mother tongue. As the Coast became increasingly isolated from France after the takeover by Spain and eventually the United States, this "old French" remained the basis of the language. The area was in something of a time warp, with the early settlers speaking what would be considered "seventeenth-century French." While some of the words may be understandable today, many are actually antiquated. In addition, Cajun French began to incorporate words for the new plants, animals, and social situations that the people encountered in this new territory. This resulted in the creation of new words and expressions that did not exist in France.

Illiteracy was another significant reason the two languages are somewhat different. Few of the people could read or write, so the language was passed on by word of mouth for over two hundred years. Speech patterns and individual accents had as much to do with what the children learned as any other factor. Since language was learned by ear, over the years some words changed into something entirely different from the original. Some words ran together while others were shortened. If a person had trouble pronouncing a particular sound, everyone who learned to speak French from that person pronounced the word with the same error. Thus the French that Cajuns spoke often resulted in the incorrect pronunciation of words and expressions passed down through the generations. Even with these differences, however, it is estimated that about 60 percent of Cajun French words are the same as standard French.[44]

The Louisiana territory and the Gulf Coast were rural and sparsely populated, so Cajun French remained the primary language until the advent of the automobile and the radio. With widespread contact, the English language began to have a greater influence on the French-speaking population. That influence was so strong that many feared the French language would be lost forever, and their fears were justified. With the development of public schools and the passing of compulsory attendance laws, eventually French would no longer be allowed in classrooms.[45] The purpose was to force the children to learn English, and therefore be more able to cope in an English-dominated society. It became illegal in some instances to speak French, and while these laws mainly affected residents of Louisiana, they had similar effects in the backwoods of Mississippi where the Cuevas family were then living.[46] As the younger generations adopted the English language, the old Coast families eventually began to lose the use of the French language altogether. Of course, there are those today who still speak Cajun French.

Living conditions on the island during the Cuevas era continued to be very primitive at best. Traditionally, large pioneer families lived in small one- and two-room houses. On Cat Island, the four-room Cuevas house was larger than most, yet the entire space was no bigger than a single great room in many of our houses today. There was normally a minimum of eight to ten people living in the house at any one time, including the parents, a number of nearly grown children, active toddlers, often a crying baby, and a slave or two at times. Occasionally there were the unexpected guests who would also sleep over, such as an itinerant priest from New Orleans or a family friend or relative. With such limited space it was not unusual for one of the older children to share his mattress with a person he hardly knew.

Blankets were the common bed cover of the period. They were most often woven of wool and varied in quality. In the rural areas of the Gulf Coast they were generally rough, while some of the blankets available in the cities like New Orleans and Mobile were made of soft wool brushed into a fine nap. The range of colors for these blankets was limited. They were usually left a natural white, but sometimes made in blue, green or red depending on the kind of dyes available. Manufactured blankets were often purchased when possible. Unfortunately none of these blankets have survived the two hundred years since the Cuevas family lived on the island. As with clothing, the blankets were used until they were completely worn out.

There were never any quilts on Cat Island, or anywhere else during the pioneer era. Quilts were not a part of American life before the 1840s.[47] Although this form of folk art is usually associated with country living, it was not until quilts' prevalent use in the latter nineteenth century that the idea of quilting in colonial times became a romanticized myth.[48] It was not practical to make quilts until there was a widespread availability of factory-manufactured cloth. The settlers had very few articles of clothing and the few pieces they had were worn until completely threadbare, resulting in a scarcity of scrap materials. The rigors of pioneer life were also too demanding on the women, who had little or no time for the tedious task of piecing bits of cloth together. In addition, the light inside the small houses was way too dim to allow for the intricate stitching associated with quilt making.

On those occasions when the weather was rainy or stormy, life in a small house was particularly trying. Although the coast enjoys mostly sunny skies, often there are spells of gloomy, drizzly weather that can last for days, keeping everyone inside. Being housebound was hard on the children, not to mention the adults who had to deal with the youngsters' pent-up energy. Since no one could read, books were not an option.

Cooking in the Cat Island Kitchen

The first chore of the day on Cat Island was to revive the fire in the fireplace. There were no such things as matches during the Cuevas era. Before matches the process of starting a fire was so tedious that the fireplace was never allowed to go out completely. Hot coals were kept burning even during the summer months as a way to reignite the fire for cooking or heating the house when needed. To start a new fire two pieces of flint rock were struck together until the resulting sparks would eventually ignite some splinters of dry wood. The technique was difficult and numerous attempts were necessary. The first friction matches were patented in 1836, but these proved to be too dangerous for popular use. The problem was solved with the introduction of red phosphorus "safety" matches in 1855, but even these were not immediately available on the Coast.[49]

Two different styles of cooking began to develop by the time the Cuevas family moved to Cat Island in 1804. Cajun and Creole foods, which began as two distinctive types of cuisine, merged through the years while still retaining a certain amount of individuality. The melting pot of cultures created a melting pot of food that even today is unmatched anywhere in the world.

The Creoles were from wealthy families of Paris, Madrid, and other major European cities.[50] Many brought their own cooks with them to New Orleans, but soon discovered that it was impossible to prepare the foods that they were used to because of the lack of necessary ingredients. The Creole ladies petitioned Bienville to improve the food supply. In response to their request Bienville called upon his own housekeeper, Madame Langlois, to work with the housewives and teach them the cooking methods she had learned from the Indians in the area.[51] She taught them the native dishes, the use of local spices, and how to apply their cooking skills to the many meats, seafood, and vegetables that were indigenous to the fertile lands and waters. The spicy food of the Spanish, the traditional sauces of the French, and the use of indigenous spices by the Africans comprise the foundation of Creole cooking. Creole is considered closer to classic French cuisine, while Cajun is characterized by a more relaxed and rural style of cooking that incorporates stronger seasonings and flavor.

Every group contributed to the "gumbo" of tastes. Choctaw Indians, who were the first Native Americans to settle in the area, shared their use of bay leaves and filé powder common to the Coast.[52] The Indians also introduced corn, beans, peas, squash, greens, onions, berries, nuts, and various kinds of fruit.[53]

During the French period, the food was mild in flavor, incorporating smooth traditional French sauces, but when Spain came into possession of the territory, pork and highly seasoned dishes using cooked onions, green peppers, tomatoes, and garlic were introduced. The Spanish not only included hot peppers in their cooking, but they were also the first to combine meat and fish in the same meal. Before that time the combination of sausage and shrimp was unheard of. Creole and Cajun cooks began serving sausage and shrimp over rice, creating such dishes as jambalaya.[54]

The African cooks made a major contribution by adding gumbo to the local scene. The name comes from the African word "gumba," meaning okra. Slaves smuggled various seeds from their native country, including yams, watermelons, okra, and several varieties of beans, so they would have food wherever they were taken. They would cultivate their crops in secret until, as cooks in the plantation kitchens, they began combining them with their masters' native foods to produce such southern cuisine as sweet potato pie and candied yams.[55]

The Africans also preferred a method of slow cooking over a low flame to intensify the blend of the different flavors. Not only did this enhance the taste, but it served a practical purpose as well. The ingredients were not always fresh, so it was necessary to cook the food for hours because of the lesser quality. They had to make meals out of vegetable parts that were generally considered inedible. They simmered such plants as collard greens, turnips, spinach, and mustard greens in oils with peppers and spices. They used the Indians' corn in a variety of dishes, creating cornbread, grits, and hush puppies.

Not only did the African cooks have to use leftover vegetables, they also had to use discarded animal parts. They developed creative and delicious ways to use the unused parts of the pig, such as the snout, ears, feet, and thighs (ham hocks). They cleaned, boiled, and fried the intestines of the pig, making what they called chitterlings or chitlins. These chitlins were also used to flavor stews and vegetables.[56]

Recipes from the 1800s collected from my grandmother and older relatives inspired me to attempt cooking the meals the way they were made on Cat Island. But I discovered that cooking in the "old way" is more complicated than I anticipated, even if the same ingredients are used. The pots today are not the same as the old cast-iron kettle that Marie used on Cat Island. The controlled heat on our modern stoves is different from the intense heat that was generated by the open fire in the large fireplace. The proportions of the ingredients are also questionable. What does it mean when the recipe calls for "butter the size of an egg"? When the recipe calls for baking soda, was that the same as the Arm and Hammer baking soda we buy in our supermarkets?

Since few people could read or write, there are no originally written recipes. It was left to later generations to put the family recipes on paper, but even then they were sketchy. Very few details were given because it was understood that whoever cooked the meal would already have the basic knowledge. When more people did begin to read and write, the recipes were not so much to describe how the meal was to be prepared, but rather to serve more as shopping lists or reminders of the necessary ingredients.

Almost everything that the Cuevas family ate was grown on Cat Island. Mainstay vegetables such as corn, okra, beans, peas, squash, cabbage, turnips, onions, pumpkins, carrots, lettuce, and sweet potatoes could be found in the Cuevas garden. Baking potatoes did not exist at the time the Cuevas family lived on Cat Island. The white potato was not popular in the United States until the late 1800s.[57] Sweet potatoes were the only potatoes eaten in the Louisiana territory and the Gulf Coast. Also, tomatoes were not used as food until after 1812 because many believed they were poisonous.[58]

The family's diet was supplemented with fish, wild game, and domestic livestock (pork and beef). The Cuevas family's front yard was the waters of the Gulf, so fish was an important part of their menu. The most common fish available were catfish (barbue), sheepshead, drum, redfish (poisson rouge), mullet, perch (patassa), turbot, eel, flounder (plie) and trout. Shellfish such as shrimp (chevrettes), crab, and oysters (huitres) were also readily available. Crawfish, which has become an iconic symbol of Cajun cooking, was mainly used for bait. Eating crawfish as a meal was not practical until the mid to late 1900s when farm-raised crawfish became the standard.[59]

The abundance of turtles in the swamps of Louisiana and south Mississippi made them a perfect food supply. Turtles, called tortue in French, were stocked on old ships sailing from Europe as a source of fresh meat. They could survive out of water with virtually no food. Turtles have a low metabolism and can live for months until they are ready to be cooked. They were easy to catch, and could also be kept in a pen just like other animals used for food. Snapping turtles were the most popular for making soup.

Homegrown fruit (figs, plums, pears, peaches, and grapes) was plentiful on Cat Island. Although traditional grapes cannot be grown on the Gulf Coast because of the weather, the families in the area began growing muscadines as a substitute. Muscadines are the grapes indigenous to the southern United States.[60] There are many varieties, but the scuppernong is the one most common on the Coast. Scuppernongs had no name in the 1800s, but were simply called "the big white grape."

Muscadine grapes grow well in a variety of soils, but they grow best in a sandy well-drained soil like that on Cat Island. The fruit grows in loose clusters of 3–40 grapes, unlike the large, tight bunches characteristic of the more traditional European and American grapes. Each grape is 1 to 1 ½ inches round with a thick, tough skin, and contains as many as five hard, oblong seeds. The fruits range in color from greenish bronze to almost black, and are abundantly juicy and deliciously sweet, with a kind of musky flavor.

The grapes within each cluster tend to ripen at different times, unlike the more traditional grape clusters that ripen as a bunch. Handpicking scuppernongs was not necessary since the grapes tend to fall on their own when they are ripe. Harvesters could spread a cloth on the ground and then vigoursly shake the vine, allowing the grapes to be collected. This was a job for the Cuevas children when the scuppernongs ripened in mid September to late October. Approximately four to six gallons of scuppernong grapes were gathered to make a batch of "white grape wine."

Wheat flour and sugar were the only food staples not grown on the island, but were purchased instead at the market in New Orleans. By 1800 the Louisiana region had become one of the major producers of sugar in the United States.[61] One of the later byproducts of the sugar industry was cane syrup (called sirop de canne), a favorite of everyone in the territory. Cane syrup, however, did not become popular until the late 1800s, so it was never used on Cat Island.

Many of the foods that we associate with the New Orleans and Gulf Coast areas were not common in 1794. Chickens, for example, did not become a widespread part of our diets until the 1800s, although chickens had been domesticated for 4,000 years.[62] Christopher Columbus brought the first chickens to the new world, but they were used mostly for egg production. Chickens were not generally kept on farms in America prior to 1800. It was not worth the time and expense involved in raising chickens for meat, because there was so much local game and fish available.

As the population increased along the eastern part of the United States, chickens became more common, eventually being used for meat as well as for their eggs. Hens that had gotten too old to lay, or that did not produce eggs consistently, were included on the dinner table. Like fish, the chicken was a perfect meal. The chicken was small enough to eat completely at one meal, which was important since the settlers had virtually no way to preserve leftovers.

"One pot" meals were common. The concept developed naturally for the settlers on the Coast and in Louisiana. Most of the dishes were gumbos, stews, and soups that were made by combining any available ingredient, including vegetables, shellfish, seafood, and wild game. These meals were slow cooked in the black iron pot that was the main fixture in the fireplace on Cat Island. The combinations that resulted from these one-pot meals led to some truly remarkable tastes. Marie cooked meat, game, and fish in the cast-iron pot. Leftovers, meats and practically anything else were dumped into the kettle. Jambalaya, stews, soups, and gumbos were not only nutritious, but also convenient. There was no attempt to recreate their European cuisine, because none of the exotic spices the Europeans knew were available in this wild new territory.

The Cuevas family raised a large herd of cattle, so milk was readily available for drinking, cooking and making cheese and butter. Cheese was an important part of the diet, and relatively simple to produce.

Coffee became popular in this country after December 16, 1773, when colonists disguised as Mohawk Indians dumped 342 chests of English tea into Boston Harbor.[63] After that time the rebellious Americans refused to drink any more tea. As a substitute they used coffee, and coffee became an overnight sensation. America never again returned to tea as its favorite drink.[64] In New Orleans, café au lait, literally "coffee with milk," became a favorite of the French people ever since coffee was first introduced. It is made by mixing an equal part of coffee and milk or crème that has been scalded rather than steamed. Café au lait was traditionally served with breakfast, while black coffee with sugar was served before breakfast and after dinner.

With the growing popularity of coffee, there were times when it was simply not available, or too expensive. Rather than do without, some people would resort to making coffee from a variety of other items, such as roasted acorns, yams, or an assortment of local grains. During those times when coffee was at a premium, the people of New Orleans and the Gulf Coast began adding chicory to stretch their supply of coffee beans. The people actually loved chicory because of the darker color and the more roasted flavor it gave to the coffee. Chicory, which was brought to the continent in the 1700s, has become synonymous with coffee, although it has a variety of other uses.[65] The leaves, for example, can be used to make a salad and the roots can be boiled and eaten like a vegetable. Many people like a cup of "coffee" made entirely of chicory. It serves as a great substitute for coffee when the roots are dried, roasted and ground. The use of chicory actually has several advantages. It contains no caffeine and it is also water soluble, which means it takes less to brew a pot.

Tea was popular in the Louisiana area before the introduction of coffee, and remained so afterward. Since tea was not available for purchase after the rebellion, the people of the Gulf Coast and Louisiana had to make their own. The most popular tea was made from the roots of the sassafras tree, a small tree indigenous to the area. It was used not only for tea, but also as flavoring, a thickener for foods, and even medicine.[66]

Breads were on the Cuevas table at every meal, but they were not easy to prepare. Flour had to be brought from New Orleans, and then some sort of yeast or starter was needed to make the dough rise. Prior to the late 1700s the only way to make bread rise was to literally beat air into the dough with eggs or egg whites. "Quick breads" were created in America with the discovery of pearlash, a refined form of potash that allowed dough to rise.[67]

Although starting the fire was a nuisance, controlling the temperature of an open fire while cooking presented an even greater challenge. Some meals required less heat than others. Since different woods burn at different speeds and temperatures, simply choosing the correct wood was an important part of food preparation. Knowing when to burn pine, oak or hickory was an art. Sometimes a direct flame was too hot and only the low heat from the embers was sufficient. To cook with these coals, the fire was started early so it would die down sufficiently to attain the correct temperature. On other occasions, simply suspending the cast-iron pots over the fire at different levels was enough to control the heat of the fire.

Kitchen cookware on Cat Island at first consisted simply of a cast-iron kettle called a chaudière (sho-dee-aire) suspended over the hearth. Almost no other pot was needed. Although this was a simple method of cooking, it was not without its dangers. There was always a threat of fire from the grease that would drip. There was also the possibility of injury from a glowing ember that could pop up.

A pail of water was warmed in the ashes during the meal so there would be hot water for washing the dirty dishes afterwards. Homemade soap and rags were used to scrub the primitive utensils. The Cuevas "kitchen" was equipped with *une huche*, or large wooden trough near the fireplace, which was necessary for mixing and kneading bread. A long-handled *pelle*, or wooden paddle, was used to remove loaves of bread from the brick oven built into the side of the fireplace.

The family was served from a large earthenware pot called a *marmite* that was set in the center of the table. It was not common to have individual place settings under these less than formal conditions, so the family simply served themselves from the marmite. The gumbos and stews that made up the majority of the meals were easy to eat without forks or knives.

The tableware pieces consisted of plates, platters, and bowls made of earthenware, pewter, or even wood. Pewter spoons and steel or iron forks were used to eat meals. Forks became fashionable in the seventeenth century, while spoons have been used for a longer time.[68] Even so, the use of one's fingers was still very much in vogue.[69]

Bowls carved out of wood were used for soup and gumbo. Later, some plates were made from pewter. Spoons were the only eating utensils, and were carved from wood or fashioned out of oyster shells. Eventually pewter was also used for spoons. The settlers did not start using forks until the Civil War. Knives, of course, were used for cutting meat, but forks were only used during the preparation of food to hold meat while it was being cut.[70]

It is not known what china was first used on Cat Island, but some of the first good china used in the country at that time was a type called "flow blue." Originally produced in the early 1800s, it began gaining popularity in America in the 1830s and remained popular until the 1900s.[71] It resembled the hand-painted oriental designs that were too costly for the average family. Flow blue used a transfer printing process that was inexpensive, and people loved the strong cobalt colors that covered the entire piece. The technique eventually became obsolete as more efficient ways to produce china were introduced. Collecting flow blue has become popular today, although it is very rare and difficult to find.[72]

The day's work on Cat Island began early, before the heat of the day. When it was light enough, Marie would send the younger children out to deliver the morning meal to Juan and the boys who were already hard at work tending the cattle. The herd was kept on the southeast side of the island, opposite from where their house stood, and where the marsh grass was plentiful for grazing. A couple of the cows were kept in a wooden pen near the house for milking. A garden was also nearby that furnished all of the fruits and vegetables that the Cuevas family needed to survive on the island. When Juan and the boys were not looking after their herd, they were hard at work maintaining the garden. The tools used for farming were few and poorly constructed, which made the work even more strenuous. Before plow irons were available, a crude wooden plow was made using a forked pole. Although the soil on the island was loose and more easily cultivated than that found on much of the mainland, such a simple plow was backbreaking at best.

There were no horses or mules on the early Coast. Instead, oxen were used when heavy work was required, and they were actually preferred over horses because of their great strength and patience. Oxen were simply bulls that were castrated when they were young to make them more manageable. They were easy to keep and did not require expensive harnesses. Oxen moved slowly, making them easy for the handlers to keep up with, and although these beasts grew to be about 2,000 pounds, which was twice as heavy as most of the beef cattle, they were gentle enough to be managed by the women and even children. The commands were simple: "gee" (turn right), "haw" (turn left), and "whoa" (stand still or stop). In addition, since the Indians did not eat oxen, they were rarely stolen.[73]

While the men worked outdoors, Marie was busy indoors, cooking, mending clothes, and washing. She even made the candles and soap for the family. Soap was mostly made from myrtle wax and had a pleasant aroma that was appealing to both sexes. The soap was gentler than common lye soap, and made an excellent softening lather for shaving.

According to the family, the Cuevas house was always clean, although not in the waxed and polished way we think of today.[74] Dusting was not a priority, but sweeping was a constant chore. The island's sandy soil was a nuisance for the family, but the cracks in the rough wood floor made it easy to keep the dirt swept to the ground below. Scrubbing was often necessary and special care was needed to remove the spills from the cooking pots. Any grease spots on the flooring were first doused with heated lye and then covered with ashes. A stiff bristle brush was used to scrub the stain, after which the floor was rinsed with hot water to wash away the lye.

The schedule for basic housework usually depended on the crops. It was important to pick the fruits and vegetables when they were ripe to prevent the birds or raccoons from raiding the food supply. Other tasks would often be put off until the harvest was complete. Laundry was a chore that required almost a full day. Not an easy task, the clothes were placed in a washtub about a third full of water with just enough soap added to cause noticeable suds, and then boiled to loosen the dirt and grime. After boiling for a while the clothes were transferred with a long wooden spoon into a second tub of clean water to cool. When the clothes were cool enough to handle, the daintier clothes were wrung out by hand. A ribbed scrub board made of wood was used to remove excess water from the heavier fabric. Once most of the water had been wrung out, the clean damp clothes were draped over the bushes outside to completely dry. The hot island sun would bleach the clothes, keeping them looking clean and smelling fresh.

After the clothes were dried they were pressed with flatirons. Two solid irons were used weighing about six pounds each. One was kept in the fireplace to heat up while Marie ironed with the other. Caution was necessary when handling these irons, because they got extremely hot in the fire. To protect against burns, a soft cotton rag was wrapped around the iron's handle. The irons also had a tendency to stick to the fabric. Common beeswax was rubbed on the surface of the hot irons to prevent damaging the material. Water was sprinkled on the fabrics to steam out wrinkles and prevent scorching.

The clothing was simple and made from homespun cloth, mostly from cotton. When the settlers first arrived, they used wool and flax to make their clothing, but the warm climate and the lack of sheep made wool impractical. In areas of Louisiana, however, some did combine wool with cotton to make a warmer cloth called "jeture de laine."[75] The plain, floor-length dresses that were the normal attire for women were made of calico (a coarse cotton cloth with bright printed patterns), gingham (a light plain-weave fabric with checks, stripes, or plaids), or a material called linsey-woolsey (a coarse cloth made from linen interwoven with wool or cotton). Linsey-woolsey was a favorite material for making shirts, trousers, dresses, petticoats, coats and jackets. Cottonade cloth (a rough grade of material made from cotton) was preferred for sheets, blankets, tablecloths, and other household items. Women also wore sunbonnets made of cottonade fabric that had been reinforced with split-cane ribs.[76] Natural dyes, such as indigo, were used to add color to the cloth when something more than the basic white was desired.

In keeping with the colonial times, Marie's entire wardrobe must have been very simple. Most of the women had only three dresses, two for everyday wear and a "dressy" one for special occasions. There were no undergarments, since women did not begin wearing underwear until the 1850s.[77] Undergarments first developed in the form of knee-length, embroidered drawers, chemises, and petticoats as protection in the colder weather. When the heavier coats were removed after people came in from the cold outside, these underclothes provided a secondary layer for warmth inside the drafty houses.[78]

Juan and the older boys likely wore pants made of cottonade cloth. Their shirts were also made of cottonade or linsey-woolsey and were usually white with no collar. Whites, beiges, earthy greens, browns, and black were the predominant colors for men's clothing. Following the French Revolution (1789–1799) the shift was from knee pants to full-length trousers, but it took a while for fashion changes to reach the Coast.[79] The pants, therefore, were usually knee length. After the beginning of the 1800s comfort and fit, rather than the cut of the pants, was the priority, and hats made of straw, split-cane, or reeds were often worn.[80]

Shoes at the time were crudely made of heavy leather and were generally very uncomfortable, since the width of the foot was not considered. Awkwardly, the same shoe was made to fit either foot. The first shoes designed specifically for left and right feet were not made until 1800, and were not available in rural areas until later.[81] The tendency was to go barefoot on Cat Island except for the difficulty of walking among the "stickers" that were so common.

Hairstyles were an individual thing, although women generally wore their hair long and men wore short hair and were generally clean-shaven. Beards and sideburns did not come into fashion until the 1850s, and became particularly popular during the Civil War.[82]

Children's clothing during the 1700s had been tight and restrictive, much like the adults' clothing of that period, but in the 1800s the designs of their clothing were moving toward more freedom of movement. Although girls' garments were becoming less restrictive, their long, relatively narrow dresses made running and playing difficult. Very young children wore tight bodices tied in the back with bands of cloth used for guiding them as they learned to walk. These bands also served to restrain more lively toddlers. Some of the girls retained the bands on their clothing long after they were needed to give the impression of continuing youth. Boys were allowed to wear trousers at the age of five or six. For some boys it was more like seven to nine, depending on the family. About that same age, girls began wearing dresses that were cut more like those of adults.[83]

Life was hard on the island and the children were expected to help with the chores. The children would milk the cows, plant seeds, and haul water from the well. Everyone had designated tasks, but the younger children loved to gather the eggs. After collecting them, they would also sort them according to size and color for cooking. Checking on the chickens took more courage than one would imagine for what one would imagine was a simple task. The roosters who were guarding their setting hens could hurt little legs and feet. They seemed to always know when the little ones were not paying attention, and would attack if they could. The job of gathering eggs could also get messy. Setting hens would not heed nature's call sometimes for hours or days when they were sitting on their eggs, but would relieve themselves immediately when lifted off the nest.

The boys learned planting, fishing, and working with wood, everything a man would need to know to assure his family's survival. Girls learned from their mothers how to maintain the home. They learned to cook and clean, as well as to spin yarn and sew. Women were experts in weaving, and they passed this skill to the children. In addition to making cloth they would also weave grass and leaves into hats, fans, and baskets.

Water was important, if not more so than food. Fortunately the water on Cat Island was sweet and clean, probably because it was filtered through the pure crystalline sand. Wells on the mainland were often contaminated by their proximity to the privies or to animal pens. Water not only was the greatest necessity of life, but it was also the cause of much of the sickness. Usually people drank from the same unwashed cup without a thought or understanding of the transmission of disease. A long-handled cup was kept by the well for all to use, and people were unaware of the danger of germs and the importance of sanitary conditions.

Doctors, Medicine and Diseases

There were no doctors on the early Coast. With the lack of medical professionals, the mother provided the necessary medicines and treatments. She filled her medicine chest with natural ingredients found in the surrounding woods. Many of the home remedies had been passed down for generations, even going back to their lives in Europe. Some of the common diseases were malaria (known as the ague), catarrh, cholera, tuberculosis, and smallpox. There were other illnesses that mostly affected the children. Those included chicken pox, diphtheria, measles, mumps, scarlet fever, whooping cough, and poliomyelitis. Survival against even the most common diseases was difficult, since the symptoms of coughing, fever, headache, diarrhea, and vomiting was common to many of the illnesses. This made it very difficult to diagnose the specific ailment, particularly for untrained professionals.[84]

There were a few doctors in New Orleans, but they usually treated only the wealthy.[85] No one, including the doctors themselves, had any real understanding of germs or why people became ill. There were no instruments for diagnosis, such as thermometers or stethoscopes, so treatments were generally devised according to guesswork or superstition. As late as 1907 most "doctors" had no formal education. Many learned by watching others or even taught themselves through trial and error. The few medical schools that existed at that time were considered by the government to be "sub-standard."[86]

Often the doctor's treatments were worse than the illness, resulting in death rather than a cure. Some of the more popular treatments included bleeding, purging, vomiting, and sweating. The doctors could only treat the symptom and not the cause, so when a person had an elevated heartbeat, for example, an herb may be administered to slow the heart. Such treatments only served to harm the patient. Most medicines of the early 1800s were totally ineffective. A treatment that was successful often worked simply because the patient "believed" it would.[87]

Family remedies were often just as effective, if not more so, than treatment by a physician. One of the most commonly used medicines in the Cuevas house was turpentine.[88] It was easily made by distilling resin obtained from the abundant pine trees in the area. Turpentine has been used medicinally since ancient times. It was applied directly to cuts and scrapes to speed healing and to reduce the pain. Mixed with animal fat, it was used as a chest rub to treat colds. It was also effective against phthiriasis (head lice), although the treatment was long and uncomfortable. The patient's hair would be completely soaked in kerosene two or three times a day, and then wrapped in a cloth for twenty-four hours. This killed not only the lice, but also the eggs. After the smelly treatment, the hair had to be thoroughly washed, and even then the odor seemed to last.[89]

The roots from the wax myrtle were a source of several medical treatments. Although the plant was never recognized officially as a drug, it was used successfully by some doctors and in some home remedies.[90] Myrtle root bark was chewed to cure a toothache, sore mouth, and bleeding gums, while powdered myrtle root bark was used to treat hemorrhages, sores, skin ulcers, and to relieve itching. The roots were also used to make tea that was gargled for sore throats. Water that had been used to remove myrtle wax while making candles was boiled further and used as a last-ditch cure for severe dysentery associated with typhoid.

The side effects were so unpleasant that the treatment was used sparingly. Some who used it reported dizziness, stomach cramps, chills, fever, depression, burning and painful eyes, dry throat, and bloating caused from gas. Some of the other popular folk medicines included paregoric to treat common diarrhea, regular vinegar to treat sunburn, and lemon juice mixed with a couple spoons of sugar was taken for a stomachache. Sassafras tea was used to shorten the length of the common cold, while a thin soup was good for "anything that ailed you."[91]

Dental problems were also an issue. Many suffered from decaying or rotting teeth. This was especially true if they ate a lot of sugar, or chewed sugar cane, common in Louisiana and on the Coast. Most people's teeth were black and many of their teeth were noticeably missing, because the common cure for toothache was extraction. Before toothbrushes people would use twigs or their fingers to try to clean their teeth, not to prevent cavities, but to remove food buildup simply as a practical matter. People did not understand the relationship between brushing teeth and tooth decay.[92]

The early families did not understand the importance of personal hygiene. They did not bathe or shower daily the way most of us do today. In fact, they often did not bath more than a few times a year. People believed that a layer of dirt actually protected them from germs. The difficulty of filling a bathtub by hauling pails of water from the well may have contributed to this way of thinking. But, when they did find it necessary, they would wash their faces, hands, arms and necks with a discarded piece of clothing dipped into a pail of water. There are so many streams and rivers along the Coast that getting wet during the course of one's day was unavoidable. These pseudo baths were helpful, although the salty waters of the Mississippi Sound only substituted one unpleasant odor for another. Everyone had the same sense of cleanliness. The people were accustomed to the bad smells associated with farm life, and that included common body odor.

With such little regard for hygienic conditions, it is a minor miracle that mothers and their babies survived childbirth. There were no medicines or drugs to ease the pain or fight infection. In fact, anesthesia was not used for childbirth until 1845.[93] Women were truly strong, enduring painful contractions in the middle of the night with only the light of a flickering candle, while shivering in the cold of winter, or soaked with sweat in the high heat and humidity of coastal summers. Along with the ordeal of childbirth itself, they had the awkward task of using a chamber pot when nature called.

It was unheard of for men in the 1800s to be present during the birth of a baby, and that included men who were doctors.[94] There were no professional midwives on the Coast, so the woman's mother or other relative would assist with the birth. Infant mortality was a real concern. Many of the families lost at least one child due to complications during the birthing process. As a precautionary measure the wife was frequently kept in bed for as much as a week after delivery. The smaller children were often sent away to stay with relatives during the last months of the pregnancy before the mother began to show. They would remain away for several weeks after the birth, mostly to help reduce the stress on the new mother, but also to avoid the question of "where babies came from." The puritan attitude of the 1800s that kept the men out of the delivery room also prohibited parents from facing the issues of sex and childbirth. The question from inquisitive children was lightly sidestepped by explaining "the stork brought them," or they were "found in a cabbage patch."

The baby's baptism was an important event. There were no churches or resident priests on the Coast, so it was common to hold group baptisms, weddings, and other sacraments at one event when a priest could visit from New Orleans or Mobile.[95] The role of godparents in the lives of their godchildren, as outlined by the church, was far more important in the

1800s.[96] The godparents took a more active role in the child's life. They were not only allowed, but encouraged to offer advice on how the child should be raised. In the event of the parent's death, which was not uncommon in the wilderness, godparents were expected not only to assure that the child receive a good Catholic upbringing, but to actually take over the physical care of their godchild.

During the years of French rule (1699–1763), Roman Catholicism was the official religion of the Louisiana territory. The Church of England, however, gained some prominence during British control of the area (1763–1780), attracting many Protestant settlers.[97] This influx continued even after Spain took over in 1781 when Roman Catholicism again became the church of state. The Catholic Church has always been an integral part of the peoples' lives. Father Michael Porter, a visiting priest from Mobile who later became that city's first bishop, held the first recorded church service at Shieldsboro (current Bay St. Louis) in 1820.[98] Juan de Cuevas was sixty years old at the time. There is no evidence that any of the Cuevas family on Cat Island attended. On July 28, 1837, Father John Mary Joseph Chanché (1795–1855) was installed as the first bishop of the Mississippi Diocese of Natchez.[99] At the time there were no Catholic churches in the entire state and the only priests in the diocese were two missionaries sent by the archbishop of New Orleans.[100]

In 1842, Bishop Chanché sent Father Guillame Labbé to oversee the Coast community.[101] He was stationed at Bay St. Louis, where he served from 1843–1844. In 1844, towards the end of his service, Father Labbé built the first Catholic Mission Church in Pass Christian.[102] On July 31, 1847, the Rev. Stanislaus Buteaux was appointed the first pastor of Our Lady of the Gulf Parish in Bay St. Louis. His parish duties included missions on Jourdan River, Pearl River, and Wolf River. These became known as the Three Rivers Missions. Present day Kiln, Mississippi, was originally known as the Jourdan River settlement. Not only did Father Buteaux serve Bay St. Louis and the Three Rivers Missions, he would also serve areas of Harrison and Jackson Counties.[103] By 1849, Father Buteaux was making monthly visits to Cat Island, taking communion to the Cuevas family, and eventually officiating at the funeral of Juan de Cuevas, who died that year.[104]

As the community continued to grow, Father Antoine Paul Guerard became the first resident priest for Pass Christian in May of 1850.[105] Father Guerard oversaw the construction of the first church in Pass Christian, and later also built a small Mission Church on the Jourdan River at Kiln. In 1861, at the end of the Cuevas era on Cat Island, there were about one hundred members of the church at Pass Christian.[106]

Survival required that every family member work, including the youngest, so there was little time for formal schooling. Nuns taught in the first public school in Shieldsboro in 1831.[10] It was not until 1870 that a uniform statewide school system was finally established. School attendance was not made compulsory until 1918.[108] The necessary skills, like making charcoal and turpentine, and hunting and fishing, were not taught in the classroom, but were handed down from father to son.

Even though the children worked long hours, they still found time to play and "just be kids." They entertained themselves with simple toys and games, or just hopping, skipping, jumping and swimming. There were no manufactured toys so the children used their imaginations to create toys from wood, scraps of cloth, corncobs, or whatever other materials they could find. It was not considered proper for older girls to participate in vigorous games such as tag or chase, so they played guessing games using common items like beans or buttons. A form of jacks was also played using marbles or small pebbles, since metal jacks were not available until probably the late nineteenth century.

The younger girls played with dolls made of cornhusks, which were made by weaving wet husks to form the doll's body, arms and legs using a technique very much like basket weaving. Usually the dolls did not have faces, but were often dressed using scraps of fabric from old clothing.

A popular game for boys and girls of that day was the very old string game, Cat's Cradle.[109] It had apparently been played in many different cultures for centuries. A long loop of string was manipulated back and forth between the player's fingers or between the fingers of more than one player to form various string figures. Sometimes the mouth or wrists were also used for more complicated moves. Names developed nationally for some of the more popular designs, such as: Jacob's Ladder, Cup and Saucer, and Hand Catch, just to name a few.

Children seem to have always played with marbles, but the marbles were not made of glass, but of clay. Glass marbles were not available until after 1846 when a German glassblower invented a way to mass-produce the little round toys.[110] The game of marbles helped children develop hand and eye coordination, and also taught them how to interact with other playmates. This was particularly true if they were playing "keepsies," in which the winner kept the loser's marbles.

A whirligig was another favorite toy.[111] It was made from a thin circular piece of flat wood or a large button. Two holes were punched in the wood about ⅜ inch from the center of the circle. A string was run through the two holes and tied to form a loop. The string was held between the thumb and forefinger of each hand. The wooden disk was twirled until it became twisted, then by pulling hard the whirligig would spin as the string unwound. By alternately pulling and relaxing the string, the piece of wood in the center could be made to spin continuously while making a buzzing sound.

The bull roarer was another ancient and universal toy.[112] A flat piece of wood was attached to a long string. By swirling the wood in circles overhead, a roaring nose was created. Sometimes the string was tied to the end of a long stick and swung to give the player more force, almost like a whip.

Children were not the only ones to play games. The adults, visiting with friends, often played cards or a game of checkers. Poker became a popular card game during this period.[113] The dice game Craps was an adult game played mostly in the bars of New Orleans. It was introduced to the city in 1813 by Bernard Xavier Philippe de Marigny de Mandeville, a wealthy Louisiana landowner, who was a gambler and politician. The name was derived from the U.S. term for a Creole person, "Johnny Crapaud." It was a simplified version of the Old English game of Hazard.[114]

There were only a few recognized holidays in the early 1800s. One of the most popular in the Louisiana territory was Mardi Gras. Pope Gregory XIII made Mardi Gras a Christian holiday when he placed it on the Gregorian calendar in 1582.[115] In 1837 the first symbolic floats made their appearance on the streets, and a secret society called the Mistick Krewe of Comus staged the first large, well-organized parade in 1857.[116]

Christmas was not a popular holiday in the early 1800s. The most important day of the season was Epiphany, January 6. In Europe it is still known as "Three Kings Day," or in Spain, "Dia de los Tres Reyes."[117] This is the day that it is believed the three Wise Men located the infant Jesus. Gifts were traditionally exchanged on Epiphany rather than Christmas, symbolizing the gifts of the Magi. In Spain today, Epiphany is still the day for exchanging gifts.

The country never had a regular national day of thanksgiving until 1863 when President Abraham Lincoln declared Thanksgiving a national holiday.[118]

The years of the Cuevas era on Cat Island saw many dramatic changes as the population of the Coast slowly increased. Small settlements from Mobile to New Orleans were beginning to develop into small villages and towns. On April 30, 1804, the United States took possession of the Louisiana territory after the area was purchased from France.[119] In 1812, the Coast counties of Hancock and Jackson were formed.[120] The area from the Pearl River to the Bay of St. Louis was named after John Hancock, the revolutionary patriot, while the area from the bay extending eastward indefinitely was named after Andrew Jackson. The state of Louisiana was created when President Madison signed an act of Congress on April 12, 1812.[121] Six days later, on the 16th, the land between the Perdido River and the Pearl River became part of the Mississippi territory. Mississippi became a state on December 10, 1817.[122] Six months later, on June 21, 1818, the first state legislature of the newly formed Mississippi incorporated the town of Shieldsboro. The name was changed officially to Bay St. Louis on March 2, 1875.[123]

There were summer resorts scattered all over the north and east in the early 1800s, but there were virtually none in the south. In 1829, the first modern hotel where guests had private rooms with their own personal keys opened in Boston, Massachusetts.[124] Florida, Cuba, and the Bermudas had yet to catch on as tourist locations, and thus had no hotels or resorts. In the string of towns and hamlets along the Mississippi Gulf Coast, however, resorts were beginning to crop up as northerners discovered the balmy weather. The warm climate of the Gulf combined with the fresh, invigorating air gave a sense of a healthy retreat. In 1836, the Pass Christian Hotel put the small village on the map.[125] Its construction was completed a full two years before the city was incorporated, and was the best hotel on the Coast before the Civil War period.

In 1837, the state legislature granted a charter to the nonexistent Mississippi City. Its promoters, John J. McCaughan, James McLauren, and Colin McRae, envisioned the resort as a potential rival to New Orleans. The city's charter made it the oldest official town on the mainland Coast.[126]

On February 8, 1838, the city of Biloxi was incorporated in Hancock County.[127] This "Gem City" of the Mississippi Gulf Coast was an energetic business city with years of history behind it. As the former capital of the French settlement of Louisiana, it developed from a small fishing village into the seat of a large seafood canning industry.

On February 5, 1839, a third county was formed on the Coast, mostly out of existing Hancock County to the west, with a small amount from Jackson County to the east. Named in honor of William Henry Harrison, the ninth president of the United States, Harrison County eventually became the most populated county on the Coast.[128]

As the tourist trade continued to grow, new hotels sprung up in almost every city along the Coast. In 1839, the Bay St. Louis Hotel, with rooms advertised at $56 per week, was the first hotel built in Shieldsboro.[129] By 1842, there were also a number of boarding houses in that city.[130] John Hohn built the Magnolia Hotel in 1847 during the steamboat era, which became the oldest running hotel on the Coast.[131] Biloxi had several other fine hotels by the late 1850s, including the American Hotel, Biloxi House, Green Oaks Hotel, and Shady Oaks Hotel, as well as many fine boarding houses.

In 1850, Dr. William Teagarden built a hotel in Mississippi City at the intersection of Teagarden Road and Beach Boulevard.[132] In addition, he built an 800-yard wharf into the sound and requested that the state build a lighthouse on shore to guide steamboats to his landing. When the government refused, he built his own private light station.

In 1853, Enoch Everitt built a hotel on Jackson Avenue called the Ocean Springs Hotel.[133] He had leased the nearby springs and advertised the medicinal value of the water.

That same year the fifteen residents of the area voted to name the town Lynchburg Springs. In 1854, shortly after the government established the Lynchburg Springs post office, the town's name was changed to Ocean Springs because of the hotel.[134]

By the late 1850s wealthy families from New Orleans along with plantation owners from Mississippi, Alabama, and Louisiana built large waterfront homes on the Gulf Coast. In the summer of 1848, the landmark Biloxi lighthouse opened, and on September 2, James Brown, from Madison County, Mississippi, purchased the property and began building what was to become Beauvoir. The construction was completed in 1852.[135]

In 1854, Father Stanislaus Buteaux founded Stanislaus College in Bay St. Louis. It began as a boarding school for boys, and was operated by the Brothers of the Sacred Heart.[136] That same year, The Chimneys community became known as Rosalie.[137]

In the late 1850s, Pierre Simon Quave, the grandson of Juan de Cuevas, operated a mercantile store at Back Bay Biloxi, now D'Iberville. The store closed on April 12, 1862, because of the Civil War, and Pierre and his brother, Christopher, joined the Confederate forces. Unfortunately both men were killed in the war. Family members reopened the store on July 2, 1870.[138] Pierre had kept a detailed journal of his customers and their purchases leaving us with a glimpse into the daily lives of the people on the Coast, the kinds of items they used, and the cost of living at the end of the Cuevas era on Cat Island (1861).[139]

Beer, Tobacco, Firearms

Beer	$0.15 / bottle
Gin	$0.40 / bottle
Gun powder	$0.60 / lb
Pipes	$0.05 each
Tobacco (smoking)	$0.40 / lb
Tobacco (chew)	$0.45 (3 plugs)
Tobacco papers	$0.05
Whiskey	$0.25 / half gallon
Wine	$0.25 / bottle
Wine	$0.80 / gallon

Building Supplies

Auger	$1.00
Axe handle	$0.25
Axe	$1.25
Barrel	$7.00
Brace and bit	$2.15
Bucket	$0.25
Coal tar[140]	$1.00 (5 gals)
Graf rope	$0.23 / lb
Lamp wick	$0.30
Lock	$1.00
Lumber	$0.50 (unknown quantity)
Lumber	$2.38 (119 feet)
Nails	$0.10 / lb
Pad lock	$0.25
Paint	$0.75
Plank	$0.50 (for one)
Plow	$1.25
Plow line	$0.15
Putty	$0.10 / lb
Rope	$0.20 / lb
Rule and level	$1.25
Ruler	$0.50
Shovel	$1.25
Spade	$1.25
Water bucket	$0.25
White lead[141]	$0.15

Cloth and Sewing Items

Bed ticking	$0.08 / yd
Buttons	$0.10
Calico[142]	$0.15 / yd
Cotton	$0.15 / yd
Cottonade[143]	$0.25 / yd
Crepe[144]	$0.20 / yd
Flannel	$0.15 / yd
Gingham[145]	$0.15 / yd
Hickory cloth[146]	$0.15 / yd
Linen	$1.50 / yd
Muslin	$0.20 / yd
Ribbon	$0.10 / yd
Thread	$0.10
Twilled cotton[147]	$0.15 / yd

Clothing

Handkerchief	$0.25
Hat	$1.50
Shirt	$1.75
Shoes (1 pair)	$1.00
Socks (1 pair)	$0.25

Food

Bacon	$0.12 / lb
Beans	$0.50
Beef	$8.00 / head

Black pepper	$0.10 / ½ lb	Lamp wick	$0.30
Bread	$0.04 / loaf	Matches	$0.10
Butter	$0.25 / ¼ lb	Picher	$0.40
Candy	$0.35	Pot	$1.20
Candy (sugar plum)	$0.40	Sifter	$0.30
Candy and cakes	$1.50	Tin dipper	$0.15
Cheese	$0.20 / lb	Tin pan	$0.35
Chicken	$0.25 (for 1)	Tin plate	$0.25
Chocolate	$0.40		
Codfish	$0.25		

Medicine

Castor oil[152]	$0.45
Paregoric[154]	$0.15
Pills (?)	$0.25 / box
Spirit of turpentine[154]	$0.25

Coffee & sugar	$1.00 (unspecified amount)		
Corn	$0.75 / gal		
Corn	$1.00 / bushel		
Corn	$6.60 / sack		

Miscellaneous

Corn (for horse feed)	$2.50	Ball	$0.10
Cream of tartar[148]	$0.25 / ¼ lb	Bridle	$2.25
Eggs	$0.30 / doz	Bridle & martingale[155]	$3.00
Flour	$6.00 / barrel	Brimstone[156]	$0.15
Fresh pork	$3.05	Cast net twine	$0.70
Garlic	$0.10	Cord of wood	$1.15
Hog head cheese[149]	$1.15 (19 lbs)	Corn for horse feed	$2.50
Lard	$0.15 / lb	Currycomb[157]	$0.25
Macaroni	$0.10	Fish hook	$0.10
Mackerel fish	$2.50	Flax seed[158]	$0.20
Meal	$1.65 / bushel	Hickory	$0.15 / yd
Molasses	$0.50 / gal	Horse collar	$0.35
Mustard	$0.15 / box	Line	$0.10
Mutton	$0.25	Spurs	$1.85 / pair
Onions	$0.15 (1 sack = $1.50)	Stirrups	$1.00 / pair
Peas	$0.50 / gal	Wood	$1.75 (one cord)
Potatoes	$0.25 / bushel		
Rice	$0.10 / lb		
Salt	$0.10		

Personal Items

Salt	$1.50 / sack	Cologne water	$0.75
Shoulder of bacon	$1.30	Fine comb	$0.25
Sugar	$0.15 / lb	Looking glass	$0.15 (a mirror)
Sweet oil (?)	$0.60 / bottle	Razor	$1.25
Sweet potatoes	$1.00 / bushel	Razor strap	$0.25
Tea	$0.15	Shaving bowl	$0.25
Vermicelli[150]	$0.20 / lb	Shaving soap	$0.10
Vinegar	$0.10 / bottle	Soap	$0.25 / bar
		Sundries[159]	$0.25
		Tuck comb[160]	$0.30

Household Items

School Supplies

Basket	$0.40		
Bowl	$0.35		
Broom	$0.25		
Candle	$0.30	Book	$ 0.15
Candle stick	$0.15	Letter paper	$ 0.15
Chamber pot	$0.40	Paper and ink	$ 0.25
Coffee mill	$0.75 (each)	Pen and handle	$ 0.20
Cups & saucer	$0.15	Pencil	$ 0.15 each
Dishes	$0.80 (for two)	Slate and pencil	$ 0.30
French tallow[151]	$0.05		

Sewing Items

Glass (drinking)	$0.05		
Jug	$0.25	Hook and eye	$ 0.05
Knife	$1.75	Needles	$ 0.10
Knives & forks	$1.25 / dozen	Silk thread	$ 0.10

Pierre Simon Quave also ran a ferry service across Back Bay. The ferry was able to continue even during the war years. Pierre recorded in his journal the following list of fees he charged to carry passengers and livestock back and forth across the Bay.[161] It is interesting to note that Pierre would also provide service occasionally to Cat Island at a cost of $3.00 per trip.

Ferry Crossing (Back Bay)

Each person crossing on ferry both ways	$0.30
1 cart crossing ferry	$0.50
1 cow crossing ferry	$0.50
1 horse crossing ferry	$0.50
7 head of sheep crossing ferry	$0.35
27 head of cattle	$13.50
83 head sheep	$4.15
1 trip to Cat Island	$3.00

Pierre "Perrique" Cuevas, son of Juan de Cuevas, and father of Pierre Simon, ran a shipyard near his son's store. Perrique paid his workers by the day. The salaries recorded were $ 1.00 per day, $ 3.00 for two days, and $ 3.40 for 4½ days. Perrique also sent his children to private Catholic school in Bay St. Louis. The tuition is recorded as $4.50 for three months, and $9.00 for three children for two months; $10.85 was spent transporting them back and forth to the school from their home in North Biloxi.[162]

The New Orleans French Market began operating in 1793, about the same time Juan de Cuevas arrived on the Gulf Coast.[163] The old market started as a trading post for Native Americans who met in the bend of the Mississippi River to exchange goods. As the market grew it spread out along the river, disrupting commerce. The Spanish officials realized there was a need to consolidate and organize the activity, so in 1891 the market was restricted to one section near Jackson Square.[164] The French Market continued to flourish, and today is the oldest trading market in the United States.[165] The world-famous Café du Monde coffee stand was established in 1862 on the original site of the old French Market. By this time, New Orleans had grown to be the nation's second-largest seaport.[166]

Throughout the Cuevas era on Cat Island, many developments were taking place in the country and the world that would change life in dramatic ways. Advances in science, medicine, industry, and the arts would eventually lift all of mankind from a simple rural existence to the modern society that we enjoy today. Unfortunately, life on the island remained as quaint and simple as always, since it took decades for many of these inventions and discoveries to become part of everyday life.

Society was also changing during those turbulent years. And, almost like the racial strife that characterized the 1960s, tensions were being felt during the first quarter of the 1800s. Native Americans were then at the center of this ethnic controversy as they were rounded up and sent to government reservations. The Cuevas family witnessed firsthand this dark period in our nation's history.

11

The Seminole Indians on Cat Island

In 1834, the Cuevas family watched as a large group of Seminole Indians was unloaded from barges in the Gulf and herded onto the beaches of Cat Island. Native American men, women and children gathered what little belongings they could carry on their backs and waded through the shallow waters from the boats to the shore. Their journey had not been by choice.

The Indian Removal Act, passed by Congress on May 28, 1830, had mandated the transportation of the Chickasaw, Choctaw, Seminole, Cherokee, and Creek Indians to the reservation set up in Oklahoma by the U.S. government.[1] These groups became known as the Five Civilized Tribes, because they had begun to adopt many of the "white man's" customs and some had even converted to Christianity. Although they were living as autonomous tribes, they were considered part of the Creek Confederacy. Many of the Indians moved voluntarily in a peaceful manner, trying in good faith to comply with the federal act, but the Seminole tribes were more difficult. They resisted the move to the Oklahoma reservation because they found themselves thrown together with other tribes who had always been their enemies.[2]

Seeing the opportunity to make a large amount of money from this government directive, an enterprising businessman in Alabama, whose name has been lost to history, orchestrated a plan that would allow him to transfer the Indians in the Alabama-Georgia area to their new home on the Oklahoma reservation. The U.S. government, which had already realized the difficulties faced in forcing thousands of Native Americans out of their lands, eagerly accepted his proposal.[3] The man contracted with the government to carry the Seminoles down the rivers of Alabama to the Gulf, where they would then be transported to New Orleans through Lake Ponchartain. From the lake they would march over to the Mississippi River to be loaded on boats waiting to take them upriver to one of the landings in Arkansas. On the final leg of the journey, they would travel on foot from the docks in Arkansas to the reservation in Oklahoma.

Most of the Indians were being moved over land, almost entirely on foot. Travel by water was a more efficient and practical method, although the journey was still too long and difficult to be completed without a stop. As part of his plan, the man suggested that Cat Island was halfway and could be used as a holding area for the Indians.[4] The government accepted the proposal and made the necessary arrangements with Juan de Cuevas to allow the Seminoles to reside temporarily on his island. Although the Choctaw Indians who had driven many of the settlers to the barrier islands were no longer a threat, such a large group of Native Americans setting up camp less than a mile from the Cuevas family home was clearly a concern.

The history of these Indians, later called Seminoles, began in the 1700s when Creek Indians from territories in what is now Alabama and Georgia began moving into northern Florida.[5] They were migrating to escape growing disputes with the Europeans who were land-hungry and encroaching on Indian territories. The Creeks were looking to replace their former land with new rich farmland abundant in Florida.[6] The Spanish encouraged the Indians to settle the old mission sites the crown had established unsuccessfully in the 1500s across southern Georgia and northern Florida. By settling in this area, the Indians created a buffer from the British in Georgia who were a growing threat to Spanish Florida. Spain protected the Indians so long as they agreed not to harass the Spanish settlements and to also consider conversion to Catholicism.[7]

The four tribes in the southeastern United States included the Choctaw, Chickasaw, Cherokee, and Creek. Although not related by blood, these bands shared the roots of a common language known as Muskhogean.[8] The Creek Indians were mostly from six villages in the Alabama-Georgia territory, Cusseta, Coweta, Areka, Coosa, Hoithle Waule, and Tuckabatchee. As they drifted into Florida they converged with other Indian groups, forming a sophisticated confederacy as a defense against the northern tribes. The Creeks accepted other tribes into the alliance who were fleeing from the tyranny of the Europeans. Eventually the band included the Coushatta, Tuskegee, Alabama, Hitchitee, and the Natchez. The member tribes who joined the Creek confederacy did not loose their individual autonomy. They were not only permitted to keep their own lands and to maintain political sovereignty, but they were also allowed to leave the alliance if and when it was to their advantage to do so.[9]

Over time the Europeans encountered so many of these Indian groups that it was difficult to separate them. In order to identify the tribes, they began giving them made-up names. Over time these "nicknames" became the official ones used by the United States in treaties and agreements, although the Indians themselves almost never used these names.[10] The British, for example, named the Creek Indians as a shortened form of the name of the Ocheese Creek along which their settlements were located. Since the Creek Indians outnumbered the other tribes in the alliance, the entire confederacy eventually became known as the Creek Indians.[11]

In the 1770s, a new tribal confederacy was formed in Florida after some of the Indians returned to lands near the Ocmulgee, Coosa, and Tallapoosa Rivers.[12] The remaining tribes became collectively called Seminoles. Most believe the name derived from "cimarron," the Spanish word for "runaway" or "separatist," since they were considered runaways from their original tribes in Georgia and Alabama.[13] Later when runaway black slaves joined the Seminole tribe, they were referred to as "maroons." This was also a derivation of the word cimarron. Some historians believe, however, that the name was not from the Spanish, but rather derived from the word ishi semoli, which was a Creek Indian word also used to describe separatists or runaways. Those who accept this interpretation contend that it was not the Spanish, but rather the Florida Indians who actually named themselves Seminoles.[14]

The few Florida Indians indigenous to the state were also included in the new Seminole tribe. There were over 100,000 in the 1500s, but their numbers were diminished after the arrival of the Europeans when they either were killed or died of disease. The few that were left were absorbed into the Creek federation. The Indians were allowed to inhabit almost the entire area of Florida, since the Spanish were originally only interested in deep-water ports along the coastline.

In addition to the soft treatment of Indians, the Spanish also offered asylum to runaway black slaves from the English colonies as an irritant to the British. The maroons found the Seminoles to be sympathetic, and were easily absorbed into the tribe. The people of the area were particularly angry when the blacks aligned with the Indians to attack plantations in Georgia.[15] Because of their actions, there was a growing desire among settlers to defeat the Seminole and to remove them from their lands. When the British took over Florida in 1763, the sanctuary offered by the Spanish ended, but Florida continued to serve as a safe destination for runaways.[16] These Black Seminoles continued to pour in, and began living on the outskirts of the Indian villages in their own independent communities. The Creek alliance treated the slaves as they did the new groups of Indians, allowing them to own their own land, elect their own leaders, and to keep their weapons. Although they were never official members of the Seminole Tribe, their knowledge of the white man's culture and language was important to the Indians. The so-called Black Seminoles also proved to be especially helpful in war, since they were ultimately fighting for their own freedom.[17]

During the War of 1812, major general Andrew Jackson was particularly angry when the Seminoles and maroons again joined forces, this time to aid the British against the United States. After a partial defeat in 1814, the Creeks signed treaties that exchanged their land in the east for government land in the west. The United States was not so trustworthy in keeping the treaties, which ultimately led to their takeover of most of the Alabama and Florida territories, as well as much of Georgia, Tennessee, Mississippi, Kentucky and North Carolina previously owned by the Indians.[18]

The First Seminole War (1817–1818) began as a result of the U.S. authorities attempting to recapture the runaway black slaves.[19] More than 3,000 soldiers under Jackson's command demolished several native villages. Facing strong resistance from the blacks and their Seminole allies, he failed in his mission to recapture the slaves or disperse the Indians. When Andrew Jackson became president of the United States in 1828, he proposed moving all of the Indians to the west of the Mississippi River from the reservation that had been specifically established for them north of Lake Okeechobee.[20] This way of thinking led to the Indian Removal Act of 1830, which made it mandatory for the Indians to move to the reservation in Oklahoma.[21] The Seminoles, however, refused to leave Florida, and hid with their families in the Everglades. This led to the Second Seminole War.

During those turbulent years, two legendary Seminole leaders emerged. The most famous was a warrior called Osceola (1804–1838), and the second was an inspirational medicine man called Abiaka (1760–1860). Osceola was born in the village of Tallassee, Alabama, to an English trader named William Powell and the granddaughter of the first white man to trade with the Creeks in Alabama, Polly Coppinger. He was a mixed breed originally named Billy Powell whose mother was part Muscogee and part Scottish. He always claimed that he was full-blooded Muscogee, since the Seminoles strictly forbade intermarriage with whites. In 1814, he moved with his mother and other Creek Indians from Alabama to Florida.

As an adult he took the name Osceola, which was an anglicized form of the Creek word *Asi-yahola,* a combination of the name of a black ceremonial drink made from the yaupon holly and a word meaning to shout or holler.[22] He was handsome and full of self-confidence, and although he had no heritage as a chief or leader of the Indian people, his skill as a public speaker allowed him to become extremely influential with the Seminoles.

Although he never led more than a small group of warriors, he masterminded several successful attacks against the United States and eventually became synonymous with the Seminoles' strong reputation for non-surrender. He was double-crossed by the United States when he was led to believe the army wanted to sign a truce. He was captured during the supposed signing on October 20, 1837, which remains one of the most disgraceful events in U.S. military history.[23] He and 200 other prisoners were transported to Fort Moultrie in South Carolina, where he died only three months later.

Osceola's death became front-page news all over the world, making him the most famous Native American, and creating his legend as a defender of the Seminole people. The old medicine man, Abiaka, born Sam Jones, never achieved the recognition of Osceola, but he is credited with keeping the Seminole resistance active after Osceola's death. Abiaka was the only major Seminole leader to remain in Florida after the Indian wars had ended.[24]

As a result of the Indian Removal Act, an estimated 100,000 tribesmen were forcibly moved westward on foot, many of them shackled.[25] In 1831 the Choctaw were the first tribe to be moved. The experience was fairly uneventful and became the model for subsequent moves. The Seminoles were next in 1832, followed by the Creeks in 1834, the Chickasaw in 1837, and finally the Cherokee in 1838.[26] The journey to Oklahoma was particularly hard on the elderly and the women with children. An estimated 4,000 Indians perished of hunger, exposure and disease on the way. The harsh trek to the west became known as the Trail of Tears because of the huge amount of suffering.[27]

Portrait of Osceola, painted from life by George Catlin, at Fort Moultrie, South Carolina, where Osceola was imprisoned and died a few months later in January 1838 (courtesy of the State Archives of Florida).

The journey to Oklahoma by way of Cat Island was not as physically taxing for the Seminoles as it was for the tribes in the north that were forced to march to the reservation over land, although confinement on the barges presented its own form of anguish. Many of the Indians were forced to stand throughout most of the passage, while the sick and infirm lay almost in stacks to make room for the large numbers on board. Restroom facilities were not even a consideration.

When the first Indian group arrived on Cat Island from Georgia, several makeshift shelters were hastily constructed similar to the chickee huts common to the Seminoles in Florida. Since Cat Island was to be a holding area, it was necessary to provide protection from the elements. The fierce storms and unpredictable weather of the Gulf made some form of shelter imperative. The Seminole-style huts were simple to construct, consisting of only a thatched roof made from the abundant palmetto branches found on the island, and supported by four corner posts. There were no walls on the huts, although cloths were

Top: Osceola was taken prisoner near Saint Augustine during the supposed signing of a truce on October 20, 1837. The incident remains one of the most disgraceful events in U.S. military history. *Bottom:* Seminole Indians in front of a chickee. Several makeshift shelters were hastily constructed on Cat Island similar to the chickee huts common to the Seminoles in Florida (courtesy of the State Archives of Florida).

hung from the frame and lowered to keep the Indians warm and dry when necessary. In the chickee huts in Florida, a floor was raised about three feet above the ground to provide protection from snakes and other creepy crawly creatures that would often invade the hut at night. Since these were temporary accommodations, no flooring was constructed in these Cat Island shelters. The Indians lay on mats made of hide or blankets directly on the sandy ground. What valuables they were able to retain, along with food rationings, were suspended from the rafters for safekeeping.

The only semblance of clothing on the men was a single square of cloth hung from a waistband in front and back. The women wore skirts woven from the palmetto leaves that were abundant on the island. With such limited clothing it was easy to see that tattoos and body paint were common on both men and women. The men's heads were shaved except for a single ponytail type length of hair hanging from the top of their scalps. The women had long hair, which they kept rolled in a bun. The warm climate and sandy soil made shoes unnecessary. The women were almost always barefoot, while most of the men wore moccasins.

To this point the removal plan seemed to be going well. The problem that would derail the operation occurred during one of the several trips down the river from Alabama. After the barge arrived on Cat Island two of the Indians became seriously ill. The undetermined disease spread among the group and before long many of the Seminoles had contracted the virus and died. The Indians, who lacked any natural immunity to many of the common diseases brought into their territories by the Europeans, were particularly vulnerable to infection because of their weakened physical condition exacerbated by the hard journey. Smallpox, measles, pneumonia, and other foreign viruses would eventually decimate as much as 75 percent of the total Indian population over a two-hundred-year period.[28]

Those who were fortunate enough to survive the illnesses on Cat Island were frightened by the medicine men, who had warned the Seminoles that the Spirits were not pleased with the relocation. As the days passed and more of the Indians were stricken, the people came to believe there was a real curse on the move.

The death toll continued to mount and shallow graves were dug in the sand to dispose of the bodies. Several skeletal remains, probably from this period, have been uncovered over the years, especially on the North Point area of Cat Island.[29] More than likely the bones of the other Indians buried there have been washed away during the fierce hurricanes that have struck during the past one hundred and fifty years.

As the situation on Cat Island continued to deteriorate the Seminoles flatly refused to go any farther to Oklahoma. It was obvious to the Alabama contractor who had devised this scheme that nothing would convince the disheartened Indians to continue. Realizing that his original objective to reach Oklahoma was no longer possible, he sought an alternative solution. After much negotiation he finally persuaded the Indians to head south towards the Everglades.[30] It was not long before these protestors were assimilated into the tribes that had remained in Florida. The ancestors of some of these Cat Island Seminoles are still living in Florida today.

While there were those somber moments in the history of Cat Island, there were also some good times. The Cuevas family became known on the coast for the great parties that were given. The one that has been most reported was the big celebration orchestrated by Juan de Cuevas shortly before his death.

12

The Last Great Party on Cat Island

On May 7, 1922, James A. Cuevas described to reporter Zoe Posey the last great party given by his grandfather on Cat Island.[1] James, who grew up on the island, was the son of Ramon Cuevas, the lighthouse keeper. The snow-white sands of its beaches and the surrounding blue-green waters provided the perfect setting for baptisms, weddings, and large celebrations. The Cuevas family was well known along the coast for giving fabulous parties, but according to his grandson, Don Juan de Cuevas threw the grandest party of all in 1844 at the age of 82. The bash was destined to become not only the greatest social event ever hosted on Cat Island, but also the old man's last.[2]

James explained how the weather was the main consideration in choosing a date for the party, since many Coast activities have been disrupted or ruined completely by a sudden and unexpected rain. Severe thunderstorms are more likely to occur in the early spring, while pop-up storms from June through August have been known to dump large amounts of water in a very short period of time. Aside from being the wettest months of the year, the sweltering heat and humidity of these summer months can also be oppressive, even with the island breezes. October was finally chosen, since the peak of the hurricane season is over in September, and the threat of any major storm is reduced.[3] Not only is October normally the driest month of the year, but in the early fall, the changing leaves and crisp clean air made the island even more glorious than ever.

Mosquitoes, sand gnats, and deerflies were another reason to avoid the summer months. This nasty assortment of biting insects was a daily challenge for the Cuevas family, who had learned to at least coexist with these little pests. In addition to the large bugs, small, almost invisible gnats called "no-see-ums" could penetrate all but the most tightly woven fabric, making it unbearable at times to stay outdoors.

October was also the month for butchering. The slaughter of animals generally took place in the fall, which assured there would be plenty of fresh meat at the party. There were no cows indigenous to America, so the only breed of cattle on the coast at that time was the "black cattle" from Andalucía.[4] The first Spanish explorers brought their wiry Moorish-Andalucian cattle with them to the Caribbean Islands, where they were set loose. The dark, thin-legged animals thrived in the wild and eventually grew into heavy-boned beef stock. Andalucian cattle were eventually brought to the Louisiana territory.[5] Juan de Cuevas raised some of the best Spanish beef and pork on the Coast, so the quality of the meat for his party was unsurpassed.

For those who preferred lighter meat, there was also an abundance of waterfowl. Along with geese, there were many varieties of wild ducks and wading birds, easily caught in the brackish waters and ponds found on Cat Island.

Pierre Guardia, the husband of Juan's daughter, Euphrosine, supervised the cooking of all the meat. He had developed a reputation on the Coast as a fine chef. Many believed he knew more about cooking than anyone in the area. Some of the men helped with the slaughter of the hogs, while others bled the chickens, geese, and ducks. These were stuffed with delicious seasonings and then baked.

The women prepared the fruits and vegetables, which were grown on Cat Island. Something in the soil there forced the most emphatically lush vegetation, providing the Cuevas family with splendid orchards of oranges, lemons, figs, plums, grapes, and peaches, as well as staples such as corn, sweet potatoes, peas, beans, pumpkins, okra, and rice. A wide variety of fish was also available just outside their door, including mullet, flounder, speckled sea trout, bull reds, and Spanish mackerel. Oyster reefs stretched out in all directions in front of the Cuevas home, while a steady supply of shrimp and blue crabs was always available in the surrounding waters.

Among the problems the guests would encounter on Cat Island were the *chouc-poulon*, or "stickers," and the prickly pear hidden in the Bermuda grass that covered many of the sandy ridges. These spiny pests made it unpleasant to walk around the island without shoes. To minimize the discomfort, the area around the immediate party site was swept and cleared.

Two large tables were constructed. One held the meats, vegetables, and other main course foods, while the other held liquors, desserts and fine delicacies. The desserts included pound cakes, teacakes, cakes covered with chocolate, and a hundred pounds of candy. Gumdrops and rock candy were the only kinds of candy made back then, but for this special occasion, the gumdrops were filled with liquor.[6] The food was abundant and fitting for the finest restaurants. According to James Cuevas, "The guests ate and drank everything including whiskey, but they never turned into a rowdy bunch because no one got drunk, they were used to the alcohol."

Everything was plentiful on Cat Island, including the wildlife. The island was always a perfect nature preserve with lazy alligators basking in the marshes, deer peeking out of the shrubs, fat squirrels chasing about, luxurious mink grooming themselves among the palmetto clumps, wild ducks and geese swimming around the ponds, and the island's namesake raccoons peering out of the dark, hiding behind their bandit masks. Large sea turtles would crawl onto the beach in May and June to lay their eggs in the sand dunes at Goose Point.

On the day of the party, two large boats ferried six loads of people from "Old Chimneys," Bay St. Louis, Pass Christian and Rotten Bayou. The visitors disembarked and made their way from the boats to the center of the party, following the sounds of the music and laughter that drifted out across the salty air. Overhead eagles swooped and circled, staying near their nests that were situated among the branches of the highest pines. Cat Island was home to some of the largest eagles in the southern United States. A couple ospreys spread their wings on nearby stumps, watching the festivities from a safe distance. These birds, a first cousin to the eagles, are more common on Cat Island than on the mainland because of the abundance of fish.

The porch of the Cuevas house served as a stage on which the musicians played. Although the music was lively, there was no rocking band, as one would expect for such an occasion. The concept of "a band" was not yet known in the mid 1800s. On some occasions a very small group of musicians, usually amateurs, were hired for a particular event, but they would disband soon after their gig.[7] The minstrel shows had begun using a "group" of musicians on a regular basis by the early 1800s, but there were still no "dance bands" even as late as 1880.[8]

A fiddle was the only instrument played at most parties in those days. Properly known as a violin, it was called a fiddle when played as a folk instrument. The only slight difference between the two is the shape of the bridge. The top of the fiddle's bridge was often cut slightly less curved than that of the violin. This allowed the dance musician to play chords. The flatter bridge also allowed the fiddler to push his instrument harder than the violinist when further volume was needed. The more rounded curve to the top of the violin's bridge allowed the classical violinist to play a single note more easily and clearly.[9]

Only a single fiddler would play at a time for most occasions, but twin fiddling was sometimes used to beef up the sound. Adding additional instruments was the only way to increase the volume before the days of electronic amplifiers. Several fiddlers were waiting to play on Cat Island. Cuevas said when one fiddler got tired another would take his place, keeping the music playing continuously throughout the week.

The influence of Cajun music was evident at the Cuevas party. The musicians had learned to use high-pitched vocals so that their lyrics could be heard in the open Gulf air. It is believed that the Indians may have contributed to the wailing and shrill singing that is common in modern Cajun style. Acadians had arrived in Louisiana with very few possessions. Since this meant they had no instruments, they could only hum or sing without musical accompaniment (*musique a bouche*). The music itself was a blend of French, Irish and Anglo-American cultures, as the different ethnic groups began sharing their European folk songs. The best melodies from the Anglo-Americans were made even better by converting the words to their own French lyrics.

A few of the younger couples that attended the party danced the risqué *calinda*. The dance had been banished from Congo Square in New Orleans a few years earlier in 1843 because of its sexual undertones and its association with voodoo.[11] The calinda originated from a very old African dance in which the men and women face each other in two lines and dance in a sexually explicit manner. The word calinda is believed to have come to Louisiana by way of the slaves from Guinea, Africa, or from Martinique. It is also possible that it derived from the Cuban-Spanish word caringa. Both words, calinda and caringa, mean dance. The spelling has been changed over the years from calinda to colinda, and has evolved into a woman's name. The popular Cajun song we know today, "Allons Danser, Colinda" (Let's Dance, Colinda), was first recorded in 1946. The lyrics have been credited to Oran "Doc" Guidry and Leroy "Happy Fats" LeBlanc.[12]

Not all songs were French in origin. "Pop Goes the Weasel" was an English country-dance song that probably dates back to the 1600s. It is a simple tune and was one of the first songs that musicians learned. The simplicity of it allowed the fiddler to do trick exhibitions by playing the fiddle behind his back, over his head, and in other flashy positions.[13] "Yankee Doodle" was another popular "fiddle" song among the French people.[14]

One of the most requested songs at the time was "Jim Crow," written in 1828. The song is recognized as America's first international hit. It is believed that Thomas "Daddy" Rice, a minstrel show performer, copied the term from a crippled, elderly black man who danced and sang the chorus: "Weel about and turn about and do jis so, Eb'ry time I weel about and jump Jim Crow." Rice would sing the song while dancing a comic jig.

Slow songs were interspersed with up-tempo "knee-slappers" to vary the pace. "Home Sweet Home," a favorite tearjerker, was written by Henry Rowley Bishop as part of the opera "Clari," or "The Maid of Milan." John Howard Payne added the emotional words in 1823 when he was homesick in Paris. "Home Sweet Home" is credited as being "the first genuine American hit," and was a frequent request.[15]

James Cuevas reported that the guests did not sleep much, and some even danced all night. They danced the back step, front step, fandango, reel, cotillion, polka, the two-step, and the waltz. As informal as life was to the pioneers, dancing was, for the most part, not as casual as it is today. All dances had their own set of moves. A good dancer would not risk making a mistake and embarrassing himself, or even worse, making his partner look bad, so it was important that he be familiar with the basic steps of the dance before starting. Along with the steps, the technique was also crucial, and the dancer was expected to at least know how to carry his hands and to position his feet.

The waltz was the original "forbidden dance." The fiery French settlers of Louisiana found the waltz exciting and quickly adapted this "wicked dance" to their own style, making it the people's choice at all their celebrations. The waltz was considered vulgar and sinful by the majority of religious leaders and by society as a whole, simply because the dance partners actually touched. Before the waltz it was unheard of for dancers to have any physical contact.[16] With its rebellious undertones, it quickly became the preferred dance of the young. It can be said that the waltz was rock 'n' roll for teenagers of the 1800s. Its lively and vigorous moves required plenty of space, perfect for the open-air party on Cat Island.

The cotillion was one of the square dances that was popular at that time. Unlike the waltz, the steps were complex and difficult to learn. Verses known as "changes" described to the dancers what steps to do next. These movements would occur up to nine or ten times during a cotillion, and consisted of such conventions as circles and various types of turns.[17]

The people also loved the Virginia reel, one of the oldest dances in America. It is the only English-style contra dance to survive here.[18] English dances and terminology lost their appeal during the War of 1812, but the negative association had diminished by the 1830s and the reel continued in popularity through the 1890s.[19]

The guests at the Cuevas party also danced the fandango, which is a native dance of Spain. Originally the fandango, which means "go and dance," was basically a courtship dance. It was all about "the chase," where boy sees girl, girl snubs boy, girl chases boy, then runs away. The movements are very simple. The woman accompanies herself with castanets while her feet stamp the time. If there are no castanets the woman snaps her fingers as a substitute. At the end of certain measures, the music stops abruptly and the dancers remain frozen until the music resumes. The music itself is played in a rapid $3/8$ time. The dancers keep the tempo with the sound of the castanets, the movement of their feet and arms, and their bodies.

Various pieces of music played at the Cat Island party were written for use by rural musicians. Many of these songs seem to have the polka's characteristics, and were probably adapted for use with the dance. The polka is a fast dance with the music played in $2/4$ time accompanied by a strong beat. First introduced in Eastern Bohemia (now part of the Czech Republic) in 1830, the *pulka* (Czech for "half-step") quickly became popular throughout Europe and the United States. It gained such popularity that many common items were named after it (e.g., "polka dots").[21]

Footwork is the most important element in step dances. The two-step originated in the 1800s as an offshoot of the minuet, and arrived in the Louisiana territory with the European immigrants. While the front step, the back step, and the two-step were all common on the Coast, the Cajun two-step was the style most preferred. It is similar to the country western form, without as many fancy spins and movements. The basic step is found in many folk dances, including the polka half-step, from which the name seems to have been derived. The dance style is relaxed although the music can be slow, medium, or fast. Along with the basic two-step movement, the dancers incorporate creative ducks, swirls, and arm and hand positions as the couple travels in a circular motion around the dance area.[22]

After eight days of continuous dancing, singing, and great food, the party gradually came to a close. As the guests began boarding the boats for the journey back to the mainland, the grey moss that hung on the trees like thick cobwebs swayed lazily in the breeze as if waving farewell, marking an end to the last great party that would ever be hosted by the Cuevas family on Cat Island.

Five short years after this memorable event, Juan de Cuevas passed away.

13

The Funeral of Juan de Cuevas

Don Juan de Cuevas died on September 24, 1849, at the age of 87. When the announcement of his passing reached the people on the mainland, a large number of friends and family made the trip to Cat Island to attend the wake. Wakes were commonly held in the home of the deceased in the 1800s, and the body was often laid out comfortably on a couch in the living room, but since the Cuevas house on Cat Island was so small, Juan's coffin was placed on the front porch to accommodate the many visitors.[1]

It was a common belief that the spirit of the deceased stayed around the house for three days after death, and around the grave for another three days more. Between death and burial it was the custom that the body should never be left alone. The vigil, therefore, was a necessary part of every funeral, along with the praying of the rosary, the traditional Catholic devotion that had started sometimes in the thirteenth century.[2] The practical reason for a wake, however, was really a precautionary one. Medicine was unsophisticated in those days, and it was not always possible to say with certainty that the person was truly dead. Some diseases such as yellow fever, which was common in the Louisiana area, reduced the pulse rate and breathing to such an extent that it was almost impossible to tell when the person died. Gruesome stories about innocent people being buried alive abounded. This horrifying mistake is not possible today because no living person could survive the modern process of embalming. Juan's body was not embalmed, since the procedure was not commonly employed until after the Civil War. President Lincoln popularized the new process as a way to preserve the bodies of the Union dead, allowing them time to be shipped back to their hometowns for appropriate burial during the war.[3]

A funeral mass for Juan de Cuevas was conducted directly from the porch. I attended a similar service in the back woods of southern Mississippi when I was very young. An occasional moan, or even one could say a howl of sorts, could be heard at times from some of the women in the crowd. It was not so unusual for mourners to be overly emotional. In fact, such display was mostly expected. Since customs did not change much among the old families of the rural coast, the funeral I attended would have been similar to the one that day on Cat Island.

Juan's funeral was typical of the funerals of the time with full mourning lasting for six months. During that period Marie and the children wore mourning clothes, as was the requirement among the Creoles. Marie wore a traditional calotte (a small, flat bonnet with a long black veil). The men wore black cravats (ties) and black bands on their hats. Some wore black crepe around their arms. After the period of full mourning it was permissible for the widow to alter her mourning clothes. So, in accordance with the tradition, Marie wore black for another six months although now edged with white collars and cuffs. It was also the custom for even children above the age of three to also wear black.[4]

Juan had been dead only two days with only another day remaining before the funeral, when the vigil was interrupted by an unspeakable event. Ramon's wife, Isabel Penalver, collapsed and died.[5]

Friends and family had been arriving from the Coast since early morning. Ramon had been greeting the guests, as well as keeping an eye on his grieving mother, when suddenly it happened. Isabel died that very day. Reports do not give the cause of her sudden death.

By the next day the family had begun to accept the horror of this untimely event. With the wake officially over, Juan's funeral proceeded as planned. The Rev. Stanislas Buteaux officiated at both services held at the Cuevas home.[6]

Father Buteaux was the first priest appointed to serve at Bay St. Louis. There was not a single Catholic church in the entire state, when the Diocese of Nachez was established in Mississippi in 1841.[7] The only two priests in the whole diocese were two missionaries sent by the archbishop of New Orleans. Father Buteaux, therefore, had a large area to cover. His parish duties included the missions on Jordan River (now known as the Kiln), Pearl River, and Wolf River. These three communities became collectively known as the Three Rivers Missions.[8] The priest had become acquainted with the Cuevas family through his periodic trips to the island to bring the family holy communion.

Along with Marie, all of the Cuevas children were in attendance at the burial with the exception of Marie Anastasia, the only child deceased. Isabel's body was also laid out on the porch of the Cuevas home for her own wake, since the mourners were already there to attend Juan's funeral.

After the service his sons took Juan's body to a shallow grave not far from the house. The digging of the grave presented a problem that was common throughout all of low-lying Louisiana and the Coast. One had only to dig a few feet to strike water on Cat Island. This meant that the water would fill into the hole almost faster than it could be dug. While this resulted in a watery grave, everyone knew it was only temporary. Arrangements had already been made to have Juan's body transferred to the new cemetery on the beachfront in Biloxi as soon as an appropriate burial vault could be completed.[9]

The family of Louis Fayard had donated the land for the Biloxi cemetery on November 27, 1844.[10] It had only been open about five years when Juan de Cuevas died. The property

The Biloxi cemetery historical marker acknowledges the burial place of Juan de Cuevas. His body was transferred from Cat Island to the new cemetery on the beachfront as soon as a burial vault was completed.

had been part of a larger grant Fayard received from the U.S. government thirty years before.[11] Although the actual recording of burials began in 1841, it is believed that many residents had already used the land as a cemetery. Some historians even believe that it may have been used as a burial ground as far back as the early 1700s, because of its location just west of the site of the proposed Fort Louis.[12]

Because New Orleans is below sea level, watery graves have always been a problem. According to records, all of the burials in the first formal cemetery in New Orleans, the St. Peter's Street Cemetery located in what is now the French Quarter, were all in-ground. The graves would often fill with water and it was not uncommon to have a coffin actually float out of its hole. Several things were tried to prevent this from happening, without much success. Heavy stones were placed in the caskets and even holes were drilled in the bottom and top to allow the water to flow through, but to no avail.

As the population grew and the St. Peter's Street Cemetery became full, a new graveyard was eventually needed. In 1789 the city established St. Louis Cemetery, which forever changed the way the area buried its dead.[13] The Spanish governor, Estéban Miró, who was

Old Biloxi cemetery is shown here heavily damaged after Hurricane Katrina in 2005. The Juan de Cuevas vault can be seen in the center left of the picture. The family of Louis Fayard donated the land for the Biloxi cemetery on November 27, 1844. It had only been open about five years when Juan de Cuevas died.

in charge of New Orleans when the new cemetery was developed, pressed the city officials to adopt the wall vault system that was popular in Spain at the time. Spain had devised an economical method of above-ground burial.[14] This worked perfectly for the wetlands of Louisiana. The practice of burial in vaults quickly became popular, particularly among the wealthier families who could afford larger and more ornate tombs. Many of these family structures took on the appearance of small houses complete with iron fences. The rows of tombs resembled city streets and quickly became known as "cities of the dead."

These old cemeteries, including the one in Biloxi, were strikingly different from the ones usually found in other parts of the country. Those more common cemeteries, with their green lawns, shady trees, and marble headstones, were nothing like the vaults in Louisiana and Biloxi. While New Orleans is not the only city below sea level, it has the highest number of above-ground burials (90 percent) in the United States.[15]

The tomb of Juan de Cuevas and his wife Marie Helene Ladner, like many of the early tombs, were made of brick because of the lack of natural stone along the Coast. Common red brick was used to construct the Cuevas vault. Plaster was applied and whitewashed to preserve the brickwork and to add a decorative touch.

It was only natural that Juan's family would choose to bury him in a Spanish vault. Not only was it the custom in his native Spain, but also the Spanish method of construction made burial quite easy. The coffin was simply placed on the ground and a vault was constructed around it. Because of the lack of natural stone along the Coast and in the Louisiana area, tombs were made of brick. Common red brick was used to construct Juan's tomb. It was the least expensive building material and the most convenient since the bricks were fired in the local brickyards. In order to preserve the brickwork and to add a decorative touch, plaster was applied and whitewashed. Marble was the only stone used in the construction. It was imported at a considerable expense and used as a door to the entrance. Once the vault was completed Juan's body was moved from his beloved Cat Island to his permanent resting place in the Biloxi cemetery.[16] According to custom his body was laid with his feet to the east and his head to the west so that he could rise facing Christ at the resurrection.

When Marie died four years later, on October 10, 1853, at the age of 78, a wake was also conducted.[17] After the perfunctory three days, her funeral service was held on the island, and her body was then transported to the Biloxi cemetery to be interred in the same vault that was built for Juan. These private above-ground tombs usually consisted of two burial spaces, although not the way one would imagine. When Juan was buried in the vault, his coffin was placed on a stone shelf inside the tomb. Below this shelf was a small pit called a

A small pit called a caveau was at the bottom of the vault. To make room for a second body, the previous remains were swept into the caveau. This allowed a small family tomb to be used many times for the interment of several generations of its owners.

caveau.[18] When it was time to bury Marie, the vault was reopened and the tomb was made ready for her body.

No one was permitted to reopen any vault for a year and a day after a burial. This was not because of any law, but rather more as a practical matter. Enough time was needed for the first body to naturally decay. The extreme temperature that developed inside these vaults aided this process. The brick and stone tombs served as ovens that would reach temperatures as high as 300° F. If there was another death within that year, the family had to rent a temporary tomb or construct another vault for the second deceased. Fortunately the Cuevas family did not have to face this possibility since there had been ample time between the deaths of Juan and Marie.

During the year after burial, the extreme heat and humidity of the Coast caused the body inside to completely decompose. When the door to the tomb was again opened, all that was left amounted to little more than bones on the shelf. Juan's remains were simply swept into the caveau below. The casket containing Marie's body was then slid into the vault in the position where Juan's had been. The entrance was sealed permanently and the marble slab was replaced. Marie's name was then chiseled in the marble along with Juan's.

The marble headstone on the tomb of Juan de Cuevas and Marie Helene Ladner was the only stone used in the construction. It was imported at a considerable expense and used as a door to the entrance.

Although the Cuevas vault only held the bodies of Juan and Marie, it was not uncommon, with this method of burial, for a small family tomb to be used many times for the interment of several generations of its owners. The remains of the last body interred would be swept into the caveau, and a new body then placed on the shelf above.[19]

The inscription on the marble entrance to the Cuevas tomb in the Old Biloxi Cemetery reads in French:

Ct— Git
JEAN COUEVE
Decede le 24 Septembre 1849
A l'age de 87 ans

Et son epouse
MARIE LADNER
Decedee le 10 October 1853
A l'age de 78 ans

Translated:

Here Lies
JUAN CUEVAS
Died 24 September 1849
At the age of 87 years
And his wife
MARIE LADNER
Died 10 October 1853
At the age of 78 years

Juan's obituary appeared in *The Daily Picayune* on September 27, 1849, with the distinction of being the only death notice posted in three languages — English, French, and his native, Spanish. With his passing, the Cuevas era on Cat Island, for all practical purposes, came to an end, although his son Ramon and his family continued to live on the island until the lighthouse closed in 1861. Juan de Cuevas remains one of the most recognizable figures in Coast history from that period. The story of his heroic deed has grown amidst controversy. The following chapter explores the origins of the tale and explains how the truth developed into the Juan de Cuevas legend.

14

How the Truth Became a Legend

The legend of Juan de Cuevas and the Battle of New Orleans includes some central facts sprinkled with hyperbole. A number of critics, however, have dismissed the whole account as pure fiction. They generally have overlooked the most intriguing question of all about the old legend. How did such a story survive for almost two centuries virtually unchanged if it is an imaginary tale? The answer goes to the very heart of the truth. Legends are not usually created out of thin air. A book about Cat Island would not be complete without an examination of what parts are true, and how the truth became a legend.

In the early 1800s, there were no newspapers in the rural settlements of America. The only way people received news about their community and the world was by word of mouth. Newsworthy information was passed along from person to person, generally spreading in the form of rumors, myths, or legends. As fantastic as some of these stories may seem to us today, they actually served as a mechanism for recording history in a time when the printed word was nearly nonexistent. These yarns were often created as ways of keeping track of historical events that could then be passed along from family to friends. The legend of Juan de Cuevas and the Battle of New Orleans was no exception.

Legends are unique. Unlike rumors or myths, which become distorted over time, legends define a specific event in a specific moment and always contain a kernel of truth. What that truth may be is often lost through the years. Legends begin as oral memory within a local community and remain essentially unchanged. Oral tradition is the property of the people, and the people did not set out to entertain, but to report and to record what they believed. Years later, when these old stories were finally written down by the educated, belief was often looked upon as some sort of fiction. During the transition from oral accounts to printed words, facets of the truth began to disappear. This is particularly true in the late eighteenth and early nineteenth centuries, when writers and reporters began to publish their view of stories that had circulated for years.

The legend began when Juan de Cuevas captured the two pirates in the Gulf off of Cat Island in July 1820 (see Chapter 8). Word of his courageous action and his reward from the government blew across the area like a summer gale, making Juan de Cuevas a household name all along the Mississippi Coast. Mr. Cuevas was a hero, and his reward from the state proved it. But his heroic act had nothing to do with the Battle of New Orleans. That remarkable story did not appear in print until over fifty years after Juan's death, although there are indications it may have begun circulating in some rudimentary form from the beginning.

Around 1907 the legend began to take shape, when word spread that Major Benjamin Harrod had purchased Cat Island from the U.S. government. As the controversy over the island's ownership grew, the heroism of Juan de Cuevas became a major issue. The *New Orleans Daily Picayune* sent a reporter to the Coast to explore the story. Mrs. Frazine Taquino, granddaughter of Juan de Cuevas and the oldest living heir at that time (1907), was interviewed along with her nephew, Lovance Smith (referred to in the article as Leonard Smith). The testimonies of Frazine and Lovance are the earliest known published account of the legend. They were very credible sources for the validity of the story because of their closeness to Juan de Cuevas. Frazine had first-hand knowledge of her grandfather's life. Her mother, Bridget, had been a teenager during the Battle of New Orleans and would have been on the island to experience the Redcoats landing on the Gulf Coast.

Mrs. Taquino told the reporter that on December 12, 1814, the Cuevas family could see the British ships, and detailed for the first time how Juan de Cuevas rowed his small boat to New Orleans to warn General Jackson of the impending attack. The article was the first printed statement that Juan de Cuevas was a hero in the Battle of New Orleans, and the first printed assertion that the island was granted by the government to Cuevas for his heroic deed in that conflict.[1]

Ramon's son, James Cuevas, added details and strength to the evolving legend. James Cuevas, a veteran of the War between the States, was known as the "Sage of Beauvoir" for his great personality and gift for telling stories. Zoe Posey (1868–1944), a freelance writer who often contributed stories to *The Times Picayune* on topics concerning the Coast, interviewed James at his residence in the old soldiers' home at Beauvoir. In her resulting article Ms. Posey states, "His grandfather was one of Jackson's veterans of the Battle of New Orleans. Cat Island, on the Mississippi Coast, was given to him for his services to his country."[2]

Fifteen years after the Posey article was published, another writer, Nannie Mayes Crump (1850–1938), interviewed James five years before his death. The article is significant because it gives the first written details of Juan's actions against the British. Ms. Crump's article is the primary source for all future references to the Hero of Cat Island.[3]

At the time of the interview, James Cuevas was the last remaining family member with direct ties to the island. Writers and historians over the years have simply retold bits and pieces of these earlier articles while continuing to add their own embellishments. One of the most prominent authors to tell of Juan's exploits was Hodding Carter, a distinguished newspaperman who won the Pulitzer Prize for Editorial Writing in 1946. Carter's prominence added impetus to the Cuevas legend. In one of his major works, *Gulf Coast Country,* Carter's gift with words allowed him to add colorful details that had never before been reported.[4]

Further articles followed. In 1956, Ray M. Thompson (1898–1977) further cemented the details of the legend in the minds of most Coastians. Thompson was a popular writer whose articles focused on historical and current events unique to the Gulf Coast. A veteran of World War I, he was born and lived in Ohio, where he had owned an advertising agency that served Ohio and Pennsylvania. After selling his business in 1940 he moved with his wife to New Orleans. In 1950, *Ford Magazine* commissioned him to write an article on the man-made beaches of the Mississippi Gulf Coast. He and his wife fell in love with the Coast and eventually moved to Biloxi. He was very interested in history, and in 1952 began contributing articles to *Down South Magazine.* Because of his interest in Coast history, he came up with the idea for a newspaper column which would be published in *The Daily Herald* and called

"Know Your Coast." The column was eventually expanded to include articles of historical interest throughout the state and the name was changed to "Know Your State."[5]

Thompson wrote a featured story in the May–June 1956 issue of *Down South Magazine* about the heroism of Juan de Cuevas. A condensed version also appeared in his "Know Your Coast" column that same year.[6] In the four-page magazine story titled "The Hero of Cat Island," he gave the most specific details of the legend to date. His sources were the Zoe Posey and Nannie Mayes Crump newspaper articles. The exploits of Juan de Cuevas were presented as fact and were accepted as fact by the many who were already conditioned to believe the story. The popularity of the magazine and the column made the story real.

Thompson wrote a second article in the July–August 1961 issue of *Down South Magazine* that continued the legend. In this piece, simply titled "Cat Island," Thompson revisited the subject. The article was a general history of some of the more colorful incidents that had occurred on the island since its discovery in 1699.[7] The legend of Juan de Cuevas, of course, was a major part of the feature. A photo of grazing cattle with a caption referring to the Cuevas era and a photo of the old Cuevas homestead, contributed by Zoe Posey, added to the authenticity of the piece.

Ray Thompson was the one person most responsible for spreading the legend, and he was also the first person to report on Juan's real act of heroism. In "Know Your Coast" (1957), Thompson told the story of how Cuevas captured the pirates and was honored by the State of Mississippi with a proclamation and a cash reward. He concluded the article with this touching sentiment, "Which ends the record of the second and lesser known heroic achievement of Jean Cuevas (or Quave) with a comment by this column:—Ironically he was rewarded for saving a cargo of silk and merely thanked for saving his country!"

In the days after the War of 1812, there was little mass communication. In the early nineteenth century, even the big events of the day went unnoticed by most of the area's population. The Mississippi Gulf Coast remained virtually undeveloped, and the barrier islands were even more remote. If anything newsworthy occurred, the information would have been slow to spread. It was entirely believable that a family living on Cat Island during the War of 1812 could, and probably did, have contact in some way with such a large invading force. But even if Juan de Cuevas was not involved with the British, something of significance did happen on Cat Island, something so big it started a legend and sparked a controversy that has lasted through several generations.

Juan's heroic capture of the pirates was the beginning. The story was big news that resonated all the way to the Mississippi capitol. The attack by the British had occurred only six years before, close enough in time that the news of the war was confused with the announcement of the heroic action on Cat Island. Over time, truth morphed into fiction and the legend of Juan de Cuevas and the Battle of New Orleans was the result.

> Legend: Juan came upon a British scouting party commandeering his cattle.
> Truth: Juan came upon two men trying to dig their boat out of the sand.
> Legend: Juan was captured and held prisoner in the hold of a British ship.
> Truth: Juan discovered the captain being held prisoner inside the ship, chained hand and foot to the cabin floor.
> Legend: Juan escaped from his captors and rowed his small boat to notify General Jackson about the impending attack on New Orleans.
> Truth: After capturing the two pirates, Juan rowed his small boat to New Orleans to notify the insurance company about the stolen goods.

> Legend: A grateful nation awarded Juan de Cuevas Cat Island for his heroic deed in the Battle of New Orleans.
>
> Truth: A grateful state awarded Juan de Cuevas a reward of $200 for his heroic deed of capturing pirates in the Gulf.

The weakness in word-of-mouth communication was the cause of the mix-up. There was no intention to create a false tale. The childhood game of Telephone demonstrates how this transformation from one story to the other could actually have taken place. In Telephone one person whispers a phrase into the ear of the next person in line, who in turn whispers what he heard to the person beside him, who then whispers it to the person next to her, and so on. By the time the last person in line hears the phrase, the result is often comical, since the ending words almost never resemble the starting ones.

The reward given to Juan de Cuevas for capturing the pirates was a big story that spread rapidly throughout the area. The people got the news that Mr. Cuevas was a hero and that he had been granted a reward for his heroic deed. But, at the same time the area was just getting details of the battle in New Orleans (1814) that had taken place not long before. With the passage of time, as the stories were told and retold, the details became confused. People passed each story along just like the kids playing Telephone.

The much-publicized reward that Juan de Cuevas received also became confused. Language added to the problem since the European immigrants who had populated the area spoke a hodgepodge of broken English, mixed with a large dose of Cajun-French, and spiced with a tinge of Spanish. The reward by the State of Mississippi for Juan's capture of the pirates was misunderstood over time as being the grant of Cat Island by the U.S. government to Juan for his heroic deed in the Battle of New Orleans. To add validity to this belief, Juan received an official U.S. patent for ownership of 1,280 acres, or the western half of Cat Island, just nine years after receiving his reward from the state for capturing the pirates. To the population on the Coast at that time, the nature of the patent was not exactly clear. The grant, an official-looking document signed by the president of the United States, Chester A. Arthur, became the proof of the story that had circulated about the Hero of Cat Island. From this point on, the legend included the belief that Juan de Cuevas had been granted Cat Island as a reward for his heroic deed in the Battle of New Orleans.

Frazina Taquino was ninety-three years old when she gave the 1922 interview. She recalled the stories, but confused the details. The Cuevas children had heard Juan's friend, Jacob Ferris, a frequent visitor to Cat Island, speak of his experiences in the war in New Orleans, details that were imbedded in their impressionable minds. The adults and Cuevas teens also told their own stories about the British on their doorsteps, adding to the young children's misunderstanding of events. The seeds of involvement in the war were thus planted, which they would later recall and attribute to their own father. But it was not these stories alone, but also the famously publicized role of Jean Lafitte in the battle that unintentionally added structure to the legend of Juan de Cuevas.

The reports about Jean Lafitte and his gallant aid to General Jackson also reached the Coast about the same time as news of the battle and the heroic act of Juan de Cuevas. The Jean Lafitte story was a key ingredient in the making of the Hero of Cat Island, and provided even more minutia to the legend of Juan de Cuevas and his confrontation with the British.

> Legend: Juan had an accurate knowledge of every inlet from the Gulf.
>
> Truth: According to testimony, Lafitte had "a more accurate knowledge of every inlet from the Gulf than any other man."

Legend: Juan had been asked by the British to guide them through the marshes to New Orleans, which he refused.
Truth: Lafitte had been asked by the British to guide them through the marshes to New Orleans, which he refused.
Legend: Juan was recognized as a hero in the Battle of New Orleans.
Truth: Lafitte was recognized as a hero in the Battle of New Orleans.
Legend: Juan was given a reward by the United States for his act of heroism in the War of 1812.
Truth: Lafitte was given a reward by the United States for his act of heroism in the War of 1812.
Legend: As a reward, the president gave Cat Island to Juan de Cuevas and his heirs forever.
Truth: As a reward, the president pardoned Lafitte and his men for their previous crimes of piracy.

As it turns out, the famous legend of Juan de Cuevas is actually a gumbo of stories mixed to form a sacredly held heroic account of one of the Coast's original pioneers. The legend of Juan de Cuevas developed into a powerful, long-running tale of heroism. But, as entertaining as the story is, Juan de Cuevas was not involved in the Battle of New Orleans. Although this explanation may blow apart the legend, it is a fact that the State of Mississippi recognized the bravery of Juan de Cuevas for his courageous capture of the two pirates in the Gulf with a public proclamation and a monetary reward. As a result, Juan de Cuevas has gone down in Gulf Coast history as the "Hero of Cat Island."

Answering the Skeptics

Many of the questions about the legend have been answered in previous chapters, but there are a few questions that have yet to be resolved. Since Juan de Cuevas of the Gulf Coast apparently could not read or write, how could an illiterate man be the son of nobility? The truth is that while his father, Don Pedro de Cuevas, was not a member of the Spanish elite, Juan de Cuevas was from a titled family. Don Pedro de Cuevas received the title of hidalgo from King Charles III in 1781.[8]

At least 10 percent of the population held some title of nobility under King Charles. This was a higher percentage than in any other European country.[9] There were several hierarchical levels in the nobility structure. The ranks included royalty, titled nobles, caballeros and hidalgos. The rank of caballeros developed during the Reconquista (Reconquest) in Medieval Spain and Portugal.[10] Caballeros were mounted settlers who were recruited by the kings with the offer of hidalguia (nobility) to any townsman who fought on his own horse with knightly arms.[11] Hidalgos were largely a rural group, mainly farmers, who lived outside the cities in small villages like Algámitas. Hidalgos in no way represented local aristocracy.[12] One was granted the title of hidalgo either directly from the king himself (hidalgo de carta) or the title was inherited through birth (hidalgo de sangre). The word hidalgo was originally a contraction of the phrase "hijo de alguno," meaning "son of somebody," due to the fact that the title was usually passed down from father to son.[13] The title of caballero, however, had to be earned, with the horseman receiving the title only by way of service.

Over time hidalgo became a title representing the lowest degree of Spanish nobility. The hidalgo was a notch above the ordinary people but well below the great lords. Caballeros were slightly above hidalgos due to their mounted service that placed them in higher favor with the court. The advantage of fighting on horseback guaranteed them the lion's share of valuables from their raids and conquests.

The rank of hidalgo had no political significance, but allowed its members certain privileges, such as the use of the title "Don" and considerable exemption from taxation. Originally, caballeros paid taxes, but eventually, through loopholes, they also gained this exemption.[14] By the 1700s, there were so many people enjoying tax-exempt status that it was putting a tremendous strain on an already burdened economy. Some estimates place the number of nobles who were free from tax obligations at over half a million. By the time Don Pedro de Cuevas received the title of hidalgo, attempts were being made to reform the title system. The pressure to revise this situation eventually led to dramatic changes in the nobility structure. By the early nineteenth century, the title of hidalgo had entirely disappeared, including the social status that acompanied it.[15] Because of these changes, Don Pedro's title was never passed down to any other member of the Cuevas family. And, even though Don Pedro de Cuevas had the title, he remained a simple farmer all of his life.

Further answers surrounding the legend involve another Spaniard. More than 120 years before Juan de Cuevas of the Gulf Coast was born, there was another man who lived in Andalucía with almost the same name. The lives of these two men have become intertwined because of the similarity of their names and their birthplace.

The legend indicates that members of the Cuevas family in Spain were great poets and writers whose works are found in libraries throughout Europe. This is true, but not about the family of Juan de Cuevas of Cat Island. It was also reported that Juan de Cuevas had received an education from specially selected tutors in the expectation that he would bring further honor and privilege to his family through his own literary accomplishments. But that is also false. Juan de Cuevas (1762–1849) of Cat Island was born of a titled family in Andalucía at Algámitas. His namesake, Juan de la Cueva (1550–1609), was born of a noble family in Andalucía at Seville — similar names, same region of Spain, but 235 years apart.

The father of Juan de la Cueva of Seville, Don Pedro Martin Lopez de Cueva, was part of the social and intellectual elite of Spanish society. His young son studied the classics under the influence and guidance of Juan de Mal-Lara (1527–1591) and Diego de Giron, and took advantage of the excellent library belonging to his cousin, Dr. Luciano de Negro, the well-known Latinist and bibliophile. De la Cueva later became a renowned poet whose main contribution to Spanish art was in the theater. He was one of the first playwrights in Spain to reduce the five-act play, which was standard at that time, to four acts. He ignored Greek and Latin traditions and developed his plots, characters, incidents, and situations with little regard to the classical model. He was also one of the first to compose dramas dealing with events in Spanish history. Among his literary works, de la Cueva composed ballads, sonnets, elegies, madrigals, and an epic about the conquest of Andalucía.[16] Juan de Cuevas of Cat Island, on the other hand, was illiterate and could not read or write.

I had the privilege of visiting the magnificent olive groves on Cuevas land in Spain.[17] I questioned how the Cuevas family came to own so much land. For an answer, one must understand the era known as the Enlightenment (1650–1800). This was a historical movement that included such philosophers and writers as Descartes, Voltaire, Diderot, and others, who believed human reason could be used to combat ignorance, superstition, and tyranny. Their aim was to build a better world by "enlightening" their peers. The key element was the notion of progress. There was a sense that everything should be directed toward the future, with the specific purpose of improving the world, society, and the individual.[18] Their principal targets were religion (embodied in the Catholic Church) and the aristocracy. Ironically, some of the earliest and most enthusiastic proponents of this movement were the idle aristocrats themselves.[19] Charles III was one of the so-called "enlightened monarchs," and he ruled Spain using the principles of that new movement.

Although Charles had no natural ability to govern, he was honestly desirous of doing a good job as king. In the spirit of the movement and with progress as his goal, Charles carried out a complete transformation of Spain. He not only reformed its agriculture and private ownership of some of the farmlands, which ultimately benefited the Cuevas family, but he also introduced the very latest in urban concepts. He changed Madrid into a modern city with elegantly designed buildings—on par with Paris, Milan, and Naples—and added running water, a sewage system, and street lighting. Although there was considerable resistance to these innovations among the populace, the nation's leaders accepted the basic plan.[20]

Juan de la Cueva de Garoza became a renowned poet whose main contribution to Spanish art was in the theater. Some details of his life have been confused with that of Juan de Cuevas of the Mississippi Gulf Coast.

The Crown's attempt to improve agriculture took a dramatic turn in 1766 when the bad harvest of that year led to famine conditions. Rising prices of bread, oil, coal, and cured meat as a partial result of the liberalization of the grain trade by the marquis of Esquilache fanned the flames of discontent. To meet the need for more grain, the king's leading economic adviser, Pedro Rodriguez de Campomanes, urged Charles to increase the number of small farmers. He, along with other enlightened thinkers, believed that small, individually cultivated farms would provide the greatest agricultural production.[21]

Gaspar Melchor de Jovellanos, one of the most respected economists of the day, believed that property should be more widely distributed. Jovellanos asked, "Why in our villages and towns are these men without land and in the countryside land without men? Bring them together and all will be served."[22] Charles agreed that private ownership would bring the greatest prosperity to the general public. As a result he began granting some of the Crown's rural property to small landowners. Don Pedro de Cuevas was one of the recipients.[23]

And finally, some have questioned whether Juan de Cuevas was banished from Spain after his arrest for smuggling. James Cuevas (c.1838–1928), who grew up on Cat Island, reported that his grandfather's involvement with the smugglers got him into trouble with the Spanish authorities. The truth is that smuggling was running rampant in Spain at that time because of the policies put in place by King Charles III. But was Juan de Cuevas involved?

In order to pay for his reforms, King Charles taxed commerce in the colonies. Other nations with no such levies were eager to trade with the American colonies, who were looking for ways to avoid paying these tariffs. In an attempt to control trade and collect the new taxes, Charles placed further restrictions on commerce. These restrictions caused the price of goods imported from other European countries to be prohibitive for the citizens of Spain as well as in the colonies. As an answer to this economic problem, an illicit trade developed. Efforts of authorities to stop the smugglers lasted most of the eighteenth century, and were likened to a war at sea. Smuggling flourished in just about all of the staples: tea, spirits, coffee, tobacco, salt, pepper, gunpowder, precious metals, and even slaves. Much romance was associated with this clandestine activity as many eighteenth-century mariners — merchantmen, fishermen, and even gentlemen sailors — indulged in a little of this "free trade."

The Cuevas family in Spain believes that Juan was most likely involved to some degree in smuggling, although the details in the legend are surely embellished.[24] The reason for his participation in this criminal act is not clear. He could have been tempted by personal profit, or motivated by a heightened sense of service to the Spanish people, as the legend suggests. His arrest for crimes against the Crown could explain why Juan de Cuevas never returned to Spain. The people in Algámitas explained that it is very unusual for anyone to ever leave the village. That was as true back in the 1700s as it is today. Although this alone is not sufficient proof that Juan was mixed up in smuggling, there are other reasons to believe that Juan was associated with smugglers, as we will see later.

According to his grandson, James, Juan returned to Biloxi some time after the scouting expedition, accompanied by a priest who was either a relative or a close friend. Evidence suggests that the priest was Father Antonio de Sedella.

Father Antonio had a direct connection to Juan de Cuevas. As a friend and parish priest, Father Antonio officiated at the baptism of Juan's oldest children as well as the wedding of Juan's first-born son. He was also called upon to issue a "Dispensation for Marriage" for Juan's son Pierre.[25] The dispensation was necessary because Pierre and his future wife were first cousins. About 1794, roughly the same time Juan de Cuevas arrived on the Gulf Coast from Florida, Father Antonio returned to New Orleans, leading to the possibility that they traveled together from the fort in Pensacola.

Father Antonio was first instituted curé of St. Louis Cathedral of New Orleans, November 25, 1785. In 1788 he was appointed commissary of the Inquisition and told to establish a tribunal of the Holy Office in New Orleans. In the spring of 1789, he contacted Governor Estéban Rodriguez Míro (1744–1802) to inform him that the Inquisition was

Over the years Reverend Father Antonio de Sedella, known as Father Antoine in New Orleans, gained the great love and respect of his congregation despite the people's original dislike of his apparent harshness as part of the Inquisition.

about to be introduced to Louisiana. He also requested that the governor make soldiers available to assist in apprehending and punishing heretics. Míro had become proprietary governor of Louisiana after serving as acting civil and military governor of the colony. The governor had been trying to promote Protestant immigration to Louisiana, so instead of responding to Father Antonio's request for assistance, he had the priest arrested and sent back to Spain. This ended the only attempt by the Church to establish the Inquisition in what is now the United States.[26]

This time the priest came, not as a torturer of the Inquisition, but as curé of St. Louis Cathedral and a simple Capuchin monk. He lived in a crude wooden hut behind the Cathedral, and for almost forty years he was a common sight on the narrow streets of the old French Quarter, clad in his habit of coarse brown cloth, a girdle of hemp, and a pair of wooden sandals. Over the years Father Antoine, as the French population in the Vieux Carré knew him, gained the great love and respect of his congregation despite the people's original dislike of his apparent harshness as part of the Inquisition. Father Antonio de Sedella (Father Antoine) became one of the best-loved men in New Orleans history, conducting himself with great piety and an showing extraordinary devotion to duty, although he continued to have bitter confrontations with the government as well as his superiors in the Church. Father Antonio died on January 22, 1829, and was buried in St. Louis Cathedral. His body was eventually moved to the "priest's tomb" in the old St. Louis Cemetery. On the day of his funeral the city council pledged to wear black crepe bands on their arms for a period of thirty days and business was suspended throughout the city.[27]

Based on the political climate of the times, the testimony of Juan's grandson James, who knew him well, and the background and association with Jean Lafitte and Antonio de Sedella (see Chapter 6), the evidence strongly suggests that Juan de Cuevas had been a smuggler for the good of Spain.

The death of Juan de Cuevas marked the beginning of the end to the Cuevas era on Cat Island. Four years later his wife, Marie, passed away, leaving only their son Ramon and his family still residing on the island. Ramon continued in his position as lighthouse keeper until it closed in 1861. The original lighthouse was one of the first on the Gulf Coast and an important part of Cuevas family history.

15

The Lighthouses on Cat Island

In 1861, Ramon Cuevas, the last lighthouse keeper, abandoned the damaged structure during a hurricane and sought refuge on the mainland.[1] Ten years later a second lighthouse was built to replace the first. By the 1950s, after years of not being in service, it had deteriorated to such a degree that it was nothing more than a wooden shell perched on top of rusted pilings. On Sunday, October 1, 1961, *The Daily Herald* reported that the lighthouse had shared the same fate as the old Cuevas homestead.[2] Careless campers staying in the building had started a fire. "A charred pile of wood and twisted metal braces" was all that remained of the last monument to early Cat Island history.

There were twelve light stations built in the United States before August 7, 1789, when the constitution finally transferred control of the nation's lighthouses to the federal government.[3] No two were built alike due to the lack of a standardized plan, but rather they evolved over centuries out of the different building techniques of the times. Each was built using local materials under local supervision.[4] Originally they were built of wood, but these were so susceptible to fire that no example remains today. Subsequent lighthouses built of stone were constructed by simply piling one stone on top of another. This resulted in a pyramid shape with a wider base to support the tower as the structure increased in height. Mortar was used to hold the stones together. Since no other bracing materials were used, these stacks of stones were unstable and often leaned and tore apart.[5]

President George Washington was originally very active with the nation's lighthouses, but quickly realized the enormity of the job for the new government's chief executive.[6] He passed the responsibility on to the commissioner of the revenue, who in turn shifted the job to the secretary of the Treasury. From 1820 through 1852 the secretary passed responsibility for the lighthouses to the fifth auditor of the Treasury.[7] This proved to be a disaster. Auditor Stephen Pleasonton knew nothing about lighthouses and did nothing to improve his knowledge over the 32 years that he served.[8] Described as a financial zealot, he would often return appropriated funds back to the Treasury without having spent them. The lighthouses built during his term were poorly constructed and in constant need of repair. His tenure has been labeled the era of "the lowest bidder" because price rather than quality determined the final product.[9] The lighting system that he employed was far less expensive than those used in Europe and much inferior.

As the Gulf Coast grew, there was an increase in boats traveling from the open waters beyond the barrier islands into New Orleans through the lakes Borgne and Ponchartrain. The traffic coming from Mobile through the Mississippi Sound also increased because the islands offered protection from high seas and wind in the Gulf. Regardless from which direction they came, most boats heading to New Orleans had to pass the western tip of Cat Island.

The government, realizing the crucial location, recognized the need for some form of marking in order to aid the vessels. In 1827, Congress approved a budget of $5,000 for the construction of a much-needed lighthouse on Cat Island. Unfortunately, the fifth auditor never acted. Instead he allowed the money to revert back to the general fund.[10] Meanwhile the need for a lighthouse on the Coast increased. Boat captains who used the waters requested that a lighthouse be constructed at Pass Christian and a lightship be anchored off Cat Island.

Lightships were basically floating lighthouses. Initially they were poor substitutes for their land-based counterparts, because for a number of years very little consideration was given to their design and construction. In principle they seemed to be an ideal solution. They could be anchored in shallow water where permanent structures would not be practical, while on the other hand they could be moved to deeper water many miles from

Stephen Pleasonton, the fifth auditor of the Treasury, knew nothing about lighthouses and did nothing to improve his knowledge over the 32 years that he served (courtesy U.S. Lighthouse Society).

shore. They also had the flexibility to be moved from one location to another as needs changed. The problems encountered, however, proved to far outweigh the benefits. Their lightweight displacement which was necessary for shallow water, caused them to rock and roll with the tides and high winds. Keeping the lamps lit during even the slightest breeze was a never-ending chore. The constant rolling motion caused frequent damage to the lanterns and their lenses, not to mention the health of the crew. Living conditions on the ships were so bad that they were hardly fit for humans. One captain likened it to being on a barrel.[11]

The customs collector in New Orleans believed the Cat Island location was too important for anything so temporary, prompting the lightship proposal to be dropped.[12] Shirley Haupt noted in her book, *Beacons in the Night: Lighthouses of the Gulf*, All the commerce of the northern Gulf Coast passes through the channels near Cat Island.[13] Not everyone agreed, however, so there were other suggestions as to where a lighthouse, or lighthouses, should be placed. Congress finally settled the matter by ordering the construction of two lighthouses, one on Cat Island and an almost identical one to be constructed in Pass Christian. On March 2, 1827, Congress authorized the secretary of the Treasury to initiate a contract for the construction of the two lighthouses.[14] Five thousand dollars each was appropriated for the projects. This was the second time that the funds had been earmarked for a lighthouse on Cat Island.

On November 22, 1830, Juan de Cuevas sold one acre on the western tip of Cat Island to the government for $75.[15] Almost a month later, on December 21, 1830, U.S. Senator Edward Livingston of Louisiana, who owned much of the Pass Christian area, and his wife Louisa sold a half-acre lot to the government for $250 on which to build the Pass Christian lighthouse.[16]

On March 5, 1831, Winslow Lewis was awarded a contract to build both lighthouses at a cost of $9,283.[17] Lewis had become a national figure when he invented what became known as the Lewis lens used for lighthouse beacons. His system incorporated a nine-inch diameter lens placed in front of the lantern, thus magnifying and reflecting the beam of light. By the end of 1812 virtually every lighthouse in the United States incorporated the Lewis lens.[18]

In 1822 Augustin Fresnel, a French physicist, invented a new order of lens which was used in light towers all along the coasts of Europe and eventually the United States.[19] The design was so superior that the lenses are still used virtually unchanged today. Since Winslow Lewis had a monopoly with his Lewis Lens, North America was late in adopting this new technology. The United States lagged far behind its European counterparts in light stations until the use of the Fresnel lens was adopted just before the Civil War.[20]

In 1827, Winslow Lewis added the construction of lighthouses to his repertoire of trades. His plans for the Frank's Island lighthouse in Louisiana were dramatically successful. This catapulted him into the nation's spotlight and as a consequence, he became the main builder in North America.[21] Having received the contract to build the Cat Island and Pass Christian light towers, he subcontracted the construction of the Cat Island lighthouse and dwelling to "master workman," Lazarus Baukens.[22]

The Cat Island lighthouse was constructed of bricks reminiscent of the New England brick towers of the time. Those towers had proven to be so durable that the same bricks were shipped from New England to be used on Cat

The Pass Christian lighthouse was almost identical to the Cat Island lighthouse. Congress ordered the two to be built at the same time. Five thousand dollars each was appropriated for the projects (courtesy U.S. Coast Guard).

Island despite an abundance of high-quality clay in the Coast area.²³ The base measured eighteen feet in diameter and tapered to a top width of ten feet and seven inches. The walls were one and a half feet thick and were covered with whitewashed stucco. The height was forty feet, a full ten feet taller than the sister light tower at Pass Christian. It was fitted with ten lamps in 14-inch reflectors characteristic of the Lewis lens. It was fueled by whale oil. The light was situated three feet above sea level and was visible for twelve to fourteen miles into the Gulf.²⁴

George Riolly of Pass Christian was appointed the first keeper of the Cat Island light tower on July 9, 1831.²⁵ Three years later he contracted smallpox on a visit to the mainland and died. Ramon Cuevas, son of the island owner, Juan de Cuevas, succeeded him. Ramon continued in that position until July 1861, when the Confederate States Light House Bureau closed it down.²⁶

The original Cat Island lighthouse was built in 1831. Ramon Cuevas, son of the island owner, Juan de Cuevas, became the second lighthouse keeper, and served until July 1861, when the Confederate States Light House Bureau closed it down (courtesy U.S. Coast Guard).

In the beginning of the 1800s the appointment and dismissal of light keepers were approved by the President.²⁷ The choices were usually political. The position did not require any formal instructions, although the person had to possess a certain level of efficiency. Winslow Lewis observed, "The best keepers are found to be old sailors, who are accustomed to watch at night, who are more likely to turn out in a driving snow storm and find their way to the light-house to trim their lamps, because in such weather they know by experience the value of a light, while on similar occasions the landsman keeper would be apt to consider such weather as the best excuse for remaining snug in bed."²⁸

The life of a light keeper was, at times, almost unbearable. Usually the tower was isolated, and the men and their families had to live under restrictive conditions. The salaries were low and many keepers had to work at other jobs to supplement their incomes. Oil was a precious commodity, and the keepers were expected to keep records of the oil used in the lamps.

In 1835, Stephen Pleasonton issued a list of duties expected of the light keepers. Those instructions were:³⁰

To the Keepers of Lighthouses Within the United States

1. You are to light the lamps every evening at sun-setting, and keep them continually burning, bright and clear, till sun-rising.
2. You are to be careful that the lamps, reflectors, and lanterns, are constantly kept clean, and in order; and particularly to be careful that no lamps, wood, or candles, be left burning any where as to endanger fire.
3. In order to maintain the greatest degree of light during the night, the wicks are to be trimmed every four hours, taking care that they are exactly even on the top.
4. You are to keep an exact amount of the quantity of oil received from time to time; the number of gallons, quarts, gills, &c., consumed each night; and deliver a copy of the same to the Superintendent every three months, ending 31 March, 30 June, 30 September, and 31 December, in each year; with an account of the quantity on hand at the time.
5. You are not to sell, or permit to be sold, any spirituous liquors on the premises of the United States; but will treat with civility and attention, such strangers as may visit the Light-house under your charge, and as may conduct themselves in an orderly manner.
6. You will receive no tube-glasses, wicks, or any other article which the contractors, Messr. Morgan & Co., at New Bedford, are bound to supply, which shall not be of suitable kind; and if the oil they supply, should, on trial, prove bad, you will immediately acquaint the Superintendent therewith, in order that he may exact from them a compliance with this contract.[31]
7. Should the contractors omit to supply the quantity of oil, wicks, tube-glasses, or other articles necessary to keep the lights in continual operation, you will give the Superintendent timely notice thereof, that he may inform the contractors and direct them to forward the requisite supplies.
8. You will not absent yourself from the Light-house at any time, without first obtaining the consent of the Superintendent, unless the occasion be so sudden and urgent as not to admit of an application to that officer; in which case, by leaving a suitable substitute, you may be absent for twenty-four hours.
9. All your communications intended for this office, must be transmitted through the Superintendent, through whom the proper answer will be returned.

>Fifth Auditor and Acting Commissioner of the Revenue
>TREASURY DEPARTMENT
>Fifth Auditor's Office
>April 23d, 1835

Ramon Cuevas was the ideal candidate to work as a lighthouse keeper. Cat Island was his home. His parents lived nearby, and some of his brothers and sisters also had homes and families scattered about the island. Most keepers were overcome by the isolation of their jobs, but for Ramon, it was little more than an extension of the only life he had ever known. While other keepers supplemented their salaries as pilots or fishermen, Ramon was able to continue what he and the family had always done, raise cattle.

On February 1, 1840, Juan de Cuevas sold ten acres of Cat Island adjacent to the lighthouse to Ramon for $200.[32] Ramon needed the property for his cattle business and wanted the land for his herd to graze.

Light keeping was usually a family affair, with the wife filling in while the husband went to the mainland for supplies. This allowed the men to at least interact with other people. The women hardly ever left the station.[33] Isolation was not a problem for Ramon and his wife, however, because the families that lived on Cat Island were large, with many children of all ages scampering about and dropping in to visit "Uncle Ramon."

The original lighthouse on Cat Island was doomed from the start. Since the lighthouses built during the tenure of Fifth Auditor Stephen Pleasanton were inferior and in constant need of repair and replacement, it is not surprising that the Cuevas lighthouse did not survive. It had been built using very little common sense. The bricks had been laid directly on the sand without any form of stable foundation. Over a relatively short period of time, the wind and waves of passing storms ate away at the bottom of the structure. Not only that, but the island itself was wearing away at the western tip. A channel was cut between the lighthouse and the rest of the island during the 1846 hurricane.[34] By 1851 the tower was only a few feet from the water.[35] On August 30, 1847, President James Polk issued an executive order reserving the lighthouse property on Cat Island, as well as parts of Horn Island, Round Island, and Petit Bois, for military purposes because of the Mexican American War.[36]

There was no railroad system in the country at that time, so the South had become dependent on lighthouses for navigation through the winding channels and shallow bays along the Gulf Coast. In 1852, a Lighthouse Board was formed as a separate branch of the Treasury Department to take an aggressive role in the operation and construction of the nation's lighthouses.[37] This nine-member board acted quickly to implement the recommendations of an 1851 investigation into the country's lighthouse operations. Congress had launched this study as a result of the numerous strong complaints it had received about the poor quality of America's lighthouses. The group, which was composed of officers of the Navy, members of the Army Corps of Engineers and civilian scientists, wanted to take advantage of new technology as well as to upgrade existing equipment. They also wanted to revise the procedures for issuing contracts. Seven districts were organized, including two on the Gulf Coast. Each of the districts had a Navy officer as a district inspector. Cat Island Light Station was under the Shieldsborough, Mississippi, Superintendency, and the post office address was Shieldsborough (now Bay St. Louis, Mississippi).[38]

A hurricane in 1855 virtually destroyed Ramon's house next to the tower, and the tower itself was severely damaged.[39] A new keeper's house was built further from shore amidst the trees and sand dunes for protection. The Lighthouse Board recommended that the tower, which was almost ready to topple, should also be moved to that location. Congress appropriated $12,000 in 1856 for a new lighthouse, but it was never built.[40]

In 1860 three hurricanes hit the Coast. It was the only time in history that three major storms hit the Gulf Coast in the same season.[41] They battered Cat Island each month for three consecutive months.[42] The first hurricane, on August 11, 1860, severely damaged the Cat Island lighthouse and completely destroyed the light keeper's dwelling.[43] Ramon and his family were forced to flee Cat Island for the mainland. Not only did Ramon lose his home, but he also lost 300 head of cattle. Up to ten feet of water swept over the mainland, killing more than 47 people.

The second storm hit almost exactly a month later, September 14, 1860.[44] The eye passed near the mouth of the Mississippi River. This hurricane destroyed the third lighthouse at Bayou St. John. Estimated damage to the area exceeded one million dollars.[45]

About two weeks later, on October 2, 1860, the third hurricane hit. Damage was severe all the way to Baton Rouge. The storm caused damage to houses, businesses, boats, and crops as far east as Pensacola. Rain total in New Orleans was over five inches."[46] The one-two-three punch of Mother Nature in 1860 seemed just as devastating then as Katrina's destruction seemed to the people of Mississippi and Louisiana in 2005.

Ramon moved his family to Shieldsboro shortly after the storms. The Confederate States Lighthouse Bureau continued to maintain, but not operate, the station until July 1861 when Ramon Cuevas received his final pay in Confederate dollars.[47] The Cuevas era on Cat Island had officially ended, but the history of the Cat Island lighthouse continued.

During the Civil War, the old brick tower continued to stand, although unused. It sustained further damage in the war when Confederate forces burned it.[48] Two gaping holes about twelve feet in length were left in its sides. The lantern was salvaged and transported to the north shore of Lake Ponchartrain to be installed in the Tchefuncte River light tower located there.

On March 3, 1871, Congress appropriated $20,000 for the construction of a new lighthouse on Cat Island.[49] It would replace the original tower last manned by Ramon Cuevas in 1861.[50] The light tower was to be a protected, screw-pile lighthouse, a design first built in England and introduced into the United States in 1850.[51] This type was specifically designed for use in protected waters such as the Mississippi Sound where wave action was fairly minimal. These were typically lightweight, square wooden houses that sat on five iron stilts. The legs resembled corkscrews and were turned into the soft sandy bottom of the sound by workers who walked them around like a mule turning a sugar cane press. This type of construction allowed the screw-pile lighthouse to be built on sites that would be unable to support the weight of the more traditional brick light tower.[52]

The new Cat Island lighthouse officially opened on December 15, 1871.[53] It was fifty feet tall, a full ten feet taller than the first. The tower/dwelling that sat atop the screw-piles was made of heart cypress. The timber siding was held in place by old-style square cut nails. A fixed fifth-order Fresnel lens system was installed. The new system cost three times that of the Lewis lamp system employed in the original brick tower. The Fresnel lens assembly required only one oil lamp whereas the Lewis system required ten. The efficiency of the new lens reduced the fuel costs by as much as 75 percent on average.[54] The Fresnel lamp shined with a fixed white light that flashed every 90 seconds. Although some lighthouses were fitted with a foghorn, neither the Cat Island lighthouse nor its sister lighthouse in Pass Christian had such a sounding device.[55]

On September 20, 1871, Sidney A. Wilkinson was appointed first keeper of the new lighthouse. His salary was $625 per year. Two years later his assistant, Charles J. Mobeny, was appointed to replace him. He served from May 9, 1873, until January 27, 1874, when he was transferred. His annual salary was $400. Henry Sherwood replaced Mobeny on January 27, 1874.[56]

The new lighthouse received its first major damage twenty-two years later when a violent hurricane struck the Gulf Coast.[57] At dusk on Sunday, October 1, 1893, gale force winds began to whip the coast. By ten o'clock in the evening water was beginning to cover the coastal islands. The eye passed over Grand Isle, Louisiana, between 11 P.M. and midnight. After midnight the winds picked up again until finally diminishing by dawn. The storm surge was as high as sixteen feet at Chandeleur Islands, causing the lighthouse there to tilt several feet. The water washed over the lantern, which was 50 feet above sea level. On Cat Island the lighthouse was severely damaged, having been knocked at an angle of about 45 degrees.[58]

On Wednesday, the first vessel, the schooner *Ventura*, left Biloxi to search for those

The second Cat Island lighthouse was built in 1871. The legs resembled corkscrews and were turned into the soft sandy bottom of the sound. The screw-pile construction allowed lighthouses to be built on sites that would be unable to support the weight of the more traditional brick light tower (courtesy of the Mississippi Department of Archives and History).

missing. The captain, John Nelson, was looking for his father, who was one of the oldest pilots at Ship Island. After a 24-hour search, the party discovered the pilot's boat, the *Chicora*, run aground on the north side of Cat Island.[59] Capt. John Nelson, Sr., and his co-pilot Capt. Joseph Lewis were found unharmed. On the following day a relief party left Biloxi on two schooners heading to Louisiana to offer their assistance. The group consisted of Captain C. Bills, A.J. Meynier, Felix and Theodore Borries, George Andrews, B. Harvey, Joseph Fayard, P. Augeida, Bud Holleman, Mike Wirovich, P.J. Dejean, A. Horn, J.C. Delamare, Tony Roderiguez and Tom Clarisse.[60] By three o'clock Thursday morning they reached Cat Island, making it their first stop. Until this time no one had visited the island since the storm had passed. The party found only three people on the island. John Duggan, one of the island's owners, was staying in the old Cuevas house about two miles from the lighthouse when the hurricane struck. As the storm waters rose, the house was completely submerged. Duggan was forced to seek refuge in the top of a tall tree. The storm's high winds whipped the branches about, tearing the skin from his arms, legs and body. It was almost impossible for him to hold on. He suffered intensely for seven hours until the storm finally subsided and he was able to come down from the tree. The searchers also found the lighthouse keeper J. Clarice and his wife defying all odds and still manning their post. The tower was severely damaged, but the light was still shining.[61]

The hurricane also caused the wreckage of two other vessels on Cat Island: an oyster and shrimp schooner from Biloxi, named the *Harriet*, was badly wrecked and stuck ashore, and a three-masted ship known as a bark was also smashed to pieces on the island. The bark's cargo of 150,000 feet of lumber was strewn with other debris all along the island's coastline. No lives were lost at Cat Island, but about 200 head of cattle were swept away.[62]

A congressional act of July 5, 1884, determined that the islands were no longer needed for military purposes and were to be returned to the public domain.[63] Before the island lands were totally released, however, a request was made by the War Department to determine if the lighthouse properties were still needed. Daniel Lamont, secretary of war, recommended to President William McKinley that the government retain the use of the lighthouses. A general order by the War Department on November 13, 1895, made it official, the Cat Island lighthouse would continued to operate.[64]

By 1900, the storms had taken their toll, and the base of the often-battered structure was in need of stabilization. Five feet of rock riprap was placed around and under the base.[65] For thirty plus years the lighthouse continued to be a part of the nation's lighthouse system, until finally on September 22, 1937, the last Cat Island lighthouse was discontinued due to the greatly diminishing number of vessels using the Mississippi Sound.[66] The land and the lighthouse were transferred to the War Assets Administration in November 1948, with the lighthouse "in general disrepair." The structure sat idle and abandoned until the federal government placed the lighthouse up for sale. Nathan Boddie, the island's owner at that time, purchased it in 1950.[67]

The last chapter in the history of Cat Island lighthouses began in the early morning hours of Sunday, October 1, 1961, when residents of Gulfport driving along the beach boulevard noticed a red glow in the Gulf coming from the vicinity of Cat Island.[68] Boddie was notified of the strange sighting. Expecting the worst the island's owner manned his boat and headed out into the sound. As he drew closer there was no doubt that there was a fire blazing on the western tip, and he saw the old lighthouse tower had burned.

The person or persons who started the fire were never caught. It could have been caused by any one of the several fishermen or hunters who used the old building for shelter. Because of the age and the condition of the structure, the fire was presumed to be an accident.[69] The era of the Cat Island lighthouses was over. By the early 1900s, Cat Island had entered the next phase of its long history with the start of the turpentine and lumber industries.

16

Turpentining and the Lumber Industry on Cat Island

There were hundreds of acres of longleaf pine on Cat Island, many of the trees sixty feet tall or more, when the Cuevas family lived there. None of the other barrier islands boasted such an abundance of this valuable timber. The virgin forest of heart pine that thrived on the island despite hurricanes and storms had never been harvested before Benjamin Harrod bought the island in 1907 and leased the turpentine rights a few years later.[1]

Longleaf pine was found almost exclusively in the southernmost portion of the United States in massive forests that stretched from Virginia to Texas. The vast quantity of trees seemed inexhaustible. The durable nature of heart pine lumber and the resin the trees produced prompted a worldwide demand for this wood. As early as the 1700s the first settlers in Jamestown depended on longleaf pine for heartwood to build their homes and furniture.[2] The farm implements and tools they made from the wood were almost as durable as metal. Furthermore, pine tar from the longleaf pine had been used as a sealant on ships since the earliest days of civilization. The British Navy found pine tar and pine tar products essential for use on their vessels, and since the United States was the only source of this valuable commodity other than Sweden, the colonies were pressured to supply their needs.[3] Because of their waterproof nature and their use on boats, pine tar, turpentine, pitch and resin became known as "naval stores" products.

The demand for pine tar diminished as the demand for turpentine increased, prompting the rise of the turpentine industry. Improved distillation processes resulted in many new uses for turpentine and other by-products of pine tar. Paint thinners, varnishes, printing inks, insecticides, soap, and many other products soon became important parts of everyone's lives. Turpentine was used for medicinal purposes as an old home remedy. It was a valuable aid in fighting infections, relieving soreness, treating burns, curing worms, controlling coughs and soothing sore throats. The Cuevas family used turpentine to control roaches and other annoying insects that were a persistent nuisance in their island home. Marie Cuevas would add a few drops of turpentine to water when washing clothes to whiten them and to make them smell sweeter. By the time the last Cuevas moved from Cat Island to the mainland, the turpentine industry that was originally centered in North Carolina, due to the large number of pines in that area, had gradually expanded through the southern states until by 1861 it was firmly established on the Mississippi Gulf Coast.[4]

In 1907, Benjamin Harrod purchased Cat Island with the idea of creating a bird sanctuary.[5] While his plan was taking shape, he brought in an expert, James R. Pickens, to explore the possibility of extracting turpentine from the huge pine trees. He was assured that turpentiners could extract the gum without killing the trees, so he reasoned he could continue to work toward his goal of forming a wildlife preserve while profiting from the sale of the turpentine. He and Pickens went over to the island together to estimate the acreage before putting the land on the market. In 1911, civil engineer J.F. Galloway, working for Pace and Morgan, a naval stores company out of Mobile, secured the first turpentine lease ever for Cat Island.[6]

Pace and Morgan planned to build a distillery on Cat Island to process not only the pine tar from trees on the island, but also to process other crude resin that would be brought in on barges from the mainland. J.B. Galloway, C.O. Galloway and William Stockton had leased large blocks of timberland in Hancock, Harrison, and Jackson counties and had contracted with Pace and Morgan to process the pine tar from these trees.[7] Enterprising businessmen, like J.F. Galloway and his associates, had formed groups known as "factors" that leased large tracts of land. After gaining control of the virgin forests, they would sublease smaller parcels to entrepreneurs who would repay the factors with proceeds from the refined resin. Local companies like Pace and Morgan generally owned the distilleries that processed the resin. Once the tar was processed into turpentine, spirit of turpentine, or rosin, the products were then shipped throughout the country.

When the 75-year-old Harrod realized it was not feasible to turn the island into a bird sanctuary, he sold Cat Island to Nathan Van Boddie in 1911.[8] Although the turpentine lease agreement expired with the sale, Boddie had already made arrangements with Pace and Morgan to renew the turpentine rights when he became the island's new owner.[9] Since the operation was already set up, the turpentiners began to work almost immediately after Boddie bought the island.

The turpentine operations began on Cat Island at the eastern edge of the pine forest just north of Little Bay where the east/west body of the T-shaped island connects with the north/south leg not far from the great sand hills. As the work progressed a wide trail, which became known as the Old Turpentine Road, was cleared through the pine forest. The crude road ran the entire length of the island from the sawmill to the Seminole staging area where the barges were loaded to shuttle the rosin to the port of Gulfport.

Upon taking control of the operations in March 1911, Pace and Morgan constructed several necessary buildings. The first was a five-room cottage for the company's general foreman, J.M. Strickland, along with a commissary building measuring 30 by 36 feet, stocked with general merchandise. Eleven tenement houses were also constructed for the employees and a barn 21 by 28 feet was built to house the mules that were sent to work on the island. A 20 by 36 feet shed was built to store the naval stores products before they were sent to the mainland.[10]

By 1913, there were up to fifty workers in the turpentine camp and at the sawmill about a mile away.[11] There were as many as 85,000 pine trees boxed on Cat Island during the turpentine operation.[12] Boxing refers to the initial method of collecting pine tar before the process was enhanced with the invention of a special metal cup in 1902 called a Herty cup. Before this improvement the only way to collect the pine tar was by cutting a deep gash at the base of the tree with a boxing ax, allowing the resin to flow into this notch and then be collected from there.

Turpentining was a physically demanding occupation that began in the spring and ran through the end of September. The heat and humidity of Cat Island was often stifling, causing many to suffer from heat-related illnesses complicated by the hordes of insects and the ever-present mosquitoes. The workers began at sunup, usually rising before 5 A.M. and working the entire day until sundown with only short breaks for breakfast and lunch. Once a week for nine months workers called "chippers" would trek through the sandy soil, making their way around and through briars, stickers, and palmetto fronds to visit each tree. These experienced bladesmen wielded a curved knife so well balanced that they could slash a cut in the tree's face in a single blow. With two quick swipes of their inch-wide blade they formed a V-shaped scar from which the pine tar would flow. The trees were not the only living things, however, that felt the sting of the chipper's blade. The snakes that slithered from the swampy areas into the path of the vigilant workers also fell victim to the special sling blade.

Tensions often ran high among the turpentine workers on Cat Island, particularly since women were also working in the camp. One day in June 1913, the first and probably only major incident was reported. Adeline Combs, who was working as a cook, got in a dispute over one of the men who had shown her attention in the food line. A twelve-year-old named Willie Pearl angered Combs by blatantly flirting with the worker. After several days of Willie Pearl's taunting behavior, Adeline finally snapped. Jumping across the wooden food table in a jealous rage, she grabbed a nearby stick and whacked the young girl repeatedly, knocking her into the sand. Tossing the stick aside, she lunged at Willie Pearl, landing on top of the screaming adolescent. Three of the men rushed to her aid, pulling the much larger woman off the girl. After the two calmed down, Adeline was arrested for violent conduct and was fined five dollars by Justice of the Peace James Fulmer. This skirmish was the only notable incident recorded in the turpentine camp on the island.[13]

Turpentining was a year-round activity although the pine tar only flowed during the spring and summer months. As the resin would flow into the cup some would dry on the face of the tree. By the fall when pine tar production had ceased, this dried resin had built up to such an amount that it could easily be harvested. Workers would use a flat iron to scrape this dried tar into scrape buckets that were pressed tightly against the tree. As the temperature dropped, the tar would harden and was easily scraped into the bucket. When the buckets were full, they were emptied into the collection barrels to be hauled to the still. The men would also use this off-season to clean up around the trees, preparing them for the next year's harvest of pine tar.

The first turpentine operation on Cat Island ended around 1913, after about two years.[14] Not all of the longleaf pine had been tapped; only the eastern grove of trees was part of this operation. When George Boddie sold Cat Island to Hernando Desoto Money,

Workers would use a flat iron to scrape the dried pine tar into scrape buckets that were pressed tightly against the tree (courtesy of the Mississippi Department of Archives and History).

under the corporate name of the Cat Island Development Company, the turpentine leases were not renewed.[15] The demand for heartwood lumber from the longleaf pine, however, created a thriving industry during this period.[16] The large number of trees found in Mississippi made the state one of the largest producers of valuable heart pine in the United States.[17] A prominent lumber company on the Gulf Coast at that time was the Cuevas Lumber Company in DeLisle. It was owned and operated by William Cuevas, a great-grandson of Juan de Cuevas of Cat Island.[18] After the turpentine operations came to a close in 1913, Nathan V. Boddie, the owner, leased the timber-cutting rights to W.B. Lundy.[19]

Lundy wasted little time in setting up his sawmill. The sawmill and boiler that powered it were brought in by boat from the mainland and unloaded at the spot on Cat Island where the Seminole Indians were once held. From there the equipment was moved by wagon along the Old Turpentine Road through the center of the island to the sawmill site. Workers with crosscut saws dropped the timber while others using axes trimmed the branches off the fallen trees. Oxen made many trips a day dragging the large logs to the mill site. Once at the sawmill, the heavy logs were moved up an incline made of squared logs to the saw table. A mechanical device consisting of a type of lever called a cant hook was used to pull the logs onto the platform. Before the invention of the "circular saw" and the introduction of steam power, a sawmill consisted of only two men with a pit saw. The work was obviously slow under such primitive conditions. Lundy, on the other hand, employed twenty-five men and was able to process as many as 1,200 feet of lumber per day.[20]

Through the 1930s sawmills were plentiful in south Mississippi and provided new jobs for people who had only been farmers. The money was good and the farmers did not have to rely on the growing season for their success. The crop of trees was there and waiting to be harvested. Although the industry appealed to many, working conditions at the sawmill were harsh. The living quarters were less than adequate, consisting of small shacks just large enough for two men and a small stove used for heat. For profit and total control the company paid the workers with tokens that could only be redeemed at the company store set up on the site.

Sawmills were usually located near the mouths of large rivers, such as the Pearl River, the Escatawpa, and the Pascagoula. In addition to the rivers, there was also a large logging operation at Handsboro on Bayou Barnard near Gulfport.[21] Initially the method for transporting logs out of the forests was slow and hard on the animals and the remaining trees. Teams of oxen would drag the logs to the water's edge, destroying almost everything in their path. Since there were no roads or even trails in most cases, the heavy logs knocked down everything they encountered, including new-growth trees and seedlings. This resulted in the destruction of future lumber supplies. A new vehicle patented in 1899 by John Lindsey of Laurel, Mississippi, made the process of hauling logs much more efficient. The eight-wheeled Lindsey Log Wagon was by the 1930s being used in almost all logging operations, including the one on Cat Island, to transport the fallen trees.[22] The wagons were easier on the animals and the environment. At the river the logs were tied together and floated like rafts downstream to the sawmills at the mouth. On Cat Island four yoke of oxen pulled the wagon loaded with logs to the sawmill site. Once the timber was cut into lumber it was hauled to a dock not far from the old Cuevas homestead. There the finished boards were loaded onto barges and shipped to the port of Gulfport eight miles away.

By the 1930s the once vast longleaf forests of the south had been virtually decimated.[23] The people of the southern states had taken this immense treasure for granted. Even though they depended so much on the lumber, they also viewed the trees as a nuisance to be

The eight-wheeled Lindsey Log Wagon was by the 1930s being used in almost all logging operations, including the one on Cat Island, to transport the fallen trees (courtesy of the Mississippi Department of Archives and History).

removed. When the new settlers moved into the area, the forests were cleared to meet their immediate need for farmland. Their lack of knowledge of the longleaf pine and its slow growth pattern resulted in poor logging methods. Their cut-and-run mentality destroyed this valuable asset that once seemed to them inexhaustible.

When Sallie Adam Boddie, the widow of Nathan V. Boddie, bought Cat Island in 1931, returning it to the Boddie family, there were still acres of these valuable trees on the island.[24] She renewed the turpentine leases and by 1933 production of turpentine and rosin was again in full operation on Cat Island. Since the trees on the eastern end of the island had already been tapped, the latest turpentine operation was moved to the thick forest near the middle of the island. By 1937, these trees were also tapped out.[25] With the end of turpentine production on Cat Island, Nathan Boddie and his sister, Sarah Boddie Buffington, Sallie's two children who by now had been given the island by their mother, leased the timber rights.[26] The longleaf pine still found on Cat Island was one of the last remaining sources of true heart pine timber in the state. For over a year, some of the most beautiful trees were cut down during this latest logging operation and the durable trees were cut into boards for market. With the last of the longleaf pine removed, the turpentine and logging operations on Cat Island ended forever.

Along with the lumber industry on Cat Island another profitable enterprise was beginning to blossom. The country was entering the Roaring Twenties and the era of Prohibition. Cat Island was the perfect hideout for the rumrunners and did not go unnoticed by the mob bosses in the north.

17

Al Capone and the Rumrunners

Prohibition had been in effect since January 16, 1919, when the National Prohibition Act was passed, making the sale of alcohol illegal in the United States.[1] Although it was a crime to sell alcoholic beverages, the demand for liquor continued to grow. At first America's thirst was filled by enterprising sailors who smuggled liquor into the United States from foreign countries. It was not long, however, before innovative Americans began to produce their own. Old solid names on the coast like Cuevas, Ladner, Nicaise, and Garriga became associated with the production and distribution of some of the best moonshine anywhere. Although only a very few members of these pioneer families were involved in the making of illegal alcohol, the success of these few backwoods entrepreneurs was so widespread that their family names continue to be associated with moonshining even today. With payoffs to public officials and law enforcement agents, the bootlegging business had gotten so relaxed that people could purchase liquor by simply walking down the street. One man made a very good living selling his homemade liquor from a baby stroller as he pushed his children from one end of Gulfport to the other. He and his wife produced a new baby every nine months to ensure the family business continued uninterrupted.[2]

On January 1, 1909, Mississippi became the first state to enact a law prohibiting the sale of alcoholic beverages.[3] By the time the National Prohibition Act was passed ten years later, the Gulf Coast had already developed a reputation for the production of the best quality whisky all the way to the Canadian border.[4] Homemade alcohol had become known as "moonshine" from a British word for any activity that was done under the cover of night. The local "moonshiners," many of whom were sawmill workers, began converting old turpentine stills into alcohol stills after the Coast's once lucrative lumber industry began to dry up. It was an understandable transition as their lumber jobs were gradually being phased out.

The rough coastline between Mobile and New Orleans was pockmarked with many bays and inlets perfect for hiding and transferring illicit goods, but of all the available places the best location for hiding treasure was on Cat Island. Whether it was pirate gold from the likes of Jean Lafitte and James Copeland, or the liquid gold of the rumrunners, Pirate's Cove on the south side of the island was the chosen place. The cove was out of sight of the mainland and was secluded enough for the rumrunners to slowly and comfortably transfer their shipments with little concern for detection.

Cat Island was perfectly situated between Cuba and New York, making the distribution of illegal alcohol to other parts of the country easy and efficient. Location, along with the high quality of the product, led the Kiln to become known as the "moonshine capital of the world."⁵ This growing reputation and ideal location did not go unnoticed by the eastern mob. Alphonse Gabriel Capone (1899–1947) controlled the bootlegging activities in Chicago and the northeast, and with the growing reputation of the liquor business on the Coast, it was not long before he became involved. There is some evidence to suggest that Al Capone controlled his local rumrunning operations from a large Spanish-style house in Ocean Springs known as Casa Flores. In June 2005, a Mississippi state employee was fishing in Davis Bayou near Casa Flores, now called Del Castle, and snagged a small leather purse containing six old coins. Engraved on the front of the coin purse were the words "Al Capone," providing provocative evidence that Casa Flores and Capone were connected.⁶

I toured Casa Flores in 1961 as a guest of the new owner, Nellie Goldsby (1890–1974).⁷ We were considering new designs to lighten the gloomy interior. The stucco house, which featured dark oak paneling and dark wood trim, was admittedly depressing, I was given some history of the old house, which was known by that time as Del Castle. Mrs. Georgette Faures Lee (1889–1979), who was originally from New Orleans, purchased the five acres of property on Davis Bayou from Mr. Leon R. Jacobs (1885–1930), a New York attorney.⁸ Georgette and her husband, Frederick E. Lee (1874–1932), moved to the Coast from Indiana in 1919 and became successful in the pecan industry. Late in 1925 the Lees began construction of their new home they called Casa Flores (the House of Flowers). They chose a design by architect Gordon Hite of New Orleans and used the Jensen Brothers Construction Company, also of New Orleans, to erect the building.⁹ After Mr. Lee died unexpectedly on September 2, 1932, Casa Flores was sold.¹⁰ Del Castle, which was already in disrepair, suffered significant damage during Hurricane Katrina in August 2005. It was demolished in March 2007, amid protests from the community which wanted the house preserved for its historical value.¹¹

With the involvement now of the East Coast crime syndicate, the Gulf of Mexico was teeming with ships carrying illegal alcohol. Aside from Al Capone, Capt. William S. McCoy was the most famous of the rumrunners. From 1900 to 1920 he worked as a legitimate excursion boat pilot in Daytona Beach.¹² With the beginning of Prohibition, he quickly realized the market potential that the new law had created. McCoy began hauling rum from the Bahamas into south Florida, without any real concern of being stopped. The Coast Guard, however, soon caught on to him and closed down his operation. Not to be deterred, he came up with an ingenious plan. It was his idea to bring the illegal alcohol in larger ships to just outside of the three-mile limit of federal jurisdiction. From there he started the practice of selling the booze to local fishermen and runners in small, fast boats that could transport the alcohol to cars or trucks waiting for the shipment on the mainland. This practice caught on and soon everyone was using McCoy's scheme. The three-mile limit became known as "the Rum Line" and the ships that were waiting were called "Rum Row."¹³ A Dutch scholar in 1703 had suggested this was an appropriate distance from the coastline to defend a country, since the maximum range of a canon was about three miles. Although that no longer applied, the three-mile limit became a standard that most nations agreed to. To help combat this sidestepping of the law, the U.S. Congress passed an act on April 21, 1924, that extended the Rum Line to a twelve-mile limit.¹⁴ This made it more difficult for the smaller boats to maneuver in the open seas.

On the Gulf Coast, the ships were unloaded beyond the twelve-mile limit and carried by speedboats back into the territorial waters of the United States to transfer points such as Smuggler's Cove on Cat Island. The shallow sandbars common in the sound offered a buffer against pursuing government agents. On Cat Island the rumrunners would transfer their loads to smaller flat-bottom boats that could carry the contraband up the Wolf or

Del Castle, originally called Casa Flores, was reported to be Al Capone's headquarters on the Gulf Coast (courtesy of Ray L. Bellande).

Jourdan Rivers to contact points in the piney woods. There, bootleggers (the name for rumrunners who carried the liquor over land instead of water) would transfer the booze to high-speed cars with drivers who knew the back roads and highways. Transportation to the northern states over land had proven to be more efficient, with lessened risk of discovery than transportation over water.

The local moonshine operation was simple, but dangerous. Moonshiners produced their alcohol in stills near creeks and streams, hidden so far in the woods that revenue agents flying in helicopters overhead were unable to spot the operation through the thick foliage. The alcohol was packaged in Mason jars before being crated for shipment. Originally opaque clay jugs were used, but Mason jars soon became the preferred containers, since these clear jars allowed the customers to see what they were buying. This was important given that unscrupulous moonshiners had occasionally duped unsuspecting buyers by cutting their liquor with water, or using additives such as syrup to give the liquid a whisky color. Capt. McCoy was one of the few runners who did not cut or dilute his alcohol, thus making his a much sought after product. It is said that the purity of his alcohol may have been one of the origins of the phrase "the real McCoy."[15] In addition to being transparent, the glass jars left no aftertaste like other types of containers.

Although shipment by land was preferred, some shipments went by sea. For those to be sent up north by ship, the jars were packed in crates, and loaded on small flat-bottom boats. The alcohol was then transported down the Wolf River into the Bay of St. Louis from as far upstream as the old Cable Bridge. Once the boat cleared the mouth of the bay, it headed through the channel between Ship and Cat Island and looped back behind Cat Island into Spit Cove (later called Smuggler's Cove because of the association with Lafitte and Copeland). If the boat's pilot had a sense of being followed, the runner would round Good Scotch Point and drift into South Bayou instead. While this location in the center of Cat Island provided total seclusion from ships in the Gulf, it was a dead end and offered no way out. If chased by agents, the runners were trapped.

One evening in 1925, one of the small rum boats named the *Nemesis* was carrying a load of Scotch from a ship past the three-mile limit off the coast of Louisiana. The shipment was to be transferred to one of Capone's boats at Cat Island for shipment up north. As soon as the boat cleared the Chandeleur Islands it was spotted by one of the boats patrolling the Mississippi Sound. The Coast Guard took chase, realizing the *Nemesis* was no fishing boat. The *Nemesis* had a substantial lead, but the pilot knew he could not outrun the larger boat. He headed for Smuggler's Cove on Cat Island while sticking as close to the shore as possible in case he had to ditch and run. As he neared what was then called Negro Point, he was suddenly thrown backwards over the stern of the boat when his small craft slammed into a sandbar just inches below the water. The impact was so great that the boat tipped, dumping its load of Scotch liquor into the Gulf. Although the pilot was apprehended, not all of the bottles of the Scotch were ever retrieved. For a long while afterward, local fishermen would occasionally discover one of the bottles bobbing up to the surface. After the incident the name of the location on Cat Island that the Cuevas family had called Negro Point became known as Good Scotch Point.[16]

Although there were many locations used by the bootleggers to transfer their illegal alcohol, Pirate's Cove seemed to have been designed specifically for that purpose. There are many stories to tell about the rumrunners of the 1920s on Cat Island, but those tales are lost in time, covered up or dismissed by the romantic adventures that defied the law, while playing hide and seek with the federal agents. On December 5, 1933, Congress ratified the Twenty-first Amendment that repealed the National Prohibition Act, virtually putting an end to the lucrative rumrunning trade.[17]

Illegal booze may have disappeared from Cat Island at the end of Prohibition, but it was replaced with legal alcohol when a group of businessmen from the Coast built a private hunting and fishing club on the south end of the island in 1928.

18

The Goose Point Tarpon Club

One July afternoon in 1927, a group of Gulf Coast businessmen were returning to Gulfport after a long deep-sea fishing trip south of Cat Island. They had caught several large fish including two tarpon. July and August are the best time for tarpon fishing in the Gulf. The fish prefer the shallow waters around Cat Island and can grow as large as eight feet long and in excess of a hundred pounds. These mighty fish always put up a fight when snagged. They will leap high out of the water struggling to get free, shaking their large heads with such force that the whole back of the boat can seem in danger. This exhausting battle between man and beast is what draws fishermen to the sport.

Tarpon have little or no food value so are usually released after the customary photos are taken. That is unless the prize fish is to be stuffed and hung over the fisherman's mantel. Sportsmen have enjoyed the outstanding fishing on Cat Island over the years, and when they were not on their boats trying to catch the "big one," they were hunting for geese and other waterfowl on the island. Hunting for blue geese has been a favorite pastime since the Cuevas era. Also known as snow geese, depending on the color of their plumage, these birds leave their breeding sites in Greenland, Canada, and Alaska sometime in late August or September and arrive on Cat Island in early October every year. So many geese have been coming to the southern tip of the island for so long that the area became known as Goose Point.

Migratory birds regularly follow the same route each year from Canada to the Gulf of Mexico. These routes are known as flyways and generally describe loosely defined zones in which the birds travel. There are four major flyways in North America: the Atlantic, the Central, the Pacific, and the Mississippi. The Mississippi flyway extends from the north Arctic polar region south to Patagonia, and generally follows the Mississippi River to the Gulf Coast. The four flyways overlap as they approach the Mississippi River valley, assuring that the region always has an abundant variety of waterfowl.[1] The honking of the geese can be heard in late August or early September as they fly overhead in their familiar V-shaped pattern, almost as if they were trumpeting their greetings to the people of the Gulf Coast.

Ducks were also popular game for hunters on Cat Island. Mallards, the ancestor of almost all of the varieties of ducks, have interbred with the American black duck to create what is called the black mallard. These ducks are only partially migratory, with some even staying all year in the coastal areas of the United States. The black mallard duck that is generally found on Cat Island is a popular game bird that presents a challenging target because of its quick speed, but also a reliable target since it has grown accustomed to humans.

The men agreed it would be nice to stay on the island for several days, since the Cat Island trips were never long enough. Unfortunately there were no facilities on Cat Island large enough to accommodate a group. There had only been a minimal number of structures built on the island since the last Cuevas left in 1860, and those buildings could only be described as fishing camps. If they had their own place, they would have more time to enjoy the hunting, fishing, and peaceful solitude that the island offered.

Bidwell Adam casually suggested the group should consider building it own lodge on Cat Island. Adam had just been elected lieutenant governor of Mississippi, and was still flush with the self-assurance that comes with winning a statewide election. At first the comment was taken in lighthearted jest, but as it was tossed around the group, the idea became more than just a fleeting fancy.

The next day Bidwell called his brother, E.J., an alderman and attorney at Pass Christian, to discuss the idea with him. Being from a prominent family on the Coast, the Adam brothers had the contacts and resources to make such a large-scale project happen. Their father, E.J. Adam, Sr., had been editor of *The Coast Beacon* newspaper, and a former mayor of Pass Christian for several terms, and the Adam brothers knew everybody who was anybody. E.J. thought the project was worth exploring, and encouraged Bidwell to move forward with the idea.[2]

Over the next few days and weeks Bidwell, along with others from the trip, met with friends and associates to discuss the feasibility of the idea. Such a large-scale project would not be easy, since there were no utilities on the undeveloped island. A call to Frank Wittmann, a prominent contractor in Pass Christian, was the first of many steps in bringing this project to fruition. After careful study Wittmann felt confident that the idea was workable. While Wittmann, who had built several of the stately mansions that face the Gulf on the beachfront road, worked on preliminary sketches, others began to discuss how financing would be arranged. It was agreed that stock certificates would be sold to finance the project.[3]

The owner of Cat Island at the time, former governor of Mississippi Lee M. Russell (1875–1943), was contacted about possibly leasing enough property to build the club. Russell had bought Cat Island in 1925 from George Boddie and proposed building a $500,000 resort on the island.[4] His plans, which included constructing a causeway over to the island, were grandiose. He even anticipated changing the name from Cat Island to Treasure Island as a marketing strategy to reflect the final development.[5] As he struggled to get investors in a slowing financial market, Gov. Russell jumped at the prospect of an exclusive hunting and fishing club on his island. He was more than willing to work out a lease arrangement with Bidwell and his group.

Bidwell Adam and his team chose "The Goose Point Tarpon Club" as the name of their new lodge and began recruiting members. It was a popular idea among the businessmen and very quickly almost fifty new members and stockholders had signed on. These included such prominent men as W.H. Raddebaugh, R.L. Malone of Meridian, and many others from the Coast. One of the most prominent club members was Barney Eaton, Sr. (1878–1944), who had moved to Gulfport in 1909 as the assistant to Judge James H. Neville, then the general counsel for the Gulf and Ship Island Railroad. In 1912 Eaton replaced Neville as the general counsel and remained in that position until 1924 when he was elected president of the newly organized Mississippi Power Company.[6] As president of the power company he had the necessary resources to install a generator and independent lighting system on the island for the club.

Another important member of the Goose Point Tarpon Club was Bernard Chotard, who had experience in the hotel industry. The Mexican Gulf Hotel, which opened June 16, 1883, was the first hotel on the Gulf Coast that was specifically designed to attract winter visitors from up north.[7] Chotard, who had worked at the luxury resort as an administrative employee, leased the hotel from the owner, Gage Clark, when Clark retired. Although the hotel was not successful under Chotard, his knowledge of hotel operations was a valuable asset to the new Cat Island club. He set up the club to run like a hotel with the guests paying for their rooms and meals just as they would at any other lodge.

Construction of the two-story building began in 1928 just before the stock market crash. The economy during the decade of the Roaring Twenties had been booming. There seemed to be no limit to prosperity in that age, when millionaires were made overnight. It was a time of wealth and excess fueled by new technologies such as the radio, the growth of the automobile, and the general expansion of air travel. Speculators made money in everything, particularly in real estate and the stock market. Although the economy was beginning to show some evidence of slowing down at the end of the decade, the investors in the Goose Point Tarpon Club saw no reason to abandon their idea. Gov. Russell's flamboyant plans for Cat Island only heightened the excitement and resolve to complete the grand project.

Frank Wittmann's design was perfect for an island retreat. It was a large-rambling, two-story building raised above the ground almost a full story to protect it from storm surges. Entry was by way of two symmetrical sets of stairs, one on the left and one on the right, leading upward and coming together in the center entry of the building on the first floor level. There has never been such an imposing structure on any of the barrier islands, with the possible exception of the casino that had been built on the Isle of Caprice some five years before.

The Goose Point Tarpon Club could be seen for miles out in the Gulf, and was a testament to the successful men who were responsible for the project. The building featured twelve bedrooms, each with its own private bath, an amenity that even some of the finer hotels did not have. There was a large dining room and kitchen staffed by an excellent cook, who prepared the meals on a large wood-burning range. As an additional benefit in the kitchen, for those guests who had had a successful day of fishing or hunting, the cook would gladly prepare their evening meals using their own fresh catch of the day.

The building faced the Gulf and featured screened galleries that ran across the entire front of the two floors. Each bedroom opened onto these long porches, allowing the guests to relax outside their rooms while enjoying the marvelous view of the Gulf without any concern for the annoying mob of mosquitoes that could be quite an irritation at some times of the year. Fishing and hunting gear was stored underneath the building along with wood for cooking and heating, and an artesian well was dug nearby to assure a continuous supply of good fresh water.

The members hired Tony Mercier, a young man from New Orleans, to be the caretaker of the Goose Point Tarpon Club.[8] Tony maintained the building year-round, making sure that the generator and all necessary equipment were in good repair. Although the club was very popular, there were many days when there were no guests on the island, and it was Tony's job to keep a watchful eye on the prestigious building. One day in 1931, on one of the rare occasions when Tony was away, a fire started mysteriously in the bottom of the building. The exact origin and cause were never fully established, but it was believed that the stacks of cooking wood, stored under the lower portion of the building, somehow

The Goose Point Tarpon Club opened in 1928 on Cat Island and featured screened galleries that ran across the entire front of the two floors. Each bedroom opened onto these long porches, allowing the guests to relax outside their rooms while enjoying the marvelous view of the Gulf.

contributed to the fateful blaze. With no one on the island, it did not take long for the fire to totally engulf the cypress structure. The fire was unable to be seen from the mainland until the smoke had risen thick and black above the island; the building burned completely to the ground before anyone was even aware that a fire had started. All the members were shocked and dismayed to learn that their wonderful weekend retreat had been destroyed.

There was some talk of trying to rebuild, but by the time of the fire, the country had experienced the stock market crash and the nation was in the midst of the terrible Depression. The stockholders, many of whom were hurt by the financial crisis facing the nation, were unwilling or unable to rebuild in such a tenuous time. The decision was made to walk away, and the membership was gradually dissolved. After only a little over three years, the once great Goose Point Tarpon Club ceased to exist.

Governor Russell's grandiose plans to develop Cat Island into a major resort died along with the club. Never able to interest investors, Russell defaulted, leaving Cat Island to be sold on the courthouse steps. Sallie Adams Boddie, the widow of Nathan Van Boddie, the first Boddie to own the island, came forward and bought Cat Island, returning it to the Boddie family.[9]

The year 1931 was a tragic year in the history of Cat Island. A few months before the loss of the Goose Point Tarpon Club, the old Cuevas homestead was also destroyed by fire. The old house that had withstood many storms and hurricanes since it was built by Juan de Cuevas in 1812 was also destroyed by a mysterious fire caused by vagrants who had taken up residence in the over one-hundred-year-old house. These two structures can never be replaced, and their historical significance, not only for Cat Island, but the entire Gulf Coast, cannot be overstated. In addition, the casino on the Isle of Caprice off the coast of Biloxi had also been destroyed by fire only a year or so before, and by 1931 the entire Isle of Caprice had disappeared below the surface of the water.

Although the hunting club was gone, a new form of hunting was about to begin. During World War II the U.S. government took over the island to train dogs for hunting, not the usual game, but rather the Japanese.

19

The Secret War Dogs of Cat Island

At 7:53 on the morning of December 7, 1941, Americans were taken completely by surprise when the first wave of Japanese planes attacked airfields and battleships at Pearl Harbor, Oahu, Hawaii. By 9:45 A.M., after a second wave of attack, 2,402 men and women had been killed and 1,282 were wounded. The next day, December 8, President Franklin D. Roosevelt signed the declaration of war against Japan. News of the sneak attack horrified the nation, causing an influx of young volunteers to join the U.S. Armed Forces, including family pets.[1]

For centuries dogs have been used in combat. The Greeks and Romans trained military attack dogs, and even during the First World War, the Germans, Belgians, French and Russians used dogs as sentries and messengers, and for other purposes. The Germans alone used as many as thirty thousand dogs in their military.[2] When the United States declared war on Japan the Army had no plans to use dogs, but prompted by patriotism and a desire to help, Arlene Erlanger, a well-known dog trainer and breeder of standard poodles, made a proposal to Washington about forming a canine support unit for the Armed Forces. She and other civilian trainers believed they could prepare dogs to aid in the support of our troops. In January 1942, Mrs. Erlanger, along with Harry I. Caesar and other leading breeders and trainers, formed a group called Dogs for Defense.[3] Mrs. Erlanger and her members in association with the American Kennel Club appealed to the public to donate their quality pets to help in the war effort. In February 1942, the Secretary of War approved the plan and authorized Dogs for Defense to serve as a clearinghouse for the donated dogs. The K-9 Program began on March 13, 1942, and in August the first War Dog Reception and Training Center was established at Front Royal, Virginia, with the Quartermaster Corps in charge of the new K-9 (canine) division.[4]

Originally, the government estimated only about 200 dogs would be needed, but that number grew as the program progressed.[5] Thirty-two breeds were accepted at first, although it was eventually limited to German shepherds, Doberman pinschers, collies, Belgian sheep dogs, and giant schnauzers. The dogs had to stand at least twenty inches tall at the shoulder, weigh more than fifty pounds and be no older than one to five years. Owners who wished to donate their pets contacted Dogs for Defense, and after a preliminary medical exam, the accepted animal was sent to one of the four newly opened training centers for a more thorough inspection. Those centers were located at Front Royal, Virginia; Fort Robinson,

Nebraska; Camp Rimini at Helena, Montana; and San Carlos, California. Only about 40 percent of the dogs passed the preliminary screening.[6]

This whole operation was experimental, since the only experience the Army had was limited to the training of sled dogs. In addition to receiving the new dogs, Dogs for Defense also supervised the volunteer trainers. These highly qualified civilians were willing to work in the program without pay, but as the demand for more dogs increased, the Quartermaster Corps began training the dog handlers, most of which were soldiers. The program was soon transferred to the Quartermaster Remount Branch, because that section had years of experience with animals.[7]

Dogs were put through a rigid military routine the same as any other new soldier. During this "basic training" period the new dogs were taught fundamental commands such as sit, stay, and come. In addition, they were trained to wear muzzles and gas masks, and to be at ease riding in military vehicles and hearing ammunition fire. It took dogs about 8–12 weeks to complete the basic program, after which they were placed in specialized training based on their temperament and abilities. These categories consisted of sentry dogs, scout or patrol dogs, messenger dogs, and mine detection dogs. The greatest majority of the dogs were used as sentry dogs and after their training were sent to military sites all over the world.[8]

In June 1942, William A. Prestre, a former Swiss army officer, wrote to President Roosevelt with an interesting proposal that had never been considered before. Prestre's theory was that different ethnic groups had different scents, mainly because of their different diets.[9] He told the president he not only could train army dogs to sniff out and attack the Japanese, but that he could train dogs to attack the enemy in packs, causing enough disruption to allow the American forces to follow in and take positions. There was so much paranoia in the country after the surprise attack at Pearl Harbor that even the most outlandish ideas were given consideration, and this was certainly one of the most far-fetched. Being a skilled salesman, however, Prestre was able to convince the Army that his proposal was plausible enough to at least be tested. The Army's Operations Division had the Swiss civilian brought from his home in Santa Fe, New Mexico, to Washington, D.C., for further discussions about his theory. After more questioning the Army felt it was worth a try and agreed to the plan. Prestre was hired with a captain's pay and placed in charge of training the dogs. Because of the sensitive nature of the experiment, the new program was classified as top secret while the dogs were being field-tested.[10]

Prestre went first to Front Royal, Virginia, to determine the quantity, quality, and breeds of the dogs at the facility. He was there also to evaluate the way the Army was then training its animals. His eccentric nature (which would prove to be difficult throughout the course of the experiment) began to show when he judged most of the army's trainers as being unfit for the project.[11] He then requested that the Army provide twenty to thirty thousand dogs for the operation. This was a staggering number of animals, particularly when one considers that out of all of the dogs already being trained by the Army at the time, his rigid inspection had found only ten to be suitable. To address this need he proposed that the military start its own breeding program to supply the large number of quality animals that would be required. The Army dismissed his idea on the basis that it would be too slow and impractical under the current war needs.[12]

In the meantime, Cat Island, which was similar to the jungle-like Pacific islands controlled by the Japanese, was chosen for the training site because of its semi-tropical climate and dense vegetation.[13] The private, uninhabited island, with its scrub oaks, palm trees,

Soldiers are shown unloading donated dogs on Cat Island for the secret mission (courtesy of Lt. Col. Robert B. Coates).

pines and marsh grasses, along with its stretches of white sand beaches and marshy lagoons, was perfect for training the dogs. During the selection process several people commented on how ironic it was that an island named Cat Island was about to be turned over to the dogs.[14]

Cat Island was very different from the other canine training facilities, not only in environment, but also in mission. Unlike the others, which were under the Quartermaster Corps Remount Division, the operations on Cat Island were placed under the auspices of the Army Ground Forces. Lieutenant Colonel A.R. Nichols was put in charge of overseeing the project.[15]

Prestre arrived on the island and immediately began to irritate the lieutenant colonel. His requirements were stringent and demanding. He would only allow dogs between one and two years old, and after inspecting almost four hundred dogs he felt none were acceptable as assault dogs. His initial plan was to employ ten dogs from each of eight breeds. He believed that the ones best suited for the mission were greyhounds, Irish wolfhounds, staghounds, Airedales, German shepherds, mastiffs, giant schnauzers, and foxhounds. Finally, forty-nine dogs donated by the public were assigned to Cat Island, not all from these breeds.[16]

After settling the dog issue and bending to Nichols' suggestion of adding bloodhounds for tracking purposes, Prestre made an almost shocking request. He told Nichols that for the experiment to work, he would need to have "live bait." Major Kimmel at the Army War College in Washington was concerned and sent a secret telegram asking for further details.[17] Prestre explained that the training would require actual people for the dogs to attack and to "kill." Since the purpose was to deploy the dogs against the Japanese, he would need twenty-four Japanese-Americans on Cat Island as targets for the dogs. Everyone involved, including Kimmel and Nichols, realized how volatile and harmful this would be to America's war effort if news ever leaked out that such experiments were being conducted, so the operation was given the highest top secret status.[18]

On November 3, 1942, Major James Lovell, under confidential orders, secretly loaded twenty-six Nisei[19] from the Third Platoon of Company B into a transport plane and left from Camp McCoy in Wisconsin to what was for them an unknown destination. The men themselves were given no explanation, nor were their fellow soldiers on the base. To their friends of the 100th Infantry, the men had mysteriously vanished with swimsuits and fishing poles. Once in the air they questioned Major Lovell about their mission, but even then he remained secretive. He simply smiled and assured them they were on their way to a nice warm place like their home in Hawaii for special training. All of the men were Nisei, but even more importantly for the experiment, they all looked like the Japanese enemy.[20]

The plane finally touched down at Keesler Air Force Base in Biloxi, but not before the entire landing area was cleared of all personnel. Large covered Army trucks were backed up to the door of the plane. The men with all of their gear jumped directly from the plane into the waiting vehicle. They were then taken to an isolated pier somewhere along the coast and transferred to a waiting boat.

After about an hour and a half the boat arrived at Ship Island, twelve miles south of the coast. Upon seeing Fort Massachusetts, the old Civil War fort located on the island, the men were sure that would be their new home. Instead, they were housed in a wooden building next to the fort. After settling in, the men spent several days doing nothing more than exploring the island, swimming, and fishing. One morning, however, the boat that had carried them to the island returned and ferried them to nearby Cat Island, where their mission would actually take place. That first trip was somewhat shaky as the dog trainer captain was trying to pilot the boat. After running aground several times they were finally able to get the boat to the island, although there was some concern they might have to swim the last part of the way.[21]

Cat Island was so different from Ship Island, which was basically flat and sandy with very little vegetation. Cat Island, in contrast, was like a jungle, lush with palmetto bushes and moss-draped oaks, pine trees and more. The lagoons that dotted the island were infested with alligators and snakes, while the swampy conditions were breeding grounds for swarms of hungry mosquitoes. Once on Cat Island the men were finally briefed about their impending mission: they were there to train dogs. Major Lovell had the unpleasant task of explaining the "special training" the men would conduct.[22]

A Coast Guard pilot was with them on the second boat trip over to Cat Island, which went without incident. On the way back to Ship Island that evening, however, the boat's motor died, leaving the men stranded in the Gulf. Since they had no radios or other means of communica-

Robert Coates' dog "Champ" (courtesy of Lt. Col. Robert B. Coates).

tion, one of the soldiers climbed the mast and set off some flares. Fortunately the Coast Guard responded quickly and towed the boat back to their base on Ship Island.[23]

The daily trips to Cat Island continued for a while without much further incident. Training began about nine o'clock in the morning and lasted for about six hours. Upon returning to Ship Island, the men would relax by fishing for the evening meal. Using handmade bamboo poles they caught white trout, enough to send back to the men at Camp McCoy. They were surprised to find that the fish were as abundant on the Gulf Coast as in the waters back home in Hawaii. They gathered oysters to roast, but for shrimp they would row out to the shrimp boats anchored in the sound, and would buy bucketfuls.[24]

The training on Cat Island began with most of the men serving as targets for scout dogs. The purpose of these dogs was to work in silence to help detect snipers, ambushes and other enemy forces. This exercise required little effort from the men, who had only to hide out in the island's swamps and wait for the dogs to find them. Each Japanese-American carried a piece of horse meat for a target, and when he was found by the dog, he would fire an air rifle into the air to condition the dog to the sound of rifle shots, place the meat against his throat and fall to the ground as if he were dead. The idea was for the dog to learn to go for the man's throat. Unfortunately the dogs did not cooperate. They

An unidentified soldier is shown training a dog on Cat Island (courtesy of the National Archives in Washington, D.C).

would grab the meat, and then playfully lick the Nisei's face as if he had just handed them a treat.[25]

Prestre had begun to use stringent forms of discipline on the dogs in an effort to convert these former family pets into vicious killers. Lieutenant Nichols found these actions to be inappropriate, and forbade Prestre from using many of these methods. The lieutenant could only imagine how the American citizens who had donated their dogs for a worthy cause would react if they knew how their pets were being used. The old Swiss complained that Nichols was interfering with the success of the program, but there was mounting evidence that the assault dog experiment was having problems.[26]

The men were allowed to write letters to their friends and family on the outside, but were prohibited from mentioning anything about "dogs" or "island." This was a top-secret operation and the government could not allow even the slightest hint about it to leak out. After awhile the men would try to be clever, writing about their experiences in Japanese and even Latin, but they were edited before they were sent.[27] The fishermen on the shrimp boats were the only other possible breach in security. They were understandably curious about this strange group of men in the Gulf. They inquired where the men were from and were simply told Hawaii. Word got out about the Japanese buying shrimp from the fishermen, prompting two government agents to investigate. After being properly briefed about the classified situation, they left Cat Island, and were the only outsiders to ever visit the operation.[28]

While the majority of Japanese-Americans were training scout dogs, six of the men were sent to the mainland to the military base at Gulfport Field to train sentry-type attack dogs. The Army Air Corps had taken over the land and the airstrip near the Gulfport airport for a military base. After the war, much of the land was later developed into the current Bayou View subdivision.[29]

Each day the men were transported back and forth to Cat Island, but on days when the weather was bad, the boat would sometimes not show up. This prompted Prestre to move the men from their base on Ship Island to permanent barracks on Cat Island. The time was growing short, and he could not afford any delays. For several days after the move, only scout dogs were trained. The men and their barracks were kept separated from the dogs on different ends of the island so the dogs would not become familiar with Japanese-Americans. Each day the Nisei had to take a barge from their end of the island to the training areas. Since there were no piers at which to dock, the barge would come only as close to the shore as the depth of the water would permit. This prompted the men to complain about having to wade to the beach in the cold water of the Gulf. One day, the pilot tried to remedy the situ-

An unidentified soldier is shown working with one of the dogs of Cat Island (courtesy of the National Archives in Washington, D.C).

ation. He gunned the motor hard, attempting to drive the barge onto the sandy beach. In so doing, he busted the engine's propeller. This ended the scout training for most of the men, although three of the soldiers were kept to continue working with the scout dogs.[30]

To begin the next phase of attack dog training, some of the men were assigned to various breeds. Two men were assigned to the Labradors and Chesapeake Bay retrievers, two were assigned to Russian wolfhounds, two had the Bouvier and Great Danes, and two others trained the Airedales. Bloodhounds had been added to the group by Lt. Nichols to be trained for tracking, and had been purchased in addition to the citizen-donated dogs. One man was left on Ship Island to edit the men's mail before it was sent out, while two others remained as cooks. The three did not participate in the actual dog training.[31]

To help Lieutenant Nichols with the project, Master Sergeant John Pierce, an Army dog trainer, was sent from California. Pierce brought his own dog to assist him on the island. The dog was somewhat of a celebrity, being the grandson of the movie star Rin Tin Tin.[32]

The most controversial part of the project began with the Japanese-Americans serving as live targets, not just to be located, but also to be "killed." Fierce competition grew between Pierce and Prestre. Pierce was able to achieve in just a few weeks. what Prestre had failed to do since the beginning of the program. Prestre had sold the government on creating packs of attack dogs, but it was Pierce's theory that a man could only effectively control two dogs at a time. Pierce was able to get his dogs to find the enemy's location and to only attack when given the command. Prestre was still trying to get his dogs to attack in packs, but they never achieved the ferocity of Pierce's dogs. So far, Prestre's Japanese experiment seemed to be crumbling apart.[33]

Although attack training was not going well, the trainers had great success with the bloodhounds. The dogs proved to be very intelligent, and soon were able to track the men without using meat. Even when they tried to elude the dogs by crossing through water, the dogs were able to pick up their scent on the other side.[34]

Boxers were to be used as suicide dogs. Dummy explosives were strapped to their collars and they were trained to go into foxholes and dugouts. Once in, the explosive was to be detonated by a radio device. Although these dogs were being trained, fortunately suicide dogs were never actually used in combat.[35]

The training period was almost at an end, with the results being somewhat mixed. The scout dogs were successful in locating their targets, and the bloodhounds were successful in tracking the soldiers, although it was not clear whether they detected their "Japanese blood," or simply the familiar scents of their trainers.[36]

On January 12, 1943, officers from the Army Ground Forces visited Cat Island to witness a demonstration of the dogs' progress. After Prestre led the dogs to the Japanese-Americans who were heavily padded for the exhibition, one of the officers, Colonel Ridgely Gaither, observed that the dogs showed no apparent ferocity or intent to do any bodily harm; he thought it seemed simply part of a routine.[37] Overall the event was characterized as nothing more than a circus animal act. Based on the demonstration, the officers pulled the plug on the failed plan. They concluded that Prestre's idea that dogs could be taught to attack in packs was apparently not workable, and his contract was ended as of February 1, 1943.[38]

Prestre was devastated and pleaded for another chance. After some effort, he was granted one more try to show what the dogs had learned. The second demonstration went no better than the first, causing officers to observe that the animals' routines seemed forced and unnatural. For Prestre, it was the end, but not before he made unfounded threats. He left Cat Island in a rage, claiming that Lieutenant Nichols had interfered with the experiment, causing it to fail. He threatened to air his complaints to the president and directly to the people. This shook the Army because it would have blown the cover of this controversial top-secret program. Nichols was called in for questioning to answer the claims. After extensive briefing the major dismissed all charges against Nichols and stated in his report, "It is believed that Mr. William Prestre is extremely eccentric and potentially dangerous subversively. It is believed advisable to acquaint the FBI with his actions and attitude, and request that he be placed under surveillance if deemed necessary."[39]

The only success out of the Cat Island experiment were the scout dogs, which was a program well underway before the Prestre debacle. The top brass agreed to continue the tracking dog program under the direction of Sgt. Pierce for another month. Ten of the original Nisei remained to complete this new assignment. After completion the men were sent to Camp Shelby near Hattiesburg, where two of them received the Legion of Merit for courageously fighting the war dogs on Cat Island.[40]

Several months after the Nisei had returned to their base in Wisconsin, men from the 828th Signal Pigeon Replacement Company took over Cat Island and began an entirely different experimental program. They tried teaming messenger dogs with carrier pigeons to improve communications between locations that could not be accessed by vehicle or on foot. The island was perfect for simulating actual combat conditions. Members of the Signal Corps designed special carrying cases to allow dogs to easily transport the pigeons. The use of the dogs combined with the pigeons proved to be very efficient, providing a valuable alternative means of communication to our troops on the battlefield.[41]

The training of dogs on Cat Island was mostly experimental and was gradually phased out at this specialized location. The first effort in the last hundred years to train dogs to attack enemy positions was also the last dog-training program sponsored by the Army

Cadre of soldiers serving on Cat Island (courtesy of Lt. Col. Robert B. Coates).

Ground Forces during World War II. Because of the lack of facilities for men or dogs, it was not practical to train large numbers of dogs on Cat Island and the Army camp officially closed on July 15, 1944.[42]

This was not the first time that Cat Island had been taken over by the government. The United States was only one of a long list of owners since the time of the first grant to Christian Ladner and Juan de Cuevas from Spain.

20

Cat Island Owners from the Past to the Present

Cat Island has changed hands many times since its discovery in 1699. The list of owners of one of the most desirable and historic barrier islands in the Gulf is long and impressive, and includes many well-known and prominent citizens of Mississippi, Louisiana, and the world. The following is a chronological list of the numerous title-holders of Cat Island since the French first discovered it, with a brief comment about each.

France

France was the first legal owner of Cat Island. René Robert Cavalier, Sieur de La Salle, claimed the Louisiana territory for the French Crown, including the Gulf Coast and Cat Island, on April 9, 1682. The initial plan was to establish a fort at the mouth of the Mississippi River, but that idea was temporarily abandoned. Six years later, the French government commissioned Pierre LeMoyne, Sieur d'Iberville, to relocate to the mouth of the Mississippi River and to colonize the area. He first visited Cat Island on February 27, 1699.[1]

Great Britain

The French owned Cat Island until the area came under the control of England. The Treaty of Paris, in 1763, forced France to surrender its territory east of the Mississippi River to Great Britain, with the exception of New Orleans, and its area west of the Mississippi to Spain. In an attempt to tighten political control over the newly acquired colonies, Great Britain organized the coastal area into East and West Florida. Cat Island was included in the west area.[2]

In 1767, a Mister Somitette (first name unknown) received a grant to Cat Island from the British.[3] He had also received a grant for Deer Island, Round Island, and 500 acres on the mainland at the same time, with the stipulation that the grants were only legal if the properties were not already in the possession of any of the French settlers. This would have made him the first private individual to own Cat Island, but since Nicholas Ladner had registered his claim three years prior, Mr. Somitette's grant to Cat Island was not deemed valid. Ladner's claim showed that he had been in possession of the island since 1745, and was using the island for pasturage several years before that. Although he had petitioned for a grant, Ladner had not yet received it. Cat Island remained in the hands of the British without a private owner.[4]

Spain

Spain became the third country to own Cat Island. The Floridas did not join in the American Revolution against England. Instead, the Spanish governor of Louisiana, General Bernardo de Galvez, watched for an opportunity to seize the territory for his own country. His plan succeeded, and by May 1781 the Coast, including Cat Island, came under the control of Spain.[5]

Nicholas Christian Ladner

Nicholas Christian Ladner became the first private individual to own Cat Island. In 1764, Ladner traveled to Mobile to pledge his loyalty to the British, who had taken control of the territory from the French. While he was there he filed a request for a grant to Cat Island, but no action was ever taken.[6] The request remained unresolved until Spain took over the territory in May 1781. Two months later, on July 31, Ladner made the same request to Spain that he had made to the British. Spain honored Ladner's petition and issued a grant to him the next day following his formal petition. On August 1, 1781, Nicholas Ladner received a grant for the entire island that had been his home for nearly 35 years.[7]

Juan de Cuevas

Juan de Cuevas was the second individual to own Cat Island. Spain issued a permit transferring the title from Nicholas Ladner to his son-in-law, Cuevas, on September 10, 1795.[8] The transaction is a matter of official record, although an actual document from Spain has never been found, and may have never existed. It was common practice for an original land grant to be passed down to the spouse or other family members without the issuance of a new grant.[9]

The Cuevas permit may have been lost with some other Spanish documents. In 1842 U.S. President John Tyler commissioned a man named José Caro to translate the records of West Florida. He was supposed to do his work on the premises at the courts, but instead, he took all of the records back with him to Pensacola. Since this was illegal, he was threatened with arrest if the records were not returned. Caro made an attempt to comply with the warning, but only returned some of the records. Historians today believe there are two to three thousand of these records still missing. The Spanish permit giving Cat Island to Cuevas is possibly one of those records that was never recovered.[10]

U.S. Government

After the Cuevas grant, the United States government briefly owned Cat Island, when it took over control of the Louisiana territory from Spain on December 20, 1803. Originally England, France, Spain, Mexico, and the Native American Indians owned all of the land that now makes up the continental United States, but as the young country grew, the federal government began acquiring land from the Atlantic to the Pacific Oceans, all part of the attitude called Manifest Destiny.[11] It was the belief of those in Washington that the inevitable providence of the United States was to stretch from ocean to ocean. To this end the government began acquiring land in several ways. Some of the land was purchased directly, like the island of Manhattan and the Louisiana territory; other land was won by treaty, like the Northwest Territories Treaty and the Guadeloupe Hidalgo Treaty. Still other land was obtained by treaty as the end result of war, like the original war for independence from

England. Once land was acquired, by whatever means, it was held by the United States government. Much of the present-day United States. was, therefore, once a part of the public domain — land owned exclusively by the federal government.[12] Cat Island was no exception, and although Juan de Cuevas had a Spanish grant, the island became the property of the United States.

Juan de Cuevas

Almost immediately, Juan de Cuevas regained title to at least a portion of Cat Island. Since it was not the intention of the United States to control its newly acquired land, it was important and necessary to recognize the legitimate "private land claims" of many of the settlers that asserted a right to ownership based on a grant, a purchase, or a settlement by another country that took place before the United States acquired sovereignty over that land. In 1819 the government began reviewing old European land grants with the intent of honoring all of those proven to be legitimate.[13]

A legal instrument had to be created by which government land could be transferred to private ownership. This vehicle is known as a land patent.[14] A patent certifies absolute and supreme title to land. Such land cannot lawfully be seized for debt and is not subject to taxation by the state, nor can state statutes enacted subsequent to the transfer have any effect on the land described in the patent.[15] The patent by its own creation lasts "forever" and belongs to the named party "and to their heirs and assigns forever." This does not mean that the property cannot be sold, but that the original owner and his family retain ownership for as long as they keep their rights to the land.

Anyone holding a European grant had to report his claim to the commissioners in order to retain title to his land. The claim had to be accompanied by some type of proof in the form of a survey, requette,[16] permission to settle, or other written evidence from the Spanish or British authorities. In some cases, however, such proof was not available even though a claim was valid. If in the opinion of the commissioners a claim appeared to be legitimate, the land in question would still be given to the holder without the documentation, but only as a "donation" from the U.S. government, not as a European grant. In such cases, the maximum amount of land any one person could receive was only 1,280 acres.[17] This was often less land than the original grant intended. Juan de Cuevas was a victim of this law.

Generally the exact boundaries of a claim were spelled out in the grant in order to protect the rights of the adjacent property owners, but the Cat Island grant was different. The original Spanish document simply granted "Cat Island" without any delineation, but with an implied understanding that it meant the whole island from shore to shore. No plat or survey ever existed because Spain did not require one for an island grant. This wording, however, was too vague for the bureaucrats in Washington. Since Juan de Cuevas had nothing more specific to back his claim than the grant itself, it was handled as a "donation" from the U.S. government. Thus, on September 28, 1830, a patent was issued to Juan de Cuevas in accordance with the law for only 1,280 acres, slightly less than half the island.

The accompanying plat clearly shows the area to be the western half of the island where the Cuevas homestead was located. The government surveyor describes the land covered by the patent[18] as being in "township nine south, of range eleven west and township nine south of range twelve west of the St. Stephens Meridian, State of Mississippi, containing twelve hundred eighty acres, and five hundredths of an acre. (1280 5/8 acres)."[19]

Many historians have taken this patent to mean that the original Spanish grant only gave Juan de Cuevas the western half of Cat Island, which we will later see is incorrect. The patent was misunderstood by almost everyone, and is the source of some of the Cuevas family's sincere belief that they can still rightfully claim ownership of Cat Island. This official document signed by the president, Chester A. Arthur, was thought by many to be a special gift from "a grateful nation" for Cuevas' heroic action in the Battle of New Orleans. This official deed seemed to verify that the legend that had been circulating since Juan's death about the "Hero of Cat Island" was actually true. Never mind that almost no one knew exactly what the patent actually said, nor did they really care about the details. If that official document did not convince the skeptics that the Cuevas heirs owned Cat Island, it at least cast enough doubt as to keep the fight alive for generations.

The U.S. Government Buys an Acre

On November 22, 1830, the United States government bought one acre on the western tip of Cat Island from Juan de Cuevas on which to build a lighthouse. It would be the first

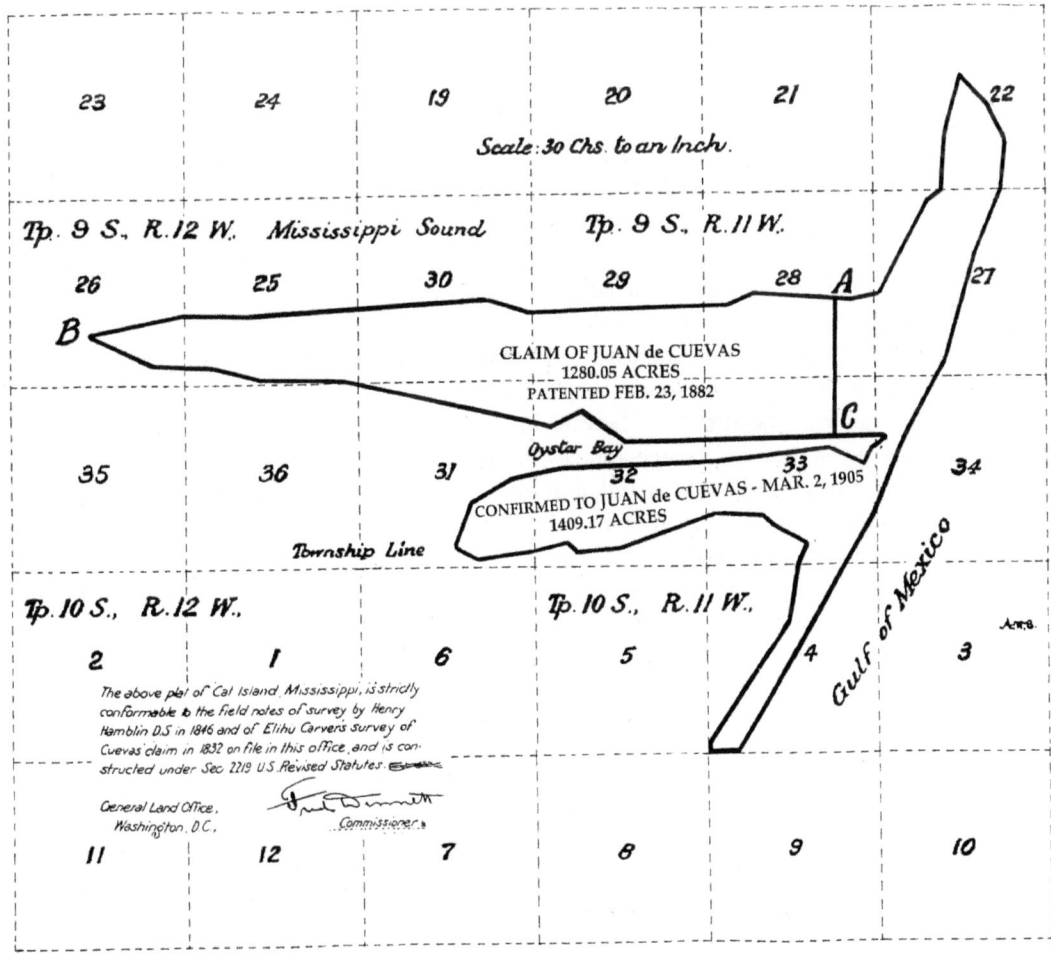

Map shows the areas of Cat Island covered by two U.S. patents granted to Juan de Cuevas. Contrary to what many have reported, Cuevas owned all of Cat Island.

lighthouse constructed on the Coast. An identical lighthouse was built at the same time on the mainland in what is now Pass Christian.[20]

Judah Philip Benjamin

Judah Philip Benjamin (1811–1884) bought Cat Island from Juan de Cuevas on March 13, 1837, for $15,000, becoming the third in a long line of individuals to own the island.[21] The amount of this sale is modest in today's dollars, but was the equivalent of a fortune in the rural society of the 1800s, where bread was 4 cents a loaf. The sale of Cat Island made Juan de Cuevas one of the wealthiest men on the Coast, by any standard. It also ended generations of island ownership by the Ladner/Cuevas families, although the last Cuevas did not leave Cat Island until 1861 when the lighthouse was closed.

In the latter part of 1836, Judah Benjamin had begun visiting Juan de Cuevas with a proposal to purchase the island. At first Cuevas was adamant he would not sell, but over time and after several visits by the eloquent young man, Juan agreed to consider Benjamin's proposal. It was obvious to all that the future for the young people was on the burgeoning Coast. The Cuevas children, with the exception of Ramon the lighthouse keeper, had already moved to the mainland, or at least had no plans to remain on the island, so Juan saw no reason to hold on to it for the family. The 26-year-old Benjamin eventually persuaded him to sell when he put together an offer that, although common today, was unique for the times. The contract would allow Juan and Marie to sell the island and still remain in their home for the rest of their lives.[22] The sale was not publicized and the transaction went virtually unnoticed. This private event is what ultimately led to doubts and suspicions concerning the island's ownership over the years, since Juan and Marie continued living in their home as before with their lives unchanged by the sale.

Judah Philip Benjamin was a brilliant man considered by many to be the "brains of the Confederacy."[23] He was born August 11, 1811, in Christiansted, St. Croix, Virgin Islands, of Jewish parents. A precocious youth, he entered Yale at the age of fourteen, but left early in his junior year. He moved to New Orleans in 1828 at the age of seventeen where he worked for a notary while studying French and law in his spare time. He was admitted to the bar in 1832 and with his friend Thomas Slidell published the *Digest of the Reported Decisions of the Superior Courts in the Territory of Orleans and State of Louisiana* (1834).[24] This enhanced his reputation as a rising young lawyer. His practice made him wealthy, allowing him to eventually become a plantation owner with 140 slaves. He was a founder of the Illinois Central Railroad, a Louisiana State legislator, and was elected to the United States Senate from Louisiana in 1852. When the slave states seceded from the Union in 1861, Confederate President Jefferson Davis appointed Benjamin attorney general, making him the first person of Jewish descent to hold a Cabinet-level office in American government.[25] He was soon elevated to the position of secretary of war. Although he was an able administrator, he was unjustly blamed for the Confederate defeats early in 1862. He resigned his office over the controversy, but was immediately appointed secretary of state. When Jefferson Davis was captured in 1865, Benjamin escaped with some difficulty to Great Britain, where he began to practice law.

Judah Benjamin was a shrewd attorney and very knowledgeable about personal property and real estate. He eventually won wide acclaim on the subject with the publication in 1868 of the book *A Treatise on the Law of Sale of Personal Property*.[26] He was appointed a Queen's Counsel the following year in 1869, and was considered one of the most learned members of the British bar until his retirement in 1883.

Judah Benjamin died May 8, 1884, and was buried in Paris, where his wife, a Louisiana Creole, and his daughter had made their home since the 1840s.[27]

James Ramsay, Laurent Millaudon, William H. Chase, and James P. Freret

Judah Benjamin had no intention of keeping Cat Island for himself. Unknown to the Cuevas family, he had been working as a broker for four wealthy businessmen from New Orleans. He was assigned to win Juan's confidence and to put the deal together. On March 25, 1837, after having the island for only two weeks, Benjamin relinquished ownership to James Ramsay for $15,000, the same amount he had paid Juan de Cuevas for the island. It was then held in trust for Ramsay's three partners, Laurent Millaudon, William H. Chase, and James P. Freret. These astute businessmen were successful land developers in Louisiana and they realized the island had great development potential. It is not known what plans they had for Cat Island, since nothing was ever done.[28]

James Ramsay

Nothing definite is known of James Ramsay's background. It appears he may have originally hailed from South Carolina, but this is not confirmed. After selling land that had been his father's, he moved first to Alabama about 1815, and then to Union Parish, Louisiana, in 1836.[29] He purchased Cat Island from Judah Benjamin the following year.

On April 29, 1837, Ramsay sold a fourth interest ($3,750) in Cat Island to each of his three partners, Laurent Millaudon, William H. Chase, and James P. Freret, while keeping a fourth for himself. Over the next sixty years, James Ramsay was the only one of these four men to retain his portion of Cat Island.

Benjamin Laurent Millaudon

Benjamin Laurent Millaudon had arrived in New Orleans from Paris in 1802. He was a wealthy investor in land, and over the years bought and sold various plantation properties, including the old McCarty sugar plantation in what was then Jefferson Parrish. The town of Carrollton developed on the site of the plantation. Laurent Millaudon and two other partners, John Slidell and Samuel Kohn, had acquired the property along with the New Orleans Canal and Banking Company in 1831.[30] In 1833 they hired Charles F. Zimpel, a surveyor, to subdivide the land to create the new town of Carrollton. Carrollton was incorporated in 1845, and it became a "bedroom" suburb of New Orleans populated by middle and upper-class citizens, and was later annexed into the city of New Orleans in 1874.[31] There was easy access to the city by road and by train. The road ran along what is now St. Charles Avenue, and the New Orleans and Carrollton Railroad ran parallel to the road. The railroad was one of the first built in the United States.[32] The only other railroads at that time were the Jefferson and Lake Pontchartrain Railroad that ran from Carrollton to Lake Pontchartrain, and a third line in New York. Laurent Millaudon was chosen as one of the first presidents of the New Orleans and Carrollton Railroad.

Millaudon purchased Cat Island six years after he purchased the McCarty plantation to start the town of Carrollton. He additionally purchased land and slaves from John Slidell sometimes in the 1800s, as part of what was known as the Houmas Plantation.[33] The Houmas Plantation house continues to be one of the most visited antebellum plantation homes near New Orleans. The architectural style of the house is a classic example of the old southern plantations. It was used as the setting for the 1964 film *Hush, Hush, Sweet Charlotte*, starring Bette Davis, as well as other well-known films and commercials.[34]

In 1856, a ship built in Cincinnati, Ohio, bearing his name, *The Laurent Millaudon*, was acquired for Confederate service and fitted out at New Orleans for the River Defense Fleet under Capt. J.E. Montgomery.[35] It is not known whether Millaudon built the ship or it was simply named in his honor. On January 25, 1862, Montgomery began to convert the boat into an ironclad ram. The newly reconditioned boat was renamed the *General Sterling Price* and was sent to Fort Pillow, Tennessee, where she was operated by the Confederacy in defense of the river approaches to Memphis. She was sunk during a battle with the Federal ram *Queen of the West*, but was later raised by Union forces and taken into federal service.[36]

William H. Chase

William H. Chase was born in Massachusetts in 1798 and attended the United States Military Academy. After graduating in 1815, he was immediately assigned to the U.S. Army Corps of Engineers, working hard to develop the town of Pensacola while also planning for its defense. The War of 1812 had shown that the forts in and around New Orleans were vulnerable and in 1819 he was given the assignment of improving these defenses. He was the chief engineer for the forts at the Rigolets, Chef Menteur, Bienvenue and the Bayou Dupre.[37]

He helped to create a new bank in Pensacola of which he became a major stockholder. The bank became the depository of federal building funds. By the 1830s he was a leading real estate promoter and became aware of the opportunity to buy Cat Island through his association with Laurent Millaudon.

In 1854 President Pierce appointed Chase superintendent of the United States Military Academy, but he resigned from the Army before taking that position. He went into the private sector, becoming the president of the Alabama and Florida Railroad Company.

During the crisis preceding the outbreak of the Civil War, he joined the Southern forces as a colonel in the Confederate Navy. Colonel Chase was made the commander of the Florida troops and put in control of the federal forts and navy yard at Pensacola. He made Pensacola his home and took an influential lead in the development of the region. He died in Pensacola on February 8, 1870.[38]

James Peter Freret

James Peter Freret was an architect in New Orleans. He became extremely popular through his accomplished use of the Queen Anne style of architecture that had been introduced to the nation at the 1876 Centennial Exposition in Philadelphia. Thomas Sully (1855–1939), who was the absolute master of the Queen Anne style in New Orleans, had designed hotels in Chattanooga, Vicksburg, Hattiesburg, and most notably the Great Southern Hotel built in Gulfport, Mississippi, in 1903.[39] Although Sully was the most influential architect of the style, Freret's fame spread and he received commissions throughout the south. Two of his more notable designs in New Orleans were the St. Charles Borromeo Church on Church Street, built in 1819, and the Charles Adams' house at 1206 Second Street, built in 1886.[40]

James and his brother William ran the Freret Cotton Press Company, which became the first large industry in the American sector of New Orleans. Their business of compressing cotton for shipment abroad was located on St. Charles Avenue between Poydras and Gravier and occupied nearly two city blocks. The size and success of their company made them highly visible businessmen and provided a stepping stone to political careers. James Freret became a city councilman from the Sixth District while his brother, William, was elected mayor of New Orleans from the Native American Party in 1840. William was defeated for re-election by Denis Prieur (1791–1857) in 1842, but was later re-elected when Prieur resigned after having served only eight months of his term. Prieur gave up the office of mayor in 1850 to accept an appointment by President Zachary Taylor as the collector of the Port of New Orleans.[41] William Freret continued in office until 1844. He is often cited as one of New Orleans' most efficient mayors due to his meticulous temperament. He was also known for his strong support for public schools and his belief in equality. His greatest achievement in office was the establishment of a free public school system.

Ramon Cuevas

On February 1, 1840, Juan de Cuevas sold ten acres of Cat Island to his son, Ramon, for $200. The property was part of the 85 acres that Juan had retained in his sale to Judah Benjamin.[42] Ramon bought the property adjacent to the lighthouse where he was employed as the lighthouse keeper. He used the land to graze cattle and to raise food. He and his family evacuated Cat Island in 1861, moving to Shieldsboro (Bay St. Louis) before a severe hurricane destroyed his home and most of his belongings. Ramon died that same year. According to the Judah Benjamin contract, any land owned by the Cuevas family would revert to the purchaser upon the death of Juan and Marie. Ramon, therefore, no longer had any claim to his land on Cat Island.

Millaudon Heirs

Laurent Millaudon died in the later part of 1886. As a consequence of his death, the taxes went unpaid on his portion of Cat Island. In March of 1887, the sheriff of Hancock County was directed to sell certain lands including Cat Island for delinquent taxes. Millaudon's heirs, who had been unaware that the taxes had not been paid, received a notice of the sale. Hoping to save their part of the island, they submitted an offer. Theirs was the winning bid at $10 and thus they were able to retain Millaudon's interest in Cat Island for an unbelievably low amount even for that time.[43] In 1896, the Millaudon heirs sold their interest in Cat Island to J.H. Duggan, Jr.

Duggan Family Owners

Over the next fifty years the ownership of Cat Island was split and transferred to several individuals, mostly in the Duggan family, until finally as many as fifteen people including two children shared possession. Ownership of Cat Island became a hodgepodge with some persons claiming as little as $1/36$ percent of the whole. The Duggan family included J.H. Duggan, Jr., T.J. Duggan, Jr., F.F. Duggan, Edith Duggan, Miriam Duggan, Isabel Duggan, Lillian A. Duggan, Louise M. Duggan, and P.R. Duggan. Other owners outside of the Duggan family included James Ramsay, John Milliken Parker, and Adele McCall Flower along with her two children, Adele and Marian, and later by default, H. Gibbes Morgan.[45]

The Duggan family was prominent in the business and social scene in New Orleans.

Mr. Thomas Smithfield Dugan (sic), patriarch of the Duggan family of Cat Island, was a real estate speculator and one of the businessmen who established the posh Garden District in New Orleans. Most of his peers had become wealthy before the age of forty and their homes served as monuments to their financial success. They flaunted their wealth as they sought public approbation to confirm their role in the community.

After the Civil War the women of the Garden District became more dominant in their households.[46] With their mounting authority within the community, these women also increased their ownership of property. By the 1860s many of the wives had their own money, having inherited substantial amounts from their fathers. Cat Island was the perfect purchase for the Duggans, who considered the ownership of the gem of the Gulf Coast barrier islands to further enhance their status with the citizens of New Orleans. The family had no plans to develop Cat Island. It was simply a luxury possession to be flaunted, and merely owning it was enough. This desire to be admired placed great emphasis on social entertainment. Louise M. Duggan, Smithfield's daughter, as a young socialite in her teens confessed that her love of pleasure was too strong for her to resist. In her diary she wrote about lavish boating parties, theater parties, and twice weekly visits to the opera.[47] Her mother also gave grand parties, including one in which an artificial fountain spewed cologne. Unfortunately, to the horror of her guests, on one occasion the unique fountain caught fire.

In New Orleans the Duggan's island getaway was well known to their friends and associates, but along the Coast few, if any, residents knew of the Duggan family, or their connection to Cat Island. This contributed to the continued assumption that Juan de Cuevas and his children were still the owners. No one in the Cuevas family or other residents of the Coast had reason to question otherwise.

Adele McCall Flower

Adele McCall Flower, a friend and neighbor of the Duggan family in the Garden District, owned 1/12 of Cat Island.[48] She was the wife of the once mayor of New Orleans Walter Chew Flower. Walter Flower married Adele McCall in 1885 and the couple had four children. Unfortunately, two of the children died in infancy. Adele and Marian, the two children that survived, were given 1/6 ownership of Cat Island despite the fact that they were minors.[49]

Adele's husband, Walter Flower, was born on his father's plantation in East Feliciana Parish, near Fort Hudson. Being well educated, he came to New Orleans and began a career in journalism as a reporter on the staff of *The Daily Picayune*. Later he studied law at Louisiana University, now known as Tulane University. After the death of his father, he began a commercial career amassing a fortune in business. He was president of the Cotton Exchange before being elected mayor and would serve New Orleans from 1850 to 1900.[50]

John Milliken Parker

John Milliken Parker owned 1/8 of Cat Island. He was from southcentral Louisiana, born March 16, 1863, in Washington, Louisiana, a village in St. Landry Parish. He was a graduate of the Eastman's Business School in New Orleans and became a prominent businessman, serving as the president of the New Orleans Cotton Exchange and the Board of Trade.[51] He was elected Louisiana governor from 1920 to 1924. He died on the Gulf Coast at Pass Christian, Mississippi, on May 20, 1939, and was buried in a tomb in the Metairie Cemetery in New Orleans.[52]

Henry Gibbes Morgan

On August 5, 1897, Henry Gibbes Morgan (1843–1925) became an owner of Cat Island by default. Morgan had loaned money to T.J. Duggan to purchase an interest in Cat Island. The mortgage amounted to $475.68. Eventually Duggan defaulted on the loan and Morgan was forced to file a suit against Duggan for the money. When Duggan could not pay, his portion of Cat Island went to Morgan as a settlement for the debt. A special commissioner's deed was issued, giving Morgan ownership of one third of one half percent interest (3/36 percent) of Cat Island and adding his name to the large group of island owners.[53]

Gibbes Morgan was a prominent attorney in New Orleans, and had served as a Confederate soldier in the 13th Louisiana Infantry during the Civil War. He studied law at the University of Louisiana, starting his career in the law office of his uncle, Judge Thomas Gibbes Morgan (1799–1861). One of the students in his law class, Edward Douglass White, became the ninth chief justice of the Supreme Court of the United States (1894).[54] Judge Morgan, Gibbes uncle, was appointed Collector of Customs of the Port of New Orleans before ascending the bench. William Freret, the brother of James Peter Freret, one of the four men who had purchased Cat Island from Judah Benjamin, had also held that position prior to him.[55]

Morgan was an unwilling partner with the Duggan family. He never expected the small loan he made to Duggan would result in his ownership of a fraction of Cat Island. He was not in the business of real estate, and wanted to sell his part as quickly as possible, but with so many individuals listed as owners, the title was a legal nightmare. He petitioned the court to force the sale of Cat Island. During the title search necessary with any real estate transaction, the serious technicality was uncovered. The original sale of the island by Juan de Cuevas to Judah Benjamin was based on the premise that Cuevas owned the entire island, but in reality, the U.S. government had erroneously granted him only 1,280 acres. The error had to be corrected if the sale of the island was to go forward.

The letter of the law had been followed concerning Cat Island, although there were questions about the government's decision from the very start. On September 29, 1830, a day after the Cat Island claim was confirmed, Jno. M. Moore,[56] the accounting commissioner of the General Land Office, received the report and suspected the error. In a letter to Stephen Pleasonton, fifth auditor and acting commissioner of the revenue, Moore pointed out that there were no marked boundaries to the claim. Since there was no specific part of the island mentioned in the grant it should be understood that the water's edge itself formed the natural property line and a more specific delineation was not necessary. Moore wrote that if the question ever came up, he believed that Juan de Cuevas owned the whole island and not just the 1,280 acres granted in the patent.[57]

Finally in 1905 when H. Gibbes Morgan became embroiled in a legal fight to sell his part of the island, it became clear to the courts that the issue of whether Juan de Cuevas owned all of Cat Island had to be legally resolved. On March 2, 1905, prompted by the lawsuit of *Morgan vs. Duggan*, a bill was pushed through Congress with the help and approval of Senator Samuel Douglas McEnery (1837–1910) of Louisiana.[58] The act, entitled "An Act for the Relief of H. Gibbes Morgan and other co-owners of Cat Island in the Gulf of Mexico," directed that a second patent be issued to Juan de Cuevas, albeit posthumously, for the remaining portion of the island (1,409.17 acres) not granted to him originally. Admitting that the government had made an error, the second patent on July 17, 1911, set the record straight.

The description given in the document is very specific about the island's remaining 1409.17 acres.

The lot one of section twenty-two, the lot one of section twenty-seven, the lot one of section twenty-eight, the lot one of section thirty-one, the lot one of section thirty-two, the lots one and two of section thirty-three, and the lot one of section thirty-four in township nine south and the lot one of section four in township ten south all in range eleven west of the St. Stephens meridian, Mississippi, containing one thousand four hundred nine and seventeen-hundredths acres.[59]

Although neither one of these patents were issued during Juan's lifetime, together they are positive proof that the U.S. government recognized Juan de Cuevas as the owner of all of Cat Island and not just a portion, as many have contended.

When the passage of the bill was announced, people misunderstood the government's actions. The title of the act was misleading, causing many to believe the government had somehow sold the island illegally to Gibbes Morgan. The government did not sell the island to Morgan, but only confirmed that Juan de Cuevas had indeed owned all of Cat Island. This new patent allowed the sale of Cat Island to proceed.

Finley S. Hewes was appointed as a special commissioner to handle the sale of Cat Island.[60] A notice of the impending sale was published in the local paper for three consecutive weeks prior to the date of the sale as stipulated by the court. Benjamin Harrod was the highest bidder at $5,000.

Benjamin Morgan Harrod

When the special commissioner, F.S. Hewes, announced the sale of Cat Island, Harrod jumped at the opportunity to make a bid. Harrod was an ardent supporter of the Audubon Society and saw this as an opportunity to fulfill his personal dream of creating a bird sanctuary on one of the barrier islands. His ownership of Cat Island presented him with a golden opportunity. Benjamin Morgan Harrod bought Cat Island from Gibbes Morgan and the Duggan family on April 1, 1907, and a special commissioner's report concerning the sale was filed with the court. Proceeds were distributed amongst the owners according to each person's share.[61]

For over a hundred years the issue of ownership had not been a question, until it was announced that Benjamin Harrod had purchased Cat Island—from the U.S. government, no less. Many of the old families along the Coast were surprised, since many still believed that the island and the Cuevas family were still connected. An article published in *The New Orleans Daily Picayune* reported that Archie Cameron, the lighthouse keeper at the time of the article, was even shocked at the report. Cameron questioned, "How could the Government sell it [Cat Island] when it belongs to the Cuevases? These are the first families of the Coast and for a century past it has been a remarkable fact that they rarely disposed of their real estate possession."[62]

The news of the reported sale jolted the Cuevas family into action. In 1908, several of the heirs filed a lawsuit in the Chancery Court of Harrison County to block the purchase.[63] Some members of the family were so sure they would win in court that they actually moved to Cat Island, living in temporary tents in anticipation of eventually setting up permanent residence there. They wanted to show that the Cuevas family may have been absent for a while, but they were back now to reclaim their island home.

With very little funds available, the family found it difficult to find an attorney, but finally the Jackson law firm of Mays and Longstreet agreed to represent them.[64] The plaintiffs rushed into court with only one purpose in mind, to stop the transfer of title. The effort was such a knee-jerk reaction to the news that the government had sold the island, that very little planning went into the overall case.

The outcome was grim. The Cuevas claim was denied, and the deed of Benjamin Harrod was certified.[65]

As a result of the Gibbes Morgan case, and the failed challenge by the Cuevas family, the U.S. government required a new title be issued for the lighthouse property previously purchased from Juan de Cuevas. As part of his purchase agreement, Mr. Harrod was required by the court to sign a new deed to confirm the government's claim to an acre on the western tip of the island for the existing lighthouse. Harrod issued a new deed for the lighthouse property on February 28, 1908.

Benjamin Harrod was born in New Orleans in 1837, and earned an A.B. degree from Harvard in 1856, and an A.M. degree in 1859. After Harvard he studied architecture and later civil engineering. In 1858, he worked for the engineers department of the U.S. Army at various forts and lighthouses along the Gulf Coast. He attained the rank of first lieutenant in the Civil War, and was an aide-de-camp to Major General M.L. Smith at the Siege of Vicksburg (May 19 to July 4, 1863). After the war he was given the courtesy title of "major" although he never achieved that rank.[66] Following his service in the Army he worked as a civil engineer and architect, developing an outstanding reputation in those fields. One of his more notable architectural designs is the Confederate monument in the Greenwood Cemetery located at 5242 Canal Boulevard. It marks a mass grave of 600 soldiers, and was the first Civil War memorial erected in New Orleans.[67]

The Fireman's Charitable & Benevolent Association had established the Greenwood Cemetery in 1852, when America was hit hard by an epidemic of yellow fever. The disease particularly devastated New Orleans, America's third-largest city at the time. The 150-acre Greenwood Cemetery provided a large burial area to relieve the other New Orleans cemeteries that were already overcrowded. The cemetery became one of the most active in the city and has the distinction of being the first to vary from the vaulted cemeteries of the past, and the first not to be enclosed by a wall made up of crypts.[68]

Benjamin Harrod was elected president of the American Society of Civil Engineers, becoming city engineer of New Orleans in 1888. When President Roosevelt created the first Isthmian Canal Commission in 1904 to study and make suggestions relative to the newly planned Panama Canal, Major Harrod was appointed as the member of the commission from the South.[69]

In May 1909, Major Harrod invited Herbert K. Job, a renowned wildlife photographer from Connecticut, to visit Cat Island and discuss his plan for a bird sanctuary. Job liked the idea and called his contacts at the National Association of Audubon Societies. Job's proposal to the association was for that group to purchase and control Cat Island. Harrod's vision was even announced in the sports publication *Forest and Stream*.[70] The president of the Audubon Association, William Dutcher, make a special trip to assess the island's potential. His conclusion was not positive. He determined that the cost of such an enterprise would far exceed the benefits, although the asking price for the island was certainly well within the group's resources. He also concluded that there was only a small strip of land on the island that would be suitable for raising the different species of birds. Therefore, he vetoed the Audubon Association's involvement, stating that the only persons who would benefit from such a venture would be the island owners, and not any conservation group.

William Dutcher's decision was a devastating blow, but Herbert Job continued to try to sell the idea. He next contacted a group of wealthy sportsmen in Boston to try to interest them in the plan. Unfortunately the investors concluded this would only be an experiment at best, and it was not considered workable.⁷¹ Benjamin Harrod was 71 years old when he purchased Cat Island, and was never able to fulfill his dream of creating a bird sanctuary.

In 1910, Major Harrod leased the turpentine rights on Cat Island to Pace and Morgan, a firm from Mobile that produced naval stores, the collective name for all products made from the gum of the pine tree. The name derives from the original use of tar as a caulking and waterproofing substance on ships — hence the word "naval." He sold the island just one year before his death in 1912.⁷² The turpentine lease between Benjamin Harrod and Pace and Morgan ended with Harrod's death, requiring that the naval stores operators would have to initiate a new lease with the island's new owner.⁷³

Nathan Van Boddie

On January 11, 1911, Nathan Van Boddie purchased Cat Island from Major Benjamin Harrod for his asking price of $10,000.⁷⁴ Nathan, born c. 1851, was married to Sallie Adams Boddie, five years his junior. They had three children, George Robert, Mary, and Sarah. This was the beginning of the five-generation ownership of Cat Island by the Boddie family.

According to his grandson, when Boddie called his bank in Gulfport for a loan, he was turned down on the grounds that it was a bad investment.⁷⁵ That did not deter him as he continued his search for a lender. In the meantime he had been talking to a group of businessmen headed by William Stockston about leasing the turpentine rights to the island, knowing that Harrod had previously made such an arrangement with Pace and Morgan. Stockton and his associates, J.B., J.F., and C.O. Galloway, arranged for the company to continue its turpentine lease on Cat Island and agreed to pay $10,500 for the turpentine rights when Boddie purchased the island. He was finally able to secure a loan from a bank in Jackson, Mississippi, for the $10,000 asking price. Boddie sold the turpentine rights to Stockton and the Galloways, and paid off the bank loan of $10,000, leaving him a clean profit of $500 and the ownership of Cat Island.⁷⁶

George Robert Boddie

George Robert Boddie, born in 1891, inherited Cat Island from his father, Nathan Van Boddie, becoming the second generation of the Boddie family to own the island. He and his wife Marie, born in 1895, had two children, Sarah and Nathan. Also living in the Boddie household at the time of the 1930 census were two black servants, Rebecca Hatchet and Lillian Ashley.⁷⁷

Cat Island Development Company

In 1917, Mississippi Senator Hernando Desoto Money (1839–1912), along with two associates, William Money and Mitchell Thomason, a retired railroad and highway contractor from Mobile, bought the island from George Robert Boddie.⁷⁸

Senator Money was born on his father's plantation in Holmes County, Mississippi. He received a law degree from the University of Mississippi in 1860, and was elected to Congress in 1875. He chose to serve only one term, and went into private practice in Washington. When Mississippi Senator James Z. George announced he would not seek re-election, Money decided to run for his seat. Senator George died, however, before the election, and Hernando

Money was appointed by Governor McLaurin to fill the seat until the meeting of the legislature in 1898. Senator Money was elected to the seat in the next election and continued to serve until 1911.

In 1863, he married Claudia Boddie, the daughter of George Boddie, the uncle of current Cat Island owner, George Robert Boddie. He invited Mitchell Thomason to visit Cat Island, and on his first trip was so impressed that he immediately recognized the tremendous potential, and teamed up with Senator Money and his brother William to purchase the island. The men came up with the idea of converting Cat Island into a seasonal resort like Catalina Island off the coast of California.[79]

Their plan was to create a biological laboratory by stocking the island with quail, pheasants, guineas, turkeys and other game birds. In addition, they planned to stock the many lakes on the island with a wide variety of freshwater fish. They would also plant oysters. One of the long slender bays on the island, which covered about 200 acres, had the perfect breeding bottom for oysters. Their studies indicated that the moderate quantity of salt water entering the fresh water in this bay combined with the character of the bottom to eliminate conchs, which are the natural enemies of the oysters. With the island stocked with fish and game, the Cat Island Development Company would build a private hunting and fishing club. The Mississippi Coast was already famous for its tarpon and other large saltwater fish, which would enhance the reputation of the Cat Island resort.

None of his great plans came to fruition, although Senator Money did try breeding Belgian hares on Cat Island. These very elegant, sleek rabbits are larger than most breeds and are built for speed. They are so fast they were called "the poor man's racehorse." They were first brought to America in 1888 and became very popular, but their popularity declined shortly after Hernando Money invested in the venture.[80] This effort was doomed from the start since Belgian hares are very difficult to breed and require a lot of personal attention. With this final failure, the Senator Money era on Cat Island came to an end. The only evidence remaining of his grand schemes was an occasional sighting of some of the Belgian hares that still populated the island for several years after.

Casino Hotel Company, Inc. Principals: F.A. Middleton, R.C. Herren, I.N. Wise, George M. Foote, and H.H. Casteel

In 1921, George M. Foote and associates purchased Cat Island from Senator Hernando Money and his partners.[81]

George Foote was a businessman in Gulfport before becoming mayor in 1909. His time in office was a period of rapid growth in the city. The board of aldermen approved the construction of shell sidewalks along the beach road where many elegant homes were being built. During his term, Gulfport got its first hospital, and the Great Southern Hotel was built becoming a major icon on the coast.

George Foote and other prominent businessmen from Mississippi and Louisiana believed very strongly that Cat Island could be transformed into a popular resort. Their vision for the island was the grandest so far, with their plan for construction of hotels, clubrooms, golf courses, amusement parks, and other entertainment venues. They were convinced they could do what Senator Money had not been able to do. The *Daily Herald* reported on January 19, 1921, that the group planned to transform Cat Island into a national attraction. Unfortunately, Mayor Foote and his corporation also failed.[82]

Lee Maurice Russell

Former governor Lee Maurice Russell bought the island in 1925 from the Casino Hotel Company, Inc., for $25,000 to be paid in yearly payments of $3,000.

Lee Russell had served as governor of Mississippi for only one term (1920–1924). He was a realtor and former lawyer born in Dallas, Mississippi, in 1875. Russell proposed to spend $500,000 on a winter resort on the island.[83] This proposal became even more grandiose when it was later reported on July 12 of that year that a $10 million dollar resort was planned on the island with a causeway reaching to Long Beach. The plan even included changing the name from Cat Island to Treasure Island for marketing purposes.[84] Because of this and other ventures in south Mississippi, Lee Russell was termed "Father of the Coast Boom." The whole Coast enjoyed prosperity. The new seawall was underway, and the new two-million-dollar Edgewater Hotel had been started, as well as the Markham Hotel in Gulfport.[85] Governor Russell was so confident in his plans he refused an offer of a million dollars for the purchase of Cat Island by Carl Fisher, a promoter who later, as a second choice, developed Miami Beach.[86] Some have speculated what the island and the Mississippi Gulf Coast would have been like if Mr. Fisher had succeeded in buying Cat Island.

The only development that was completed on Cat Island was the Goose Point Tarpon Club (see Chapter 19). This was a roomy, two-story structure with upper and lower galleries, twelve bedrooms with baths, a huge dining room and kitchen, and its own electricity. It was a private club of about fifty members that included Bidwell Adam, a prominent Coast attorney, and then lieutenant governor of Mississippi. The club burned down sometime in 1931 and was never rebuilt.[87]

Governor Russell's great plans never materialized, due to a lack of investors. Without the anticipated money, he fell behind on the mortgage. He was given until November 19, 1930, to catch up a $3,000 payment. He was not able to meet the deadline, so Chancellor Dan M. Russell granted a $10,000 judgment against Russell and his wife, and he was forced to put the island up for sale.

Finances were only part of Governor Russell's escalating problems. A former stenographer charged him with breach of promise and seduction after a torrid affair. He was tried in a federal court with the jury ruling in his favor. Although he was acquitted of the charges, he never recovered personally or financially. Governor Russell defaulted on the mortgage and the island was about to be sold on the courthouse steps.

Sallie Adams Boddie

Sallie Adams Boddie, widow of Nathan Van Boddie, the first Boddie to own the island, wanted to return the island to the Boddie family. When she realized that the island was about to be sold, she bought Cat Island back from Governor Russell on February 6, 1931, for $11,000, returning the island to the Boddie family.[88] Her son George, who had sold the island to Senator Hernando Money, was now deceased, so Sallie Boddie transferred the ownership of Cat Island to her two grandchildren, Nathan and Sarah, George's only two children.

Nathan Boddie and Sarah Boddie Buffington

The two children of George Robert Boddie, the man who had allowed the island to slip out of the possession of the Boddie family, were given the island by their grandmother, Sallie

Adams Boddie, in 1935, just four years after she had bought the island back from Governor Russell. Young Nathan and his sister, Sarah, were each given a 50 percent share of the island, with the exception of the land and lighthouse structure still owned by the government.[89] Nathan and Sarah were the owners when the federal judge ruled against the Cuevas family in 1962 over the ownership of Cat Island. On February 9, 1949, Nathan bought the lighthouse and property back from the U.S. government, which was in the process of liquidating unused public land.

In the late 1960s and early 1970s, Senator Trent Lott was an administrative assistant to U.S. Representative William Colmer, a veteran congressman from south Mississippi. Lott was given the job of taking the preliminary steps toward turning the group of barrier islands in the Gulf into a national park. From the very beginning Cat Island was considered to be the crown jewel of the whole project. Nathan Boddie was very supportive of the government's efforts to protect the natural environment of the barrier islands at first, but whether due to the slowness of the government to act, or a failure to reach a financial agreement, negotiations with Boddie eventually fell through.[90]

Threatened by the prospect of losing his island by eminent domain, Nathan knew something had to be done. He set out to show that his plan for private development was already underway. He did this by dredging a series of channels on the east end of the island, and subdividing the property along the channels. He then sold about 20 lots to individual investors, making up about six acres of the island. A bulkhead and a house were constructed, forming the foundation of Boddie's development plan. This along with extensive lobbying in both Mississippi and Washington successfully frustrated the government's attempts to take over Cat Island at that time.[91]

The U.S. government was not Nathan's only looming problem. In 1959, Mrs. Jack William Keen of Abita Springs, Louisiana, a descendant of Pierre Baptiste "Perrique" Cuevas, the tenth child of Juan de Cuevas, launched the most aggressive attempt thus far to win back the island for the Cuevas family.[92] The Shell Oil Company had contacted Mrs. Keen, expressing a desire to lease the mineral rights to Cat Island. Their preliminary title search raised doubts about the validity of the current owner's deed, and the company believed that the Cuevas family might very well have a legal claim to the island. It was suggested that if the title could be cleared, the oil company would be willing to sign a lucrative oil and mineral lease with the Cuevas heirs.

Many in the family believed that the 1909 attempt to stop Benjamin Harrod's claim to Cat Island was lost as a result of corruption. They were convinced the new "owner" exerted an influence over the chancery court through his "buddies" in local politics. They believed their only chance of regaining Cat Island was in an impartial federal court. By taking the case out of the local jurisdiction, they believed they would surely win what was rightfully theirs. In 1968, the heirs of Juan de Cuevas got the opportunity to present their case to a federal judge.[93]

Spearheaded by Mrs. Keen and her attorney, Joseph F. Keogh of Baton Rouge, an all-out effort was begun. Notices concerning the Cat Island lawsuit were published in local papers announcing several organizational meetings to be held in communities along the Coast.[94] Large numbers of curious and enthusiastic family members came together as word spread about the impending case. Family support was overwhelming.

The federal suit was filed June 21, 1962, in the United States District Court, Southern District of Mississippi in Biloxi.[95] The defendants, Nathan Boddie and his sister, Sarah Boddie Buffington, traced their claim to the 1837 deed from Juan de Cuevas to Judah P. Benjamin, while Mrs. Keen and the Cuevas heirs disputed the validity of that deed. They contended the alleged sale to Benjamin was fraudulent because Juan de Cuevas had signed with an "X," although he was described by some reports of that era as a learned man.[96] The suit additionally asserted that the family had a claim under a reservation in the deed of 100 arpents to Cuevas and his heirs and that adverse possession would be an issue. They further contended that a 1905 congressional act that allegedly conveyed the property to H. Gibbes Morgan and co-owners was a violation of the U.S. Constitution in that it deprived the descendants of property without due process of law. They asserted that the United States could not legally give to Morgan land that had been previously granted to Juan de Cuevas by the U.S. and Spanish governments.[97]

On March 11, 1968, Judge Dan M. Russell, Jr., issued his decision, stating: "The court finds that the heirs at law of Juan de Cuevas have no interest whatsoever in and to 'Cat Island.'"[98] Judge Russell's federal ruling ended any hope that the family had to ever regain ownership of the island, but it did nothing to appeasing many of the Cuevas family who to this day believe that Cat Island still rightfully belongs to them.

Nathan Boddie and his sister Sarah Boddie Buffington owned the island together for fifty years. Nathan Boddie died in 1985, leaving his half of the island to his son, George, and daughters, Cala and Elizabeth. Shortly after Nathan's death, Sarah transferred her half of the island to her only child, Nancy Ann Buffington Reece.[99] Sarah died at her home in Canton, Georgia, on May 10, 2005, at the age of 87.[100]

George Robert Boddie

(his children)
Nathan Van Boddie, Sarah Ann Boddie, Patrick Pierce Boddie, Sandra Pierce Boddie,

Cala Boddie Colbert

(her child)
Sanders Whitworth Colbert

Elizabeth Boddie Adair

(her children)
Carleton L. Adair, Joseph Adams Adair, Charles Nathan Adair, Cala Susan Adair

Nancy Ann Buffington Reece

(no children)

The Boddie family owned Cat Island for almost 100 years, yet the family has never lived on the island as their home. According to Cala, the only significant building on the island was a house her brother built, modeled after the Horn Island lighthouse. It was destroyed by Hurricane Katrina in 2005, the same way that a house built by their father, Nathan, had been destroyed by Hurricane Camille in 1969.[101]

Arrival of the casinos to the Gulf Coast in August 1992 resulted in an incredible economic boom to the area. With the growth of a vibrant tourism industry, and with visitors now coming from all over the nation and the world, there was growing pressure on the Boddies to either develop the island commercially or to preserve its pristine condition.

In 1998, the National Park Service and the Trust for Public Land reopened discussions with the four Boddie heirs about the possible purchase of the island. The Trust for Public Land is the fifth-largest environmentalist organization in the United States. Based in San Francisco, it works throughout the country to help structure, negotiate, and complete land transactions that create protected natural areas. The group serves as an independent agent that buys land from willing landowners, to be later transferred to a public agency.[102]

After careful consideration the Boddie family decided they did not want to see the pristine natural beauty of their island destroyed by large-scale commercial development and concluded that the best way to protect the island was to sell it to the National Park Service. In November 1999, The U.S. House passed a bill to include Cat Island in the Gulf Islands National Seashore, but because of the constraints of the congressional budget, the island was to be sold in two parts.[103]

The Trust for Public Land

On March 28, 2002, the Trust for Public Land (TPL) completed the scheduled purchase of a little more than half of Cat Island at a cost of $13 million. The first of what was supposed to be a two-part deal included the property beginning at the western tip of the island and extending eastward for about three miles, including a one-mile portion from Goose Point northward.[104] This is essentially the western half of Cat Island that was originally granted to Juan de Cuevas in his first patent. That land includes the sites of the old Cuevas homestead and lighthouse, and Goose Point on the southern tip of the island.[105]

The remaining portion of the island was to be purchased by TPL over the next several years for an additional $12 million. When completed the total purchase price of Cat Island by the National Park Service would amount to $25 million. The sale would include the

These are the areas of Cat Island now owned by the National Park Service.

entire island with the exception of 150 acres to be retained by the Boddie family for their personal use along with several separate lots owned by other private individuals.

National Park Service

On March 28, 2002, the National Park Service bought approximately one half of Cat Island from the Trust for Public Land, to be included in the Gulf Islands National Seashore. (GINS)[106] The purpose of the GINS was to preserve the Gulf Coast barrier islands and the coastal defense fortifications, and to understand the bayou ecosystem, while providing these resources for public use and enjoyment. Eventually included in the Gulf Island National Seashore were Ship, Petit Bois, and Horn Islands in Mississippi; the eastern portion of Perdido Key in Florida; Santa Rosa Island in Florida; the Naval Live Oaks Reservation in Florida; Fort Pickens and the Fort Pickens State Park in Florida; and the Pensacola Naval Air Station in Florida that includes the Coast Guard Lighthouse, Fort San Carlos, Fort Barrancas, and Fort Redoubt. Cat Island, considered by the government to be the "gem of the barrier islands," was not originally included because of Nathan Boddie's refusal to sell.

The Boddie Family Retains Half of Cat Island

Bureaucratic delays brought an end to the Boddie's agreement to sell the remaining half of Cat Island to the Park Service. Exasperated after six years of negotiations and a failure of the Trust for Public Land to exercise its option to purchase the remaining portion of Cat Island, the Boddies withdrew their offer to sell in April 2004. According to Superintendent Jerry Eubanks of the Gulf Islands National Seashore, the process broke down because of the length of time the agency's appraisal arm was taking.[107] The failure not only meant that the remaining eastern half of the island remains in the hands of the Boddies, it also lifted any restrictions that would have limited development on their land. The family has stated that it hopes to keep the island in its pristine condition, but they also acknowledge they are considering other options.[108]

The Boddies have not closed the door on future discussions with the National Park Service, but with the boom in growth along the Mississippi Gulf Coast, there will be tremendous pressure to extend that development onto the island. Only time will tell whether Cat Island's natural beauty will be preserved. The Cuevas family no longer has any claim to the island, but the connection will never be broken. In their hearts and minds, Cat Island will always be the Cuevas family home.

The old Cuevas house is gone from Cat Island, but the original home of Juan de Cuevas still exists in his hometown of Algámitas, Spain. I had the pleasure and honor to meet and visit with the Cuevas family who still live in the original home.

21

A Visit to the Cuevas Homestead in Spain

The house where Juan de Cuevas lived in Algámitas, Spain, still exists. The building is over 250 years old, and continues to be occupied by members of the Cuevas family. Although a visit to Spain is not directly related to the history of Cat Island, knowledge of the Cuevas house would be of historical interest to so many on the Gulf Coast, that I am including this chapter as part of the untold story.

The village of Algámitas is located about forty-five minutes due north of Ronda, and less than half an hour away from the small towns of Campillos, Osuna and Olvera in the province of Seville. It is situated on the slopes of the Sierras in a valley between two large mountains, the largest of which is known as El Peñón (The Rock). The village was originally called Hagalmi by the Hebrews, and later translated to Algameca by the Arabs, evolving over time into Algámitas, which also means "The Rock."[1] The grand Moorish cities of Córdoba, Granada and Seville are only an hour and a half away by car, as is Málaga on the Mediterranean coast known as the Costa del Sol.[2]

Algámitas is in the heart of Andalucía, the largest and most colorful of the country's seventeen autonomous regions. Each region is different in personality, but Andalucía more than any of the others is the essence of Spain. It is the birthplace of the guitar, flamenco music, bullfights, and almost every other cultural image that comes to mind when one thinks of Spain.[3]

Algámitas is no Camelot, but in a romantic sense for the Cuevas family, there are similarities. Like Camelot, Algámitas seems to be a place so far back in time that it may as well be fictitious. Both towns have existed in the dim light of history as fabled places, each the home of a heroic figure. Although not on the same scale as King Arthur, Don Juan de Cuevas has also become a character of legend. Arthur was a brave military leader who defended his country against the Anglo-Saxons.[4] Juan was a brave individual who defended his island home against the descendents of the Anglo-Saxons—the British. King Arthur had his Merlin. Don Juan had his Father Antoine. Merlin was a wizard; Father Antoine was a priest.

When Juan de Cuevas lived in Algámitas, the population was less than 100 people. Today the population has grown to about 1,400. There are now at least thirty Cuevas families living in the village, a sizeable number for a town so small.[5] Many of the old traditions that have been lost elsewhere survive in this rural area amidst the beautiful countryside. Life in

Andalucía is the largest and most colorful Spain's seventeen autonomous regions. Each region is different in personality, but Andalucía more than any of the others is the essence of Spain.

Algámitas goes on much as it has for generations. It remains a working village well off the beaten path. Donkeys and sheep can still be seen in the streets and on the mountainsides. It is not uncommon today to see farmers heading to the fields with a couple of mules rather than a tractor. This is the real Andalucía.[6]

It has always been an agricultural community, producing mostly olives, as well as mixed cereals and sunflowers. These are still the main crops of the city, with a third of the world's olive oil coming from this warm and dry region. The weather usually remains mild in the daytime with temperatures ranging pleasantly from 70° to 84° during the summer months and 48° to 66° during the colder winter months. The possibility of rain is greater during the months of November and December.

The five oldest buildings in Algámitas stand in a row in the center of town. The wealthiest families originally lived in these houses, and in fact, some still do. One of the oldest of the five is "The Cuevas House," the original home of Juan's father, the hidalgo Don Pedro de Cuevas. It was Juan's home before coming to America. A nobleman's house and all that it implied symbolized the wealth, status, and continuity of the family. Regardless of its size or location, the hidalgo's home was of such importance that the house was retained and passed down from generation to generation, and thus has remained in the Cuevas family since the time of Don Pedro.[7] I had the pleasure of meeting the current owner, whose mother gave me a tour.[8]

The three-story townhouse (adosado) is typical of the majority of homes in Algámitas. It is in such good shape one would never guess its age. The basic structure of the home is still much the way it was during the time that Juan and his family lived there. The whitewashed exteriors, ornate doors, and red tiled roof are representative of the style most common throughout southern Spain, which gave rise to the name *pueblos blancos* or the "White Villages of Andalucía."[9]

The stone walls of the Cuevas house, like the other *pueblos blancos* are covered with stucco and then painted with a thick coat of whitewash. Whitewash is especially effective on adobe-like materials because it is absorbed easily and the resultant chemical reaction hardens the surface. The exteriors of the houses reflect generations of paint, and every year after the spring rains have ended, all of the houses are meticulously whitewashed again to a state of pristine splendor.

White has always been the prevailing color in the Mediterranean not only because it

The eight provinces of Andalucía. The village of Algámitas is located about forty-five minutes due north of Ronda, and less than half an hour away from the small towns of Campillos, Osuna and Olvera in the province of Sevilla.

reflects the sun, but also because it was cheap to produce. Few things change in Andalucía and it is quite common to watch a homeowner mixing the whitewash in exactly the same way as his grandfather and his great-grandfather did before him. The annual whitewashing is a ritual that ushers in a season of rebirth after the drab dead of winter. Sunlight and shadows bounce off the clean white walls of these houses, creating a brilliant backdrop for the bright red and yellow flowers dripping from the balconies.

The windows and doors of the Cuevas house are protected by ornate wrought iron bars called rejas, which are the same variety found on most of the houses in Andalucía. The village blacksmith still uses the ancient Iberian craft of iron forging to make these black grills. Some are simple while others are quite complicated in their design. The elegant, shiny black gate in the foyer of the Cuevas house is one of the most attractive in the village.[10] Quite often the window and doors are painted green or blue, a Mediterranean custom that supposedly repels flies.

The Muslims who conquered Andalucía in 711 not only introduced the white villages, but they also influenced other architectural details. The Koran forbade them from using the representation of animals or people in architectural ornamentation. It also prohibited the use of precious metals, so the ever-resourceful Muslims turned to ceramics for decoration. They developed the craft of ceramics into an art form. Unglazed tiles had been around since the time of the Romans, but the Muslims introduced a method of sealing the clay with thin coatings of glass. The Malagueños kept the composition of these iridescent tiles a carefully guarded secret.[11] To this day, ceramic tiles dominate virtually every place in Spain, from public places to private homes.

The complicated patterns of the tiles that were used to enliven the walls and floors became known as the Mudéjar style, a name coined in 1859 by José Amador de los Ríos (1818–1878), an Andalucían historian and archeologist.[12] The geometrical character of these patterns eventually appeared not only in tile, but also in other inexpensive materials like brick, wood, plaster, and ornamental metals. The sophistication of this elaborate work has never been surpassed.[13]

Glazed tile wainscoting called alicatado is a common feature both inside and outside

The Cuevas house in Spain is typical of the "White Villages of Andalucía." The whitewashed exterior, ornate doors, and red tiled roof of the buildings gave rise to the name *pueblos blancos*. A woven *esparto* mat can be seen hanging in the front door to let in the breeze, while sheltering the interior from the sun.

of many of the buildings in southern Spain. The glazed tiles themselves are called azulejos. This beautiful tilework is a focal point of the foyer in the Cuevas house, and is particularly exquisite. The original purpose of the tiles was not merely decoration, but rather to protect the walls from the animals that would brush against the sides as they were herded down the narrow streets and through the front of the house to the stables in back.[14]

The local craftsmen who built the houses of Spain made use of the materials that were available. This meant using mostly terracotta tiles for the roof and common stone for the walls, but certain fine stones are found in various areas throughout the country. There is alabaster in Aragón, pinkish marble in Alicante, and serpentine in Almería. Much of these beautiful stones was carried away to the big cities to be used in the construction of the palaces and cathedrals, although some of the best stones did find their way into the local houses, including the Cuevas house. Other areas in Spain had to use rubble stone, sun-dried adobe bricks, clay, wood, and *pisé*—a method of ramming a mixture of dried earth, clay, straw, and gravel tightly into an external form to produce a petrified wall of earth.[15]

The climate in Spain is generally hotter and drier than that of the surrounding European countries, so the stone walls of the Cuevas house and others in the region were built thicker than normal to provide coolness in the summer and warmth in the winter. The solid walls are the reason the houses have survived in such good condition for centuries, but were impossible to penetrate when electricity was eventually added. The wires that are hidden in the walls of most normal construction had to be attached directly to the front of these old buildings. The few houses that have air conditioning rely on window units.

In the 1700s, farmhouses served as shelters for both the family and their animals, with humans and horses living under one roof. The front doors of the houses were arched to allow for their horses, which were led through the front door and down the center of the home to the stable at the rear of the building. A woven *esparto* mat hanging over the opening of the wooden doors serves as a screen that lets in the breeze while sheltering the interior from the sun.

Francisca Cuevas (foreground) with her sister Concepcion in the foyer of the Cuevas house. The village blacksmith still uses the ancient Iberian craft of iron forging to make the elegant gates found in the foyer of most homes. The one in the Cuevas house is one of the most attractive in the village.

Originally the Cuevas house had the living area on the ground floor and a second level above that was used to store hay and grain for the horses. This remains basically the same, but renovations over the years have converted the second story hayloft into sleeping quarters, and the stable has become a garage for the family car. A third garden floor was also a later addition. The first room entered from the foyer is the dining room. The formal table is set with a white lace cloth and a vase of flowers. Old World paintings adorn the walls. The master bedroom is off to the left of the dining room. Through the stained glass double doors is the living area. The kitchen and bath area are to the left of the living room.

The floors are covered with highly polished marble laid in a green and off-white checkerboard pattern. The floors are complemented by elegant green drapes that grace the double doors leading from the living room into the courtyard. The traditional focus of family life in Andalucía is the terrace outside the back door. Whether it was a small patio or a garden courtyard like in the Cuevas house, water has been a central feature since the days of the Muslims. The Cuevas patio is lush with green plants and flowers.

The garage is to the right of the courtyard. It was originally the stable. The entire enclosure is painted with the familiar whitewash, including the rough-hewn beams that are visible in the ceiling. The garage door opens to a small street behind the house. When Juan lived there, a small canal ran where the paved road now exists. The flowing water has long since been covered over by the road, but it still runs under the street in huge aqueducts, although what once was a large stream is now only a trickle.

Behind the house and directly across the road, there is an old outbuilding originally used as a second stable. It is in serious need of repair, and is too unstable and dangerous for current use, but it offers a unique glimpse of the architecture of these old houses. The stone walls of the building have never been plastered, allowing one to see the original color and construction. The hand-cut beams supporting the roof clearly show the age of the structure.

As a historian I was deeply moved by the experience. The Cuevas family in Spain believes I may be the first relative to return to the home since Juan de Cuevas left Spain in the late 1700s.

Notes

Preface

1. "Historic Cat Island Lighthouse Destroyed," *The Daily Herald* (Gulfport/Biloxi Mississippi), October 5, 1961.

Chapter 1

1. Robert A. Morton, "Historical Changes in the Mississippi-Alabama Barrier-Island Chain and the Roles of Extreme Storms, Sea Level, and Human Activities," *Journal of Coastal Research* 24, no. 6 (2008): 1587–1600.
2. "Beautiful Phenomena," *The Daily Herald*, February 5, 1901.
3. "On Cat Island," *New Orleans Daily Picayune*, 15 September 1907.
4. Published in *The Daily Herald* (Gulfport/Biloxi), January 25, 1890.
5. Ray M. Thompson, "Cat Island," *Down South*, July-August 1961.
6. Frank Heiderhoff, "All about Cat Island," *The New Orleans Times*, June 4, 1871.
7. "Park Service Buys Coveted Cat Island: Casino Developers Had Eyed the Barrier Island off the Gulf Coast. (Park Expansion)," *National Parks Magazine* 76, nos. 3–4 (April 1, 2002).
8. J.R. Suter and S. Pendland, "Evolution of Cat Island," *Coastal Sediments '87*.
9. Jon Frank, "Cat Island Holds Promise," *The Daily Herald*, June 24, 1983.
10. According to Geology.com, meteorologists working in the Pacific during World War II began using women's names for storms. This method of naming storms was so easy that in 1953 the National Hurricane Center adopted it for use on storms originating in the Atlantic Ocean. Once this practice began, public awareness of hurricanes increased dramatically. Earlier hurricanes were unnamed and were only designated by the latitude/longitude points representing the location at which they originated.
11. C. Paige Gutierrez, *The Mississippi Coast and Its People—A History for Students*. Book 8: Marine Discovery Series, 1987. Produced by C. Paige Gutierrez and the Department of Wildlife Conservation, Bureau of Marine Resources.
12. Gambling Vertical File, *Down South Magazine*, May–June 1952 and September–October 1958.
13. National Oceanic and Atmospheric Administration, U.S. Department of Commerce.
14. "Biographies: Bernard 'Bernie' Goldstein, Founder (1929–2009)," Islecorp.com, http://www.islecorp.com/management-goldstein.aspx (accessed May 26, 2010).
15. Ray M. Thompson, "Isle of Caprice, the Coast's Little Island That Isn't There," *Down South,* May–June 1962, p. 7.
16. Walter Fountain, "Below Waves Lies Once Luxurious Isle of Caprice," *The Daily Herald* (Gulfport/Biloxi), 1972.

Chapter 2

1. Charles E. O'Neill and Marcel Giraud, "A History of French Louisiana: An Essay Review of a History of French Louisiana. Volume One. The Reign of Louis XIV, 1698–1715" (Lafayette: Louisiana Historical Association, Summer 1975), vol. 16, no. 3: pp. 303–306.
2. Andrew Lossky, *The Nature of Political Power According to Louis XIV* (New York: Doubleday, 1967), p. 110.
3. Bernard De la Harpe, *The Historical Journal of the Establishment of the French in Louisiana* (Lafayette: University of Southwestern Louisiana, 1971), p. 218.
4. Mémoire de Estrées Margry, *Découvertes et Establissements des Français* (1614–1754), vol. 4, pp. 95–289, and *The Journal of Iberville*, Historical Collections of Louisiana, vol. 2, pp. 31–142.
5. Charles L. Sullivan and Murella Hebert Powell, *The Mississippi Gulf Coast, Portrait of a People* (Sun Valley, CA: American Historical Press, 1999), p. 12.
6. Captain Chateau, who was in command of one of the boats, reported this in his journal on the first visit to the island.
7. Nothing further is known about Father Anastasias.
8. The journal of Captain Chateau is the only source for the men's stopover on Cat Island.
9. "De Oyster and de Coon—The Experience of a Hungry Coon Who Went Oyster-hunting on Cat Island," *New Orleans Daily Picayune*, October 21, 1887.
10. Iberville to the Ministry, August 11, 1699, Archives des Colonies, C13A, f. 101–05.
11. For more information on compte de Maurepas read "Historical French Documents of the Eighteenth Century; From the Archives of Jean-Frédéric Phélpeaux Compte de Maurepas," *Parke-Bernet Galleries,* 1962.
12. The journal of Iberville, *Historical Collections of Louisiana,* 3, p. 236.
13. Richebourg Gaillard McWilliams, *Fleur de Lys and Calumet Being the Pénicaut Narrative of French Adventure in Louisiana* (Baton Rouge: Louisiana State University Press, 1953), p. 58.
14. John B. Hattendorf, *England in the War of the Spanish Succession: A Study of the English View and Conduct of*

Grand Strategy, 1702–1712, Modern European History (New York: Garland Pub., 1987), pp. 277–279.
  15. Ibid.
  16. Peter J. Hamilton, *The Founding of Mobile, 1702–1718, Studies in the History of the First Capital of the Province of Louisiana* (Mobile, AL: Colonial Mobile Book Shop, 1946), p. 33.
  17. Philomena Hauck, *Bienville: Father of Louisiana* (Lafayette: Center for Louisiana Studies, University of Southwestern Louisiana, 1998), p. 155.
  18. Ibid., p. 24.
  19. Kat Bergeron, "Tricentennial," *Sun Herald,* February 7, 1999, pp. 16–17.
  20. Charles Gayarré, *History of Louisiana* (New York: W.J. Widdleton, 1867), p. 201.
  21. Charles L. Sullivan, *Hurricanes of the Mississippi Gulf Coast* (Biloxi, MS: Gulf Publishing, 1986), p. 49.
  22. John Carswell, *The South Sea Bubble* (Stanford, CA: Stanford University Press, 1960), pp. 274–279.
  23. Andrew Lossky, *The Nature of Political Power According to Louis XIV* (New York: Doubleday & Company, 1967), pp. 46–47.
  24. Guy Walton, *Louis XIV's Versailles* (Chicago: University of Chicago Press, 1986), pp. 191–193.
  25. Lossky, *Nature of Political Power,* p. 146.
  26. O'Neill and Giraud, "A History of French Louisiana"
  27. Antoin Murphy, *John Law: Economic Theorist and Policy-maker* (Oxford: Clarendon Press, 1997), pp. 335–339.
  28. Ibid., p. 167.
  29. Emerson Hough, *The Mississippi Bubble* (New York: McKinlay, Stone & Mackenzie, 1902), p. 139.
  30. Ibid., p. 141.
  31. Ibid., p. 142.
  32. Ibid., p 153.
  33. Gayarré, *History,* p. 101.
  34. Ibid., p. 168.
  35. Ibid., p. 231.
  36. Albert Phelps, *Louisiana* (New York: Houghton, Mifflin, 1905), p. 63.
  37. Laville Bremer, "Amichel, a Narrative History of the Gulf Coast," *The Times-Picayune New Orleans States,* January 2, 1944, magazine section.
  38. According to the 1810 U.S. census New Orleans had a population of 10,000, making it the fifth-largest city after New York, Philadelphia, Boston, and Baltimore. In the next thirty years New Orleans grew faster than any other American city so that by the 1830 census it had become the third-largest American city behind New York and Baltimore.
  39. Charles L. Sullivan, *The Mississippi Gulf Coast: Portrait of a People* (Northridge, CA: Windsor Publications, 1985), p. 22.

Chapter 3

  1. Frank Heiderhoff, "All about Cat Island," *The New Orleans Times,* June 4, 1871, magazine section.
  2. I have been unable to find a source to verify Heiderhoff's statement that the bricks were similar to those used throughout France at the time.
  3. Gilles Proulx, *Between France and New France: Life Aboard the Tall Sailing Ships* (Toronto: Dundurn Press Limited, 1984), p. 42.
  4. Mémoire de Estrés, August 21, 1679, Margry, *Découvertes et établissements des Français (1614–1754)* vol. 4, p. 284.
  5. There are no known dates for Remy Reno, but d'Iberville's journal states that Reno was the architect that accompanied the men on the ship, *La Badine,* on the initial voyage to the Gulf Coast. It was his assignment to build Fort Maurepas.
  6. If there were a fort built on Cat Island, Remy Reno would have been the only man to design it. He was the only architect on the voyage.
  7. Sir Reginald Blomfield, *Sébastien le Prestre de Vauban, 1663–1707* (New York: Barnes & Noble, 1971), pp. 289–291.
  8. According to the Virginia Lime Works Company in Madison Heights, Virginia, burned oyster shell lime has been used in building construction, both as masonry mortar and plaster, but also in limewashes and other applications, for centuries. The lime is made by burning oyster shells in a kiln.
  9. This is conjecture on the part of Heiderhoff. It is not reasonable to think that he could identify the type of weapons used in the fort from the scant evidence he observed.
  10. Blomfield, *Sébastien,* p. 28.
  11. Ibid., p. 74.
  12. Ibid., p. 75.
  13. Refer to the accompanying illustration to understand this revolutionary design.
  14. Blomfield, *Sébastien,* p. 146.
  15. F.J. Hebbert, *Soldier of France: Sébastien le Prestre de Vauban, 1633–1707* (New York: P. Lang, 1990), pp. 233–235.
  16. Ibid., p. 196.
  17. Ibid., p. 224.
  18. Margry, *Découvertes,* p. 384.
  19. Samuel Wilson, *Colonial Fortifications and Military Architecture in the Mississippi Valley* (Urbana: University of Illinois Press, 1965), p. 77.

Chapter 4

  1. Randall Ladnier, *Jean Baptiste and Hentiette, A Creole Tragedy* (Sarasota, FL: Ladnier, 1995), pp. 42–43. The incident was described in a letter from the governor of Louisiana, Louis Billouart, Chevalier de Kerlerec, to the king's minister, Peirine de Moras, on October 2, 1757.
  2. Joseph G. Dawson, *The Louisiana Governors: From Iberville to Edwards* (Baton Rouge: Louisiana State University Press, 1990), p. 23.
  3. From a letter sent to the French minister of marine on August 15, 1763, from Redon de Rassac, a Louisiana official. University of Notre Dame Archives (UNDA), Notre Dame, Indiana.
  4. Catholic Church, Archdiocese of New Orleans Collection (ANO), University of Notre Dame Archives (UNDA), Notre Dame, Indiana.
  5. Dawson, *Louisiana Governors,* p. 53.
  6. Herbert Asbury, *The French Quarter: An Informal History of the New Orleans Underworld* (New York: Alfred A. Knopf, 1936), p. 38.
  7. Rupert Furneaux, *The Seven Years War* (London: Hart-Davis MacGibbon, 1973), pp. 133–134.
  8. Ibid., p. 136.
  9. Asbury, *French Quarter,* p. 39.
  10. Ibid., p. 41.
  11. Ladnier, *Jean Baptiste,* p. 42. Taken from a letter dated October 2, 1757, written by Governor Kerlerec to the king's minister Peirine de Moras documenting the difficulties he was facing on Cat Island.
  12. John McCormack, *One Million Mercenaries: Swiss Soldiers in the Armies of the World* (London: L. Cooper, 1993), pp. 125–126.
  13. Ibid., p. 134.

14. Ladnier, *Jean Baptiste*, p. 42.
15. Ray M. Thompson, "Cat Island," *Down South*, July–August 1961.
16. Albert James Pickett, *History of Alabama, Chapter XVI, Horrible Death of Beaudrot and the Swiss Soldiers* (Sheffield, AL: Republished by Robert C. Randolph, 1896), p. 304.
17. Asbury, *French Quarter*, p. 41.
18. Ladnier, *Jean Baptiste*, p. 42.
19. In a petition by Nicholas Christian Ladner to the Spanish government dated July 31, 1781, for a grant to Cat Island, Ladner stated he had been living on the island for the past thirty-five years.
20. Ladnier, *Jean Baptiste*, p. 2.
21. Pickett, *History of Alabama*, p. 304.
22. Nap L. Cassibry, II, *The Ladner Odyssey* (Gulfport, MS: Cassibry, 1987), p. 693.
23. Ladnier, *Jean Baptiste*, p. 32. The rough draft of King Louis XIV's pardon of Jean Baptiste Baudrau, II, is dated October 20, 1747. Titled "Letter of pardon from the sentence to the galleys for Jean Baptiste Baudreau," there is no indication of the date of the actual pardon, but it can reasonably be assumed to be sometime in 1747.
24. Eric Beerman, "Arturo O'Neill: First Governor of West Florida during the Second Spanish Period," *The Florida Historical Quarterly* 60, no. 1 (Florida Historical Society, July 1981): 29–41.
25. Ladnier, *Jean Baptiste*, p. 42.
26. Pickett, *History of Alabama*, p. 304.
27. Asbury, *French Quarter*, p. 38.
28. Pickett, *History of Alabama*, p. 304
29. Ibid., p. 305.
30. Ibid.
31. Ibid.
32. Ladnier, *Jean Baptiste*, p. 42.
33. Pickett, *History of Alabama*, p. 306.
34. Thompson, "Cat Island."
35. Pickett, *History of Alabama*, p. 304.
36. Asbury, *French Quarter*, p. 39.
37. M. Bossu, *Travels through That Part of North America Formerly Called Louisiana* (London: Printed for T. Davies, 1771), vol. 1, pp. 320–325.
38. Asbury, *French Quarter*, p. 39.
39. Breaking on the wheel was a barbaric form of execution that began during the Middle Ages in France. The prisoner was placed on a large wagon-type wheel with his arms and legs stretched out along the spokes. As the wheel was slowly turned, the executioner would swing a club, striking the victim's limbs over the spaces between the spokes and breaking the bones. Sometimes fatal blows known as *coups de grâce* were mercifully ordered. The club would strike the victim's chest, causing death. Without these lethal strikes the criminal could live for hours or even days. In France, the person could sometimes be granted a retentum, a form of mercy in which the condemned was strangled after the second or third blow. At the end, the victim's arms and legs were woven through the spokes of the wheel. The wheel, with the body still attached, was then lifted onto a tall pole for the birds to eat. After undergoing such harsh torture, the victims were usually dead, but occasionally the criminal was still alive to endure a slow and agonizing death.
40. Pickett, *History of Alabama*, p. 307.
41. In *History of Alabama*, James Pickett claimed to have French letters in his possession that described this execution.
42. Asbury, *French Quarter*, p. 39.
43. National Public Radio covered the event live with on-air commentary by Hobbs Allan, a descendent and one of the organizers.

Chapter 5

1. Daniel Defoe, Charles Johnson, and Manuel Schonhorn, *A General History of the Pyrates* (Columbia: University of South Carolina Press, 1972), pp. xvi–xxii.
2. Harry Van Demark, "Pirates of the Gulf," *Texas Magazine*, May 1910.
3. According to the Oxford English Dictionary, 2nd ed. (New York: Clarendon Press, 1989), a "letter of marque and reprisal" gives permission to cross an international border to take some action or reprisal against an attack or injury. The letter of marque was authorized by an issuing jurisdiction to conduct reprisal operations outside its borders.
4. Asbury, *French Quarter*, p. 55.
5. William C. Davis, *The Pirates Laffite: The Treacherous World of the Corsairs of the Gulf* (Orlando, FL: Harcourt, 2005), p. 238.
6. Asbury, *French Quarter*, p. 155.
7. Davis, *Pirates Laffite*, p. 32.
8. Jean Lafitte, *The Journal of Jean Laffite: The Privateer-Patriot's Own Story*. (New York: Vantage Press, 1958), p. 68.
9. Jack C. Ramsay, Jr., *Jean Lafitte, Prince of Pirates* (Austin, TX: Eakin Press, 1996), p. 87.
10. Davis, *Pirates Laffite*, p. 26.
11. I have not found any books on Jean Lafitte that agreed on his birthplace. The majority seem to believe that he was born in France, although the exact location is questionable. It is my opinion that no one knows for sure where Lafitte was born.
12. Ramsay, *Jean Lafitte*, p. 88.
13. Ibid., p. 89.
14. Lyle Saxon, E.H. Suydam, and Carl H. Pforzheimer, *Lafitte, the Pirate* (New York: Century, 1930), p. 72.
15. Ramsay, *Jean Lafitte*, p. 48.
16. Saxon, *Lafitte*, p. 12.
17. Ibid., p. 34.
18. Ramsay, *Jean Lafitte*, p. 94.
19. Jean Laffite, *The Memoirs of Jean Laffite: From Le Journal de Jean Laffite*, translated by Gene Marshall (Philadelphia: Xlibris, 1999), p. 31.
20. Asbury, *French Quarter*, p. 159.
21. Saxon, *Lafitte*, p. 50.
22. Ibid.
23. Ibid., p. 136.
24. Ramsay, *Jean Lafitte*, p. 90.
25. Asbury, *French Quarter*, p. 137.
26. Ramsay, *Jean Lafitte*, p. 44.
27. Le Page du Pratz, *Histoire de la Louisiane* (Baton Rouge: Published for the Louisiana American Revolution Bicentennial Commission by the Louisiana State University Press, 1758), p. 289.
28. John Andrechyne Lafitte, *The Journal of Jean Laffite: The Privateer-Patriot's Own Story* (New York: Vantage Press, 1958), p. 120.
29. du Pratz, *Histoire*, p. 227.
30. Lafitte, *Journal of Jean Laffite*, p. 121.
31. Harris Gaylord Warren, *The Sword Was Their Passport; A History of American Filibustering in the Mexican Revolution* (Baton Rouge: Louisiana State University, 1943), p. 81.
32. *Memoirs of Jean Laffite*, translated by Gene Marshall.
33. Demark, "Pirates of the Gulf."
34. *The Hancock County Eagle*, Bay St. Louis, August 1958, souvenir centennial edition, p. 3.
35. Local oral and published reports.
36. Saxon, *Lafitte*, p. 73.

37. Asbury, *French Quarter*, p. 137.
38. Ramsay, *Jean Lafitte*, p. 49.
39. Ibid., p. 182.
40. du Pratz, *Histoire*, p. 339.
41. Ibid., p. 327.
42. Letter from Andrew Jackson to President James Madison dated January 21, 1815 (Library of Congress).
43. du Pratz, *Histoire*, p. 328.
44. Lafitte, *Journal of Jean Laffite*, p. 38.
45. Ramsay, *Jean Lafitte*, p. 88.
46. Warren, *Sword Was Their Passport*, p. 34.
47. Folklore handed down in the Cuevas family and corroborated by newspaper reports.
48. Catherine Garriga Cuevas, discussion with the author, June 26, 1958.
49. Buried treasure on Cat Island has been alluded to in several articles, including "Cat Island to Be Fully Developed," *The Daily Herald*, December 3, 1919, and "Cat Island May Hold Treasure," *The Daily Herald*, March 23, 1925, p. 8.
50. "Body Found," *Bay St. Louis Gazette*, March 27, 1869.
51. Heiderhoff, "All about Cat Island."
52. Copeland made a confession to the sheriff on October 30, 1857, just before his execution at Augusta, Mississippi. He not only admitted his crimes, but he also described an island off the coast as the depository for much of his ill-gotten cash. Many of the old settlers believe he meant Cat Island, since it is the only barrier island with suitable topography. Refer to "Cat Island May Hold Treasure," *The Daily Herald*, March 23, 1925, p. 8.
53. Linda Simpson, "Outlaws, Rascals and Ruffians," presented by the Mississippi Local History Network, http://www.rootsweb.ancestry.com/~msalhn/Outlaws/copeland youth.html (June 27, 2000).
54. Extracted from the Perry County, Mississippi, WPA files.
55. J.R.S. Pitts, *Life and Confession of the Noted Outlaw, James Copeland*. (Jackson: University Press of Mississippi, 1970), p. 37.
56. As told to Pauline's son Francois Basquez, born July 8, 1838, on Cat Island, and passed down as family lore.
57. Pitts, *Life and Confession*, p. 103.
58. Thompson, "Cat Island," p. 12.
59. Pitts, *Life and Confession*, p. 127.
60. Ibid., p. 133.
61. "Treasure Tales, Mississippi," presented by the Okie Treasure Hunter, http://okietreasurehunter.blogspot.com/2008/03/treasure-tales-mississippi.html (March 5, 2008).
62. Ramon Cuevas, who lived on the island until 1961, often told his friends and family that he believed the markings were made by members of the Copeland gang, but no one could verify their origin.

Chapter 6

1. I have compiled the legend of Juan de Cuevas from several oral sources passed down within the Cuevas family, as well as from several printed articles that include Ray M. Thompson, "The Hero of Cat Island," *Down South*, May–June 1956; Zoe Posey, "Gulf Coast Reminiscences of Jas. A. Cuevas of Days before Sixties," *The Times Picayune*, May 7, 1922, magazine section, p. 4; Nannie Mayes Crump, "Tortured Cat Islander Helped Save City from British, Says Grandson," *The Times-Picayune*, January 10, 1937; Thompson, "Cat Island"; and Hodding Carter and Anthony Ragusin, *Gulf Coast Country* (New York: Duell, Sloan and Pearce, 1951), p. 52. Almost every article about Juan de Cuevas has mentioned some parts of the legend, but a complete version has never been published.

2. Edward Gaylord Bourne, *Spain in America* (New York: Barnes & Noble, 1962), p. 297.
3. City Archives, New Orleans Public Library, *Digest of the Acts and Deliberations of the Cabildo: Ecclesiastical— Father Friar Antonio Sedella*.
4. Condé Benoist Pallen, John Joseph Wynne, Charles F. Wemyss Brown, Blanche M. Kelly, and Andrew A. MacErlean, *The New Catholic Dictionary. A Complete Work of Reference on Every Subject ... of the Church* (London, 1929).
5. Ibid.

Chapter 7

1. Ray M. Thompson, "Know Your Coast, Another Tale of Jean Cuevas," *The Daily Herald*, September 27, 1957.
2. Posey, Magazine Section, 4.
3. Posey, "Gulf Coast Reminiscences," p. 4; "An Act for the Relief of John Quavre," *Journal in the House of Representative of the Fifth Session of the General Assembly*, State of Mississippi. Signed by Cawles Mead, speaker of the House of Representatives, and James Pattan, lieutenant governor and president of the Senate, November 24, 1821.

Chapter 8

1. *Edinburgh Magazine* was published in England by William Blackwood from 1817 to 1980.
2. G.R. Gleig, *The Subaltern* (London: J.M. Dent & Sons, 1915).
3. The full title of the book by Lt. George Robert Gleig is *Narrative of the Campaigns of the British Army at Washington and New Orleans under Generals Ross, Pakenham, and Lambert, in the Years 1814 and 1815; with Some Account of the Countries Visited*.
4. Gleig, *Subaltern*, pp. 249–351.
5. Dale Greenwell, *Twelve Flags Triumphs and Tragedies* (Ocean Springs, MS: Greenwell, 1968), p. 168.
6. Posey, "Gulf Coast Reminiscences."

Chapter 9

1. Murella H. Powell, "Biloxian Was a Part of Golden Era of Postcards," *The SunHerald* (Mississippi), October 12, 2003.
2. Susan Brown Nicholson, *The Encyclopedia of Antique Postcards* (Radnor, PA: Wallace-Homestead, 1994), p. 3.
3. Richard Carline, *Pictures in the Post: The Story of the Picture Postcard and Its Place in the History of Popular Art* (London: Gordon Fraser Gallery, 1971), p. 59.
4. Powell, "Biloxian."
5. Thompson, "Cat Island."
6. Archie Cameron was the lighthouse keeper from 1904 to 1914. The keeper's house was surrounded by water when he took the position. He and his wife Nellie, with their three children, Hazel, Eugene, and Gladys, moved into the old Cuevas house two miles away from the lighthouse. While living in the Cuevas house, Archie also served as a watchman for the owners of cattle that grazed on the island. Source: Murella H. Powell, Biloxi Public Library.
7. Vernacular architecture refers to a form of folk houses that were built by carpenters and builders who had no formal architectural training, but instead built houses based on ethnic heritage, local standards, or tradition. These building traditions and designs can be traced to European sources, and were passed from one generation to the next with almost no change in appearance, size, shape,

materials, or methods of construction. The word vernacular when referring to architecture has the same meaning as vernacular when referring to language. That is to say vernacular language is the common everyday language spoken by people of a certain region as opposed to a formal literary language. The same is true of vernacular architecture.

8. Henry Chandlee Forman, *The Architecture of the Old South: The Medieval Style, 1585–1850* (Cambridge, MA: Harvard University Press, 1948), pp. 134–143.

9. John Francis McDermott, *The Spanish in the Mississippi Valley, 1762–1804* (Urbana: University of Illinois Press, 1974), pp. 69–72.

10. Ronald W. Hasse, *Classic Cracker: Florida's Woodframe Vernacular Architecture* (China: Pineapple Press, 1992), pp. 37–40.

11. Fred Kniffen, *Folk Housing: Key to Diffusion* (Baton Rouge, LA: Association of American Geographers, 1965), p. 561.

12. Mary Ellen Alexander, *Rosalie and Radishes—A History of Long Beach, Mississippi* (Gulfport, MS: Dixie Press, 1980), p. 5.

13. Ibid.

14. Cuevas family description.

15. "On Cat Island," *New Orleans Daily Picayune*, September 15, 1907.

16. Ibid.

17. Ibid.

18. L.L. Ingram, M.C. Templeton, G.W. McGraw, and R.W. Hemingway, "Knot, Heartwood, and Sapwood Extractives Related to VOCs from Drying Southern Pine Lumber," *Journal of Wood Chemistry and Technology* 20, no. 4 (2000): 415.

19. Hasse, *Classic Cracker*, pp. 37–40.

20. Forman, *Architecture*, p. 113.

21. Ibid., p. 79.

22. Oszuscik, p. 57.

23. Barry Jean Ancelet, Jay Dearborn Edwards, and Glen Pitre, *Cajun Country* (Jackson: University Press of Mississippi, 1992), pp. 111–113.

24. Interview with Ella Malina Favre Cuevas by the author on September 22, 1959, from descriptions by her mother, Emelina Cuevas Favre.

25. Ben Earl Looney, *Cajun Country* (Lafayette, LA: USL Press, 1974), p. 56.

26. Heiderhoff, "All about Cat Island," 27. Lawrence S. Cooke, *Lighting in America: From Colonial Rushlights to Victorian Chandeliers* (New York: Main Street/Universe Books, 1976), pp. 187.

27. Lawrence S. Cooke, *Lighting in America: From Colonial Rushlights to Victorian Chandeliers* (New York: Main Street/Universe Books, 1976), pp. 187.

28. Charles F. Millspaugh, *American Medicinal Plants: An Illustrated and Descriptive Guide to Plants Indigenous to and Naturalized in the United States Which Are Used in Medicine* (1892) (New York: Dover Publications, 1974), pp. 71–74.

Chapter 10

1. Arnold Toynbee, *The Industrial Revolution* (Boston: Beacon Press, 1956), pp. 147–148.

2. Henry Varnum Poor, *Manual of the Railroads of the United States for 1870–71* (New York: H.V. & H.W. Poor, 1870), p. xxviii.

3. Toynbee, *Industrial Revolution*, p. 149.

4. Ibid., p. 151.

5. Frances Gies and Joseph Gies, *Daily Life in Medieval Times: A Vivid, Detailed Account of Birth, Marriage, and Death; Food, Clothing, and Housing; Love and Labor, in the Middle Ages* (New York: Black Dog & Leventhal Publishers, 1999), p. 96.

6. Nap L. Cassibry, II, *Early Settlers and Land Grants at Biloxi* (Gulfport, MS: Cassibry, 1986), vol. 1, p. 2.

7. Pintado Papers, Mobile County Historical Library, Mobile, Alabama.

8. Charles L. Sullivan, *The Mississippi Gulf Coast: Portrait of a People* (Northridge, CA: Windsor Publications, 1985), p. 23.

9. Ibid.

10. Estéban Rodríguez Miró y Sabater served under Charles III and Charles IV of Spain. He was the interim governor from 1782 to 1785 while Bernardo de Galvez was in Cuba. One of Miro's first acts as governor was to issue an order for a census of the Gulf Coast area. The census was taken on April 30, 1791.

11. Nicholas Ladner dit Christian had eleven children: Jean Baptiste, Nicholas II, Marie Louise, Michel, Pierre, Francois, Claude, Joseph, Magdelene, Marie Helene, and Genevieve. There were only ten listed on Cat Island in the census because his eldest daughter, Marie Louise, was married to José Morin and, therefore, listed as Morin's wife.

12. Ephraim Kirby sent a report to U.S. president Thomas Jefferson on May 1, 1804.

13. Charles L. Sullivan and Murella Hebert Powell, *The Mississippi Gulf Coast—Portrait of a People* (Sun Valley, CA: American Historical Press, 1999), pp. 34–35.

14. Thomas Jefferson and Paul Leicester Ford, *The Works of Thomas Jefferson, Federal Edition* (New York: G.P. Putnam's Sons, 1904–5), vol. 10, p. 214.

15. Sullivan, *Mississippi Gulf Coast*, p. 34.

16. Mary Ellen Alexander, *Rosalie and Radishes—A History of Long Beach, Mississippi* (Gulfport, MS: Dixie Press, 1980), p. 8.

17. Sworn statement made at Shieldsborough, Mississippi, on August 9, 1847, by Madam Louise Ladner, widow of Jacques Ladner (1778–?).

18. Sworn statement by Marselite Ladner, oldest child of Jacques Ladner, at Shieldsborough on August 9, 1847.

19. Several depositions in the lawsuit of *Laroisini v. the Heirs of John B. Carco* were taken on July 19, 1847. All stated that few people lived in the (Biloxi) area in 1815; that the land was uncleared and uncultivated and only 2 footpaths existed before Lameuse Road was constructed in 1836; and that there were no horses, carts or wagons in Biloxi before 1836.

20. C. Ray Brassieur, "Louisiana Boatbuilding: An Unfathomed Fortune," Louisiana Folklife Festival booklet, 1989.

21. Ibid. C. Ray Brassieur is an oral historian/folklorist. For more information about Louisiana's boatbuilding traditions, see Ray Brassieur's essays in the Louisiana Folklife Photo Gallery. Select Material Culture × Boats and Boatbuilding. http://www.louisianafolklife.org/FOLKLIFEimagebase/photogallery.asp (1999–2003).

22. Looney, *Cajun Country*, p. 123.

23. Brassieur, "Louisiana Boatbuilding."

24. Howard Irving Chapelle, *The History of American Sailing Ships* (New York: W.W. Norton, 1935), p. 66.

25. Ibid., p. 68.

26. In a letter handwritten in French in 1866 by Pierre Quave (Cuevas), son of Juan de Cuevas, Pierre writes that he has his goélette for sale.

27. Posey, "Gulf Coast Reminiscences."

28. Mary Bellis, "The History of Steamboats," http://inventors.about.com/library/inventors/blsteamship.htm (2008).

29. Robert H. Thurston, *Robert Fulton—His Life and*

Its Results (New York: Dodd, Mead, and Company Publishers, 1891), p. 121.

30. Sullivan and Powell, *Mississippi Gulf Coast*, p. 64.

31. *The Sea Coast Echo* (Bay St. Louis, Mississippi), May 28, 1978, heritage edition; vol. 87, no. 43.

32. Harry Sinclair Drago, *The Steamboaters, from the Early Side-wheelers to the Big Packets* (New York: Dodd, Mead, 1967), pp. 224–227.

33. R.A. McLemore, *A History of Mississippi* (Jackson: University and College Press of Mississippi, 1973), pp. 57–60.

34. Dunbar Rowland, *Encyclopedia of Mississippi History*, vol. 1 (Madison, WI: Brant, 1907), p. 843.

35. Dunbar Rowland, *Memoirs of Mississippi, Vol. I, Mississippi Legislative Journal of the Senate, 1817–1818* (Jackson: Mississippi Archives, 1817–1818), p. 490.

36. George Washington Cable, *Old Creole Days* (New York: Charles Scribner's Sons, 1883), pp. 59–60.

37. William Faulkner Rushton, *The Cajuns: From Acadia to Louisiana* (New York: Farrar Straus Giroux, 1979), pp. 98–102.

38. Sir Arthur G. Doughty, *The Acadian Exiles; A Chronicle of the Land of Evangeline* (Toronto: Glasgow, Brook & Co., 1916), p. 285.

39. Ibid.

40. Ibid., p. 286.

41. Rushton, *Cajuns*, p. 140.

42. Randall P. Whatley and Harry Jannise, *Conversational Cajun French I* (Gretna, LA: Pelican Publishing Company, 1978), p. viii.

43. Whatley and Jannise, *Conversational Cajun French*, p. ix.

44. Jules Daigle, *Cajun-Self Taught* (Ville Platte, LA: Swallow Publishing, 1992), p. 12.

45. Ron Thibodeaux, "Vive le francais," *The Times-Picayune*, July 17, 2001.

46. Daigle, *Cajun-Self Taught*, p. 12.

47. Adelaide Hechtlinger, *American Quilts, Quilting, and Patchwork: The Complete Book of History, Technique & Design* (New York: Galahad Books, 1974), pp. 134–137.

48. Ibid.

49. Joshua Pusey, "Fascinating Facts about the Invention of Book Matches," http://www.ideafinder.com/history/inventions/matches.htm (revised 2005). Joshua Pusey was a well-known lawyer in Pennsylvania before the turn of the century. Pusey invented book matches in 1889 and sold his rights to the Diamond Match Company for $4,000.

50. Jess DeHart and Melanie DeHart, *Creoles & Cajuns: The Two Faces of French Louisiana* (Folsom, LA: Hamlet House, 1999), pp. 199–203.

51. Philomena Hauck, *Bienville: Father of Louisiana* (Lafayette: Center for Louisiana Studies, University of Southwestern Louisiana, 1998), pp. 146–148.

52. Filé powder is made from ground dried sassafras leaves. The powder is a gray-green color with a pungent and aromatic flavor. It is used primarily as a thickening agent in gumbo as well as a seasoning.

53. Fred Bowerman Kniffen, *The Indians of Louisiana* (Baton Rouge: Louisiana State University and Agricultural and Mechanical College, 1945), pp. 73–74.

54. Ruby Le Bois, *Cajun: The Authentic Taste of Spicy Louisiana Cooking* (London: Southwater, 2004), pp. 177–186.

55. Denis Kelly, *Creole and Cajun Cooking* (Vancouver: Raincoast Books, 1993), pp. 166–167.

56. Terry Thompson-Anderson, *Cajun-Creole Cooking* (Tucson, AZ: HPBooks, 1986), pp. 256–258.

57. William Stuart and Kary Cadmus Davis, *The Potato; Its Culture, Uses, History and Classification* (Philadelphia: J.B. Lippincott, 1937), pp. 279–284.

58. Sam Cox, "I Say Tomayto, You Say Tomahto..." http://www.landscapeimagery.com/tomato.html (accessed August 2004).

59. LSUAgCenter, "A Brief History of Crawfish Farming in Louisiana," http://www.lsuagcenter.com/en/our_offices/research_stations/Aquaculture/Features/extension/Classroom_Resources/History+of+Crawfish+Aquaculture+in+Louisiana.htm (accessed March 2009).

60. F.C. Reimer, *Scuppernong and Other Muscadine Grapes: Origin and Importance* (West Raleigh: North Carolina Agricultural Experiment Station of the College of Agriculture and Mechanic Arts, 1909), p. 18.

61. H.C. Prinsen Geerligs; R.J. Geerligs, *The World Cane Sugar Industry, Past and Present* (Manchester, England: Altrincham, 1912), p. 256.

62. American Poultry Journal Publishing Company, *Origin and History of All Breeds of Poultry: Trustworthy Information regarding the Origin and History of All Recognized Varieties of Chickens, Ducks and Geese* (Chicago: American Poultry Journal, 1908), pp. 25–28.

63. Benjamin Woods, *The Boston Tea Party* (New York: Oxford University Press, 1964), p. 188.

64. Williams H. Ukers, *The Romance of Coffee; An Outline History of Coffee and Coffee-Drinking through a Thousand Years* (New York: Tea and Coffee Trade Journal Co., 1948), p. 63.

65. Sean Paajanen, "Chicory," http://coffeetea.about.com/cs/coffeesubstitutes/a/chicory.htm (accessed February 2001).

66. Ernst Lehner and Johanna Lehner, *Folklore and Odysseys of Food and Medicinal Plants* (New York: Tudor Publishing, 1962), p. 144.

67. Quick bread is the name given to bread which has been leavened by chemical agents, such as baking powder or soda. Potash is the residue that is left over after all the water has been drained off the lye solution that resulted from the leaching of wood ashes.

68. Alain Charles Gruber, *Silverware* (New York: Rizzoli, 1982), p. 77.

69. Catherine Garriga Cuevas, discussion with the author, October 12, 1959.

70. Dorothy Denneen Volo and James M. Volo, *Daily Life in Civil War America* (Westport, CT: Greenwood Press, 1998), pp. 102–103.

71. Mary Frank Gaston, *The Collectors Encyclopedia of Flow Blue China* (Paducah, KY: Collector Books, 1983), p. 42.

72. Ibid., p. 45.

73. "Life on the Trail — Draft Animals," Heritage Gateways, http://heritage.uen.org/resources/Wcdb79b3effa80.htm (accessed May 6, 2006).

74. According to Catherine Garriga Cuevas, one of the characteristics of the Cuevas family in general is their reputation for being obsessively clean. The family on Cat Island was reportedly no exception. Discussion with the author, May 23, 1958.

75. Barry Jean Ancelet, Jay Dearborn Edwards, and Glen Pitre, *Cajun Country* (Jackson: University Press of Mississippi, 1992), p. 39.

76. Edward Warwick, *Early American Dress: The Colonial and Revolutionary Periods* (New York: B. Blom, 1965), pp. 92.

77. Ibid., p. 246.

78. Alice Morse Earle, *Two Centuries of Costume in America* (New York: Macmillan, 1903), p. 81.

79. Edwin Adams Davis, *Louisiana the Pelican State* (Baton Rouge: Louisiana State University Press, 1959), p. 187.

80. Ibid.

81. Russell Ash, *Fantastic Millennium Facts* (New York: DK Publishing, 1999), p. 74.
82. Victoria Sherrow, *Encyclopedia of Hair: A Cultural History* (Westport, CT: Greenwood Press, 2006), p. 177.
83. Earle, *Two Centuries*, p. 78.
84. John Duffy, *Epidemics in Colonial America* (Baton Rouge: Louisiana State University Press, 1979), pp. 135–136.
85. Laurie Trask Mann, *Changing Medical Practices in Early America*. http://dpsinfo.com/wb/medhistory.html (updated December 3, 2008).
86. C. Keith Wilbur, *Revolutionary Medicine: 1700–1800* (Chester, CT: Globe Pequot Press, 1980), pp. 178–179.
87. Bobbie Kalman, *Early Health and Medicine*. The Early Settler Life Series (New York: Crabtree Publishing Company, 1991), pp. 58–59.
88. My father, Oliver John Cuevas (1892–1973), kept a small bottle of turpentine in the medicine chest at all times to relief the pain of common cuts and to aid in the healing process. I have used turpentine and have found it to be very effective.
89. Kalman, *Early Health*, p. 97.
90. Ibid., p. 101.
91. According to the family, the soup was made by cutting about a pound of beef into small pieces and boiling the meat in two quarts of water. After the mixture was reduced to about a pint of liquid, a little salt was added. It was served one cup at a time.
92. Chicago Dental Society, "Brushing through the Ages: Even the Pharaohs Cleaned Their Pearly Whites."
93. Carol and John Williams, "Those Were the Days," www.440international.com (1995–2002).
94. "The History of Medicine—1800–1850," Minnesota Wellness Publications, Inc., http://www.mnwelldir.org/docs/history/history03.htm (accessed July 14, 2003).
95. The Rev. Leo F. Fahey, "Bay St. Louis (A History of Hancock County's Catholic Institutions)," *The Sea Coast Echo*, Golden Jubilee Edition (Bay St. Louis, MS: 1942).
96. The Rev. William Saunders, "The Role of Godparents," *Arlington Catholic Herald*, 2003. Father William Saunders is dean of the Notre Dame Graduate School of Christendom College and pastor of Our Lady of Hope Parish in Sterling, Virginia. Father Saunders is also the author of *Straight Answers*, a book based on 100 of his columns and published by Cathedral Press in Baltimore.
97. Randy J. Sparks, "Religion in Mississippi," *Mississippi History Now* (an online publication of the Mississippi Historical Society), http://mshistory.k12.ms.us/index.php?id=96 (November 2003). Randy J. Sparks, Ph.D., is an associate professor of history at Tulane University, and director of its Regional Humanities Center. He is the author of *Religion in Mississippi*, from which this article is extracted, and *On Jordan's Stormy Banks: Evangelicalism in Mississippi, 1773–1876*.
98. The Rev. Leo F. Fahey, "Bay St. Louis (A History of Hancock County's Catholic Institutions)," *The Sea Coast Echo*, Golden Jubilee Edition (Bay St. Louis, MS: 1942).
99. Mary Bellan Eidt, "Biographical Sketch of John Mary Joseph Chanche," St. Mary Basilica Archives, Natchez, Mississippi.
100. Fahey, "Bay St. Louis," 1942.
101. St. Mary Basilica Archives, Natchez, Mississippi.
102. Ibid.
103. Research conducted at the Church of the Annunciation, Kiln, Mississippi, by Nap L. Cassibry II with the help of Reverend Austin Walsh, S.T., then the priest at the Church of the Annunciation.
104. Zoe Posey, "Gulf Coast Reminiscences of Jas. A. Cuevas of Days Before Sixties." Typed article submitted to *The Times-Picayune*, May 7, 1922.
105. Research conducted at the Church of the Annunciation, Kiln, Mississippi, by Nap L. Cassibry II with the help of Reverend Austin Walsh, S.T., then the priest at the Church of the Annunciation.
106. Ibid.
107. Ray M. Thompson, "Bay St. Louis: Its History in a Hurry," *The Daily Herald*, Bay St. Louis Centennial Edition, p. 4A (Biloxi, MS: 1958).
108. "Mississippi," Microsoft<reg> Encarta<reg> Online Encyclopedia 2000, http://encarta.msn.com..
109. Bab Westerveld, Joost Eiffers, and Michael Schuyt, *Cat's Cradles and Other String Figures* (New York: Penguin Books, 1979), pp. 104–109.
110. Charise Mericle Harper, *Imaginative Inventions: The Who, What, Where, When, and Why of Roller Skates, Potato Chips, Marbles, and Pie and More!* (Boston: Little Brown, 2001), p. 165.
111. Donald Simanek, "Physic Lecture Demonstrations," http://www.lhup.edu/~dsimanek/scenario/demos.htm (accessed June 3, 2007).
112. Alfred Cort Haddon, *The Study of Man* (New York: G.P. Putnam's Sons, 1898), p. 267.
113. Ash, *Fantastic*, p. 81.
114. Asbury, *French Quarter*, p. 88.
115. Harry L. De Vore and Martin Yoseloff, *City of the Mardi Gras* (New York: Beechhurst Press, B. Ackerman, 1946), p. 117.
116. Ibid., p. 216.
117. Maymie Richardson Krythe, *All about American Holidays* (New York: Harper and Row, 1962), pp. 89–93.
118. Margaret Sabo Wills, "Founder of the Feast: The Story of the Victorian Magazine Editor Who Helped Make Thanksgiving Our National Holiday," *Country Living*, November 1988, pp. 164–165.
119. R.J. Claire and Katy Claire, *History of Pass Christian* (Pass Christian, MS: Lafayette Publishers, 1976).
120. Irene S. Gillis, *Biographical and Historical Memoirs of Mississippi* (Greenville, SC: Southern Historical Press, 2005), p. 132.
121. Isaac J. Cox, *The West Florida Controversy, 1798–1813* (Baltimore: Johns Hopkins Press, 1918), pp. 156–157.
122. Ibid., p. 157.
123. Rowland, *Memoirs*, p. 843.
124. Ash, *Fantastic*, p. 79.
125. Dan Ellis, *Pass Christian Discovered* (Pass Christian, MS: Ellis, 1997), p. 5.
126. Sullivan and Powell, *Mississippi Gulf Coast*, p. 53.
127. Federal Writers' Project, *Mississippi, the Magnolia State*. American Guide Series. (New York: Hastings House, 1938), p. 81.
128. Glen Lyle Swetman and Glen Robert Swetman, *Biloxi, a Banker's Daybook*. (Baltimore: Gateway Press, 1994), p. 80.
129. *The Sea Coast Echo*, Bay St. Louis, MS, May 29, 1977, Heritage Edition; vol. 87, no. 43.
130. Ibid.
131. Sullivan, *Mississippi Gulf Coast*, p. 58.
132. Ibid., p. 54.
133. Ibid., p. 63.
134. Ibid.
135. Dr. Val Husley, *Biloxi: 300 Years* (Virginia Beach, VA: Donning Company/Publishers, 1998), p. 31.
136. Sullivan, *Mississippi Gulf Coast*, p. 59.
137. Alexander, *Rosalie*, p. 12.
138. Pierre Quave Store Journal (1857–1862), Archives of the Biloxi Public Library, Biloxi, MS).

139. Ibid.

140. Coal tar is a viscous black liquid containing numerous organic compounds obtained by the destructive distillation of coal. It is used as a roofing, waterproofing, and insulating compound, and as a raw material for many dyes, drugs, and paints.

141. White lead is a heavy white pigment used as a base in paint. It is one of the oldest paint pigments used by man. When used in paints it is first ground into a fine powder and mixed with linseed oil. It covers better than most white pigments, but because it is basically lead carbonate, it is extremely toxic.

142. Calico is a printed cotton cloth, coarser than muslin, and it is characterized by an overall pattern, usually floral.

143. Cottonade cloth is a heavy, thick fabric made of cotton or mixed fibers that resembles wool. It was commonly used for work clothes.

144. Crepe is a light, soft, thin fabric of silk, cotton, wool, or another fiber, with a crinkled surface.

145. Gingham is a kind of cotton or linen cloth in which the pattern, usually stripes or checks, is woven into the fabric rather than printed directly onto the cloth. With gingham the yarn is dyed before it is woven.

146. Hickory cloth is a very durable cotton twill similar to denim and used for work clothes.

147. Twilled cotton is a slightly ribbed fabric woven to have a surface of diagonal parallel ridges.

148. Cream of tartar is a white crystalline substance, with a gritty, acid taste, and is used largely as an ingredient of baking powders.

149. Hog head cheese is not a cheese at all, but rather a sausage made from the meaty bits of the head of a calf or pig (sometimes a sheep or cow) that are seasoned, combined with a gelatinous meat broth and cooked in a mold. When cool, the sausage is removed from the mold and thinly sliced. It's usually eaten at room temperature. In French it's called *fromage de tête*.

150. Vermicelli is the flour of a hard and small-grained wheat made into dough and forced through small cylinders or pipes to make a slender, wormlike form. Macaroni is made when the paste is forced through larger tubes.

151. French tallow is a kind of soap made from olive oil instead of animal fats.

152. Castor oil is a vegetable oil obtained from the castor bean. It was valued chiefly as a laxative and as a treatment for lacerations and other skin disorders such as psoriasis.

153. Paregoric was a household remedy in the eighteenth and nineteenth centuries. The main ingredient is morphine, and the medicine was used to calm fretful children, to treat diarrhea, and to suppress coughs.

154. Turpentine is a fluid obtained by the distillation of resin obtained from trees, mainly pine trees, and used in the early days for cuts.

155. Martingale is a strap fastened to a horse's girth, passing between his forelegs, and fastened to the bit, or now more commonly ending in two rings, through which the reins pass. It is intended to hold down the head of the horse and prevent him from rearing.

156. Brimstone is a hard gritty stone used to sharpen knives. In biblical times, it was used to sharpen swords, and in more peaceful times, plowshares.

157. Currycomb is a wooden, rubber or metal oval comb with rows of dull teeth, which is used to clean a horse, mule or ox's coat.

158. Flax seed comes from a plant that has a single, slender stalk, about a foot and a half high, with blue flowers. The fiber of the bark is used for making thread and cloth, called linen, cambric, lawn, lace, etc. Linseed oil is expressed from the seed.

159. Sundries are miscellaneous small articles, details, or items.

160. A small comb of bone or wood, usually with six to eight teeth, and used to secure women's hair in certain styles, such as in a bun.

161. Pierre Quave Journal (1857–1862), Archives of the Biloxi Public Library, Biloxi, MS.

162. Ibid.

163. Martha Reinhard Smallwood Field, *The Story of the Old French Market, New Orleans* (New Orleans: Compliments of the New Orleans Coffee Co., 1916), p. 38.

164. Ibid., p. 52.

165. Ibid., p. 66.

166. Husley, *Biloxi*, p. 35.

Chapter 11

1. The Indian Removal Act, published May 28, 1830, "Chapter CXLVIII: An Act to Provide for an Exchange of Lands with the Indians Residing in Any of the States or Territories, and for Their Removal West of the River Mississippi." Taken from: *The Cherokee Removal: A Brief History with Documents*. Edited by Theda Perdue and Michael D. Green (New York: St. Martin's Press, 1995), pp. 116–117.

2. Ibid.

3. Ray M. Thompson, "When the Seminoles Were on Cat Island," *The Daily Herald*, August 18, 1964.

4. Ibid.

5. Jerry Wilkinson, "History of the Seminoles," presented by the Historical Preservation Society of the Upper Keys, http://www.keyshistory.org/seminolespage1.html (accessed January 2002).

6. Gerald Forbes, "The Origin of the Seminole Indians," *Oklahoma Historical Society's Chronicles of Oklahoma* 15, no. 1 (March 1937): 102–108.

7. Wilkinson, "History."

8. "Muskhogean Indian Family History," Access Genealogy, http://www.accessgenealogy.com/native/tribes/muskhogean/muskhogeanhist.htm (accessed June 2001).

9. "Creek Indians," http://www.creekindian.com (accessed October 2003).

10. Transcribed documents from the Sequoyah Research Center and the American Native Press Archives.

11. Ibid.

12. Glen Welker, "Tuskegee Literature," Indigenous Peoples' Literature, http://www.indigenouspeople.net/tuskegee.htm (accessed April 1999).

13. Wilkinson, "History."

14. Ibid.

15. Kevin Mulroy, *Freedom on the Border: The Seminole Maroons in Florida, the Indian Territory, Coahuila, and Texas* (Lubbock: Texas Tech University Press, 2003), p. 12.

16. Ibid., p. 14.

17. Ibid., p. 47.

18. Robert Coulter, "Seminole Land Rights in Florida," *American Journal of the Institute for the Development of Indian Law* 4, no. 8 (1978): 2–27.

19. "First Seminole War," http://www.u-s-history.com/pages/h1129.html (accessed March 2005).

20. Wilkinson, "History."

21. The Indian Removal Act, published May 28, 1830.

22. Obituary: Osceola (Asi-Yahola, Bill Powell, Talcy), January 30, 1838, "This Day in History," http://nativenewsonline.org/history/hist0130.html (accessed August 2001).

23. Charles H. Coe and Charlton W. Tebeau, *Red Pa-

triots: The Story of the Seminoles. Bicentennial Floridiana Facsimile Series (Gainesville: University Presses of Florida, 1974), p. 89.

24. Glen Welker, "Oceola, (Black Drink)," Indigenous Peoples' Literature. http://www.indigenouspeople.net/osceola.htm (accessed April 1999).

25. Forbes, "Origin," p. 104.

26. "Indian Removal, 1814–1858," Resource Bank, PBS Online, http://www.pbs.org/wgbh/aia/part4/4p2959.html (accessed October 2001).

27. Gloria Jahoda, *The Trails of Tears* (New York: Holt, Rinehart and Winston, 1975), pp. 87–89.

28. Guenter Lewy, "Were American Indians the Victims of Genocide?" George Mason University's History News Network, http://hnn.us/articles/7302.html (accessed January 2005).

29. Skeletal remains have been discovered on various parts of Cat Island. Some of these locations are designated on old maps of the island.

30. Thompson, "When the Seminoles Were on Cat Island."

Chapter 12

1. Zoe Posey, "Gulf Coast Reminiscences."

2. According to the marker on his burial vault, Don Juan de Cuevas died five years after the great party.

3. Weather information is based on monthly averages for Louisiana and the Mississippi Gulf Coast from meteorologist Bob Swanson, *USA Today*'s assistant weather editor, April 11, 2007.

4. I.L. Mason, *A World Dictionary of Livestock Breeds, Types, and Varieties* (Wallingford, Oxon, UK: CAB International, 1996).

5. Ibid.

6. Posey, "Gulf Coast Reminiscences."

7. Gig is now considered slang for a booking engagement for musicians, but originally it came from the Old French word *gigue* meaning a fiddle or a jig (dance), or possibly from *giguer* meaning to dance.

8. There were "Dixieland Bands" in New Orleans, which incorporated a variety of instruments. Later called "jazz" bands, these groups were usually made up of a violin, cornet, and trombone playing the lead with a piano, banjo and tuba forming what we would now call the rhythm section.

9. John Broadhouse, *Facts about Fiddles. Violins, Old and New* (London: W. Reeves, 1879), pp. 177–181.

10. Barry Jean Ancelet, *Cajun Music: Its Origins and Development* (Lafayette: Center for Louisiana Studies, University of Southwestern Louisiana, 1989), p. 93.

11. Raymond E. François, *Ye Yaille, Chere: Traditional Cajun Dance Music* (Lafayette, LA: Thunderstone Press, 1990), p. 171.

12. François, *Ye Yaille*, p. 172.

13. Denes Agay, *Best Loved Songs of the American People* (Garden City, NY: Doubleday, 1975), p. 93.

14. Stuart Murray, *America's Song: The Story of "Yankee Doodle"* (Bennington, VT: Images from the Past, 1999), pp. 193–194.

15. Ash, *Fantastic*, p. 78.

16. Eduard Reeser, *The History of the Waltz* (Stockholm: Continental Book Co., 1947), p. 155.

17. Ralph G. Giordano, *Social Dancing in America: A History and Reference* (Westport, CT: Greenwood Press, 2007), p. 159.

18. A contra dance, or longways dance, is a type of folk dance in which couples are arranged in a line facing one another.

19. Giordano, *Social Dancing,* p. 177.

20. Michael Herman, *Folk Dances for All* (New York: Barnes & Noble, 1947), p. 73.

21. William G. Falkowski, *Polka History 101* (Buffalo, NY: Polish Community Center, 1980), p. 44.

22. Ryan A. Brasseaux and Kevin S. Fontenot, *Accordions, Fiddles, Two Step & Swing: A Cajun Music Reader* (Lafayette: Center for Louisiana Studies, 2006), p. 112.

Chapter 13

1. B.L. Morrison, *Louisiana's Funeral Customs, Graves & Graveyards* (Gretna, LA: Gulf South Press, 1983), p. 26.

2. H. Thurston and A. Shipman, "The Rosary," *The Catholic Encyclopedia* (New York: Robert Appleton Company, 1912). Retrieved June 25, 2010, from New Advent: http://www.newadvent.org/cathen/13184b.htm.

3. Robert G. Mayer, *Embalming: History, Theory & Practice* (New York: McGraw-Hill, 2000), pp. 69–74.

4. Morrison, *Louisiana's Funeral Customs,* pp. 77–80.

5. The obituaries for Juan de Cuevas and his daughter-in-law, Isabel Penalver, appear together in *The Daily Picayune,* September 27, 1849.

6. The Rev. Leo F. Fahey, "Bay St. Louis, a History of Hancock County's Catholic Institutions," *The Sea Coast Echo* (Bay St. Louis, Mississippi), Golden Jubilee Edition, 1942.

7. Ibid.

8. Research conducted at the Church of the Annunciation, Kiln, Mississippi, by Nap L. Cassibry II with the help of Reverend Austin Walsh, S.T., who was then the priest at the Church of the Annunciation.

9. Posey, "Gulf Coast Reminiscences."

10. Mississippi Gulf Coast Historical and Genealogical Society, "The Biloxi Cemetery," special issue 7, August 2002, Introduction. Compiled by Julie Suarez.

11. Harrison County Deed Book 3, pp. 36–37.

12. Mississippi Gulf Coast Historical and Genealogical Society, "The Biloxi Cemetery."

13. Morrison, *Louisiana's Funeral Customs,* p. 62.

14. "Cities of the Dead," Cemeteries, http://cache.zoominfo.com/CachedPage/?archive_id=0&page_id=61851855&page_url=%2f%2fwww.explore-neworleans.com%2fcemeteries_uk.html&page_last_updated=11%2f26%2f2002+9%3a46%3a04+AM&firstName=Esteban&lastName=Miro (accessed February 2010).

15. Morrison, *Louisiana's Funeral Customs,* p. 88.

16. Posey, "Gulf Coast Reminiscences."

17. According to religious customs.

18. Morrison, *Louisiana's Funeral Customs,* p. 101.

19. Ibid.

Chapter 14

1. A feature article entitled "All about Cat Island" (*The New Orleans Sunday Times,* June 4, 1871), written by Frank Heiderhoff only twenty-two years after Juan's death, describes in detail the discovery and early history of Cat Island, but did not mention Juan de Cuevas or the Battle of New Orleans. His son Ramon, the lighthouse keeper, was featured, however. The absence of any reference to Juan de Cuevas or his noble stand against the British seems to indicate that the story had not spread at that time. An act of such historical importance would have certainly figured prominently in Heiderhoff's article.

2. Posey, "Gulf Coast Reminiscences."

3. Nannie Mayes Crump, "Tortured Cat Islander Helped Save City from British, Says Grandson," *The*

Times-Picayune (New Orleans), January 10, 1937, sect. 2, p. 2.
  4. Hodding Carter and Anthony Ragusin, *Gulf Coast Country* (New York: Duell, Sloan and Pearce, 1951).
  5. University of Southern Mississippi — McCain Library and Archives, [Ray M.] Thompson Papers, Collection #M8, dates: ca 1837–1972.
  6. Ray M. Thompson, "The Hero of Cat Island," Know Your Coast, *The Daily Herald* (Biloxi, MS), June 6, 1956.
  7. University of Southern Mississippi — McCain Library and Archives, [Ray M.] Thompson Papers, Collection #M8, Dates: ca 1837–1972. Box 1, folder 5 (1956).
  8. Information from a discussion on September 10, 2006, with the Cuevas family who still lives on the original Spanish grant in Algámitas, Spain.
  9. Frank Edward Manuel, *The Enlightenment* (Englewood Cliffs, NJ: Prentice-Hall, 1965), p. 36.
  10. The Reconquest was a campaign by the Christians to recapture territory from the Muslims (Moors) that was believed to have originally been Christian-controlled states.
  11. David Abulafia, *The New Cambridge Medieval History* (Cambridge: Cambridge University Press, 1999), p. 313.
  12. Alfonso García Valdecasas, *El Hidalgo y el Honor* (Madrid: Revista de Occidente, 1958), pp. 167–168.
  13. Fernando González-Doria, *Diccionario Heráldico y Nobilario* (San Fernando de Henares, Madrid: Trigo Ediciones, 2000), pp. 265–266.
  14. Since horses, arms and wealth were heritable, and also considered property, the tax exemption could apply. Towards the end of the title system the distinctions between hidalgo and caballero families became increasingly blurred.
  15. Valdecasas, *El Hidalgo*, p. 168.
  16. William Rose Benét, "Juan de la Cueva de Garoza," *The Reader's Encyclopedia* (New York: Thomas Y. Crowell Company, 1965).
  17. September 10, 2006, discussion with the Cuevas family who still lives on the original Spanish grant in Algámitas, Spain.
  18. Sir Charles Petrie, *King Charles III of Spain; An Enlightened Despot* (New York: J. Day, 1971), pp. 133–136.
  19. Alfred Cobban, *The Eighteenth Century: Europe in the Age of Enlightenment* (New York: McGraw-Hill, 1969), pp. 99–104.
  20. Charles C. Noel, "Madrid: City of the Enlightenment," *History Today* 45 (October 1995).
  21. Manuel, *Enlightenment*, p. 202.
  22. Petrie, *King Charles III*, p. 189.
  23. Information from a discussion on September 10, 2006, with the Cuevas family who still lives on the original Spanish grant in Algámitas, Spain.
  24. Ibid.
  25. Saint Louis Cathedral Marriage Book 4, p. 106, A 483.
  26. Asbury, *French Quarter*, p. 55.
  27. Ibid., p. 54.

Chapter 15

  1. Cassibry, *Ladner Odyssey*, p. 66.
  2. "Historic Cat Island Lighthouse Destroyed," *The Daily Herald* (Gulfport/Biloxi, MS), October 5, 1961.
  3. On August 7, 1789, the Ninth Act of the first Congress, and the first Public Works Act, provided for the transfer of the twelve existing lighthouses in the United States from the individual states to the federal government.
  4. Samuel Willard Crompton and Michael J. Rhein, *The Ultimate Book of Lighthouses: History, Legend, Lore, Design, Technology, Romance* (San Diego, CA: Thunder Bay Press, 2000), p. 67.
  5. Crompton and Rhein, *Ultimate Book of Lighthouses*, pp. 67–71.
  6. United States Coast Guard, "Lighthouses: Then and Now," http://www.uscg.mil/history/articles/h_lighthouses.asp (accessed July 2000).
  7. Ibid.
  8. Ibid.
  9. Ibid.
  10. Dan Ellis, *Lighthouses and Islands of the Gulf* (Pass Christian, MS: Ellis, 2000), p. 65.
  11. Willard Flint, *Lightships of the United States Government: Reference Notes* (Washington, D.C.: Coast Guard Historian's Office, U.S. Coast Guard Headquarters, 1989), p. 91.
  12. Ellis, *Lighthouses*, p. 65.
  13. Shirley Haupt, *Beacons in the Night: Lighthouses of the Gulf* (Lake Charles, LA: Port of Lake Charles, 1999), p. 27.
  14. Ellis, *Lighthouses*, p. 61.
  15. Deed filed in Harrison County Record Book B, pages 225 and 226.
  16. Ibid.
  17. Ellis, *Lighthouses*, p. 61.
  18. David Melville, *An Expose of Facts, Respectfully Submitted to the Government and Citizens of the United States, Relating to the Conduct of Winslow Lewis, of Boston Superintendent for Lighting the United States' Light Houses, an Accredited Agent of the Treasury Department: Addressed to the Hon. the Secretary of the Treasury* (Providence, RI: Miller & Hutchens, 1819), pp. 155–157.
  19. Bruce Watson, "Science Makes a Better Lighthouse Lens," *Smithsonian* 30, no. 5 (August 1999): 30. Reproduced in Biography Resource Center.
  20. Watson, "Science," p. 31.
  21. Haupt, *Beacons*, p. 77.
  22. Ellis, *Lighthouses*, p. 65.
  23. U.S. Coast Guard Historian's Office, U.S. Coast Guard Headquarters, 2100 Second Street, SW, Washington, D.C. 20593-0001.
  24. Ibid.
  25. Ellis, *Lighthouses*, p. 65.
  26. Ibid., p. 66.
  27. Excerpt from National Parks Service, "A Keeper's Life," http://www.nps.gov/history/maritime/keep/keep19th.htm.
  28. *Report of I.W.P. Lewis Reproduced in Public Documents and Extracts from Reports and Papers Relating to Light-Houses, Light-Vessels, and Illumination Apparatus, and to Beacons, Buoys, and Fog Signals 1789–1871* (Washington, D.C.: Government Printing Office), p. 370.
  30. Excerpt from National Parks Service, "A Keeper's Life," http://www.nps.gov/history/maritime/keep/keep19th.htm.
  31. Several years later, Pleasonton struck out no. 6 of the instructions and modified no. 7 to replace "contractors" with "Superintendent."
  32. Harrison County Deed Book of Records, no. 6, pp. 134 and 135.
  33. Haupt, *Beacons*, p. 58.
  34. Ellis, *Lighthouses*, p. 66.
  35. Sullivan, *Hurricanes*, p. 49.
  36. From a report by M. James Stevens, December 11, 1975, prepared for the feasibility committee of Gulf Islands National Seashore considering acquisition of Cat Island.
  37. Flint, *Lightships*, p. 92. Flint was the official Coast Guard historian and author of *Lightships and Lightship Stations of the U.S. Government*, published by the Coast Guard

in 1989 and now considered a primary source of American lightship information.
38. Ibid.
39. Ellis, *Lighthouses*, p. 66.
40. Ibid.
41. Sullivan, *Hurricanes*, p. 49.
42. Ibid., p. 50.
43. Ibid., p. 52.
44. Ibid.
45. Ibid., p. 54.
46. Ibid.
47. Ellis, *Lighthouses*, p. 66.
48. United States Coast Guard Historian's Office.
49. An act of Congress for sundry civil expenses of the government for the fiscal year ending June 30, 1872.
50. Ibid.
51. United States Coast Guard Historian's Office.
52. Ibid.
53. Ibid.
54. Ibid.
55. Ibid.
56. National Archives.
57. David Roth, National Weather Service. This information was provided as a public service by NOAA's National Weather Service (NWS).
58. Ibid.
59. "Death Work at Biloxi," *The Daily-Picayune*, October 7, 1893.
60. Cassibry, *Ladner Odyssey*, p. 66.
61. "Lighthouse Keeper Clarisse and Wife Still on Duty," *Daily Picayune*, October 7, 1893, p. 2.
62. Ibid.
63. "An Act to Provide for the Disposal of Abandoned and Useless Military Reservations," General Orders by United States War Dept., United States, Adjutant-General's Office, United States, Military Secretary's Dept. (July 5, 1884).
64. "An Act to Provide for the Disposal of Abandoned and Useless Military Reservations," General Orders by United States War Dept., United States, Adjutant-General's Office, United States, Military Secretary's Dept. (November 13, 1895).
65. Riprap is the term for rock or cement used to reduce water erosion. The angular pieces resist the hydraulic forces, thus dissipating the energy caused by the waves.
66. Ellis, *Lighthouses*, p. 67.
67. Ibid.
68. "Lighthouse Destroyed by Fire," *The Daily Herald*, October 1, 1961.
69. "Historic Cat Island Lighthouse Destroyed," *The Daily Herald*, October 5, 1961.

Chapter 16

1. "Lumber Manufacturers May Cut up Timber Supply on Cat Island," *The Daily Herald* (Gulfport, MS), September 7, 1907.
2. Heart Pine Reserve, Specialists in Antique Heart Pine, "America's Love of Wood," http://heartpinereserve.com/heritage_pg.html (accessed June 7, 2007).
3. *Dictionary of American History*, s.v. "Naval Stores," http://www.encyclopedia.com/doc/1G2-3401802913.html (accessed July 2005).
4. Robert B. Outland, *Tapping the Pines: The Naval Stores Industry in the American South* (Baton Rouge: Louisiana State University Press, 2004), pp. 120–121.
5. "Island to Be Sold," *The Daily Herald* (Gulfport, MS), December 19, 1908.
6. "Turpentine Rights on Cat Island," *The Daily Herald* (Gulfport, MS), February 2, 1911.
7. "Pine Trees on Cat Island to Be Tapped," *The Daily Herald* (Gulfport, MS), March 9, 1911.
8. Deed from Benjamin M. Harrod to Nathan V. Boddie, January 11, 1911, Harrison County, Mississippi, Deed Book 95, pp. 514–515.
9. Thompson, "Cat Island," p.13.
10. "Naval Stores Firm Busy on Cat Island," *The Daily Herald* (Gulfport, MS), April 5, 1911.
11. Thompson, "Cat Island," p. 13.
12. "Naval Stores Firm Busy on Cat Island."
13. "Had Trouble on Cat Island," *The Daily Herald* (Gulfport, MS), June 23, 1913
14. Old maps of Cat Island indicate turpentine operations that had begun when Nathan V. Boddie purchased the island, in 1911, ended around 1913. The lumber business began on the island about the same year that the turpentine had been depleted.
15. "Features Planned for Cat Island," *The Daily Herald* (Gulfport, MS), September 20, 1920.
16. The L.N. Dantzler Collection at the University of Mississippi is a good source of information about the lumber industry on the Gulf Coast during the first quarter of the 1900s.
17. Glenn Hughes, *Longleaf Pine in Mississippi*, Publication 2201, Extension Service of Mississippi State University, cooperating with U.S. Department of Agriculture. Published in furtherance of acts of Congress, May 8 and June 30, 1914.
18. "William Cuevas Engaged in Lumber Business," *The Daily Herald* (Gulfport, MS), December 2, 1910.
19. Thompson, "Cat Island."
20. Ibid.
21. Nollie W. Hickman, *Mississippi Harvest: Lumbering in the Longleaf Pine Belt, 1840–1915* (Jackson: University Press of Mississippi, 2009), p. 34.
22. Ibid., p. 104.
23. Tony Howe, "Growth of the Lumber Industry, (1840–1930)," *Mississippi History Now* (an online publication of the Mississippi Historical Society), http://mshistory.k12.ms.us/articles/171/growth-of-the-lumber-industry-1840-to-1930 (accessed May 2003).
24. The acres of trees still available on Cat Island in 1931 led to profitable businesses in turpentine and later heartwood pine.
25. The timber rights were leased in 1937, which indicates the trees were no longer producing pine tar for turpentine.
26. Thompson, "Cat Island," p. 20.

Chapter 17

1. The National Prohibition Act (P.L. 66–66, 41 Stat. 305), also known as the Volstead Act, was adopted by Congress to implement the recently ratified Eighteenth Amendment to the Constitution of the United States.
2. My father, Oliver John Cuevas, who was this bootlegger's cousin, often spoke to me about the man's activities, which were well known on the Gulf Coast.
3. James K. Vardaman, "Prohibition for Mississippi — Thank God," *The Issue* 1, no. 49 (January 2, 1909).
4. Sullivan, *Hurricanes*, pp. 140–141.
5. Kelli Bozeman, "Where in Mississippi Is ... Kiln?" *Mississippi Magazine*, May–June 2005.
6. *The Ocean Springs Record*, June 9, 2005, p. B8.
7. Jackson County, Mississippi Record of Deeds Book 199, p. 489.
8. Jackson County, Mississippi Record of Deeds Book 56, pp. 644–645.

9. *The Jackson County Times*, November 21, 1925, p. 5.
10. *The Daily Herald*, September 3, 1932, p. 2.
11. Steve Phillips, "Ocean Springs Mayor Vetoes Demolition Permit," WLOX, ABC Channel 13, http://www.wlox.com/Global/category.asp?C=1702&nav=menu40_1 (accessed May 27, 2009).
12. Ronald Williamson, "The Real McCoys," *The Daytona Beach News-Journal*, October 2, 2010.
13. Ian Williams, *Rum: A Social and Sociable History of the Real Spirit of 1776* (New York: Nation Books, 2005), p. 305.
14. R.R. Churchill and A.V. Lowe, *The Law of the Sea* (Manchester: Manchester University Press, 1983), p. 67.
15. Williamson, "The Real McCoys."
16. Local lore.
17. Herbert Asbury, *The Great Illusion: An Informal History of Prohibition* (New York: Greenwood Press, 1968), pp. 144–145.

Chapter 18

1. Eugene V. Connett, *Wildfowling in the Mississippi Flyway* (New York: Van Nostrand, 1949), p. 2.
2. Bidwell Clayton Adam, discussion with the author, Gulfport, Mississippi, June 15, 1961.
3. Ibid.
4. Thompson, "Cat Island," p. 13.
5. Zoe Posey, "Cat Island Owner Lee M. Russell to Spend $500,000 on Winter Resort," *The Times-Picayune*, April 30, 1925.
6. John H. Lang, *History of Harrison County, Mississippi* (Gulfport, MS: Dixie Press, 1935), p. 145.
7. Dan Ellis, "The Mexican Gulf Hotel, A Grand Winter Hotel on Davis Avenue," Hotels Past, http://hotels.passchristian.net/mexican_gulf_hotel.htm (accessed June 13, 2007).
8. Ray Thompson, "Goose Point on Cat Island," *The Daily-Herald*, January 23, 1959.
9. *The Mississippi Guide*, February 6, 1931.

Chapter 19

1. Michael G. Lemish, *War Dogs: A History of Loyalty and Heroism* (Washington, D.C.: Brassey's, 1999), p. 41.
2. Tom Newton, "K-9 History: The Dogs of War!" *A Special Presentation from Hahn's 50th AP K-9, West Germany*, http://community-2.webtv.net/Hahn-50thAP-K9/K9History/ (accessed May 18, 2000).
3. Lemish, *War Dogs*, p. 36.
4. Joseph J. White, "Day to Honor Our Loved War and Service Dogs," http://k9magazinefree.com/k9_perspective/iss36p7.shtml (accessed June 14, 2009).
5. K.M. Born, "Archives of the U.S. Army Quartermaster Museum & Quartermaster Historian, Fort Lee, Virginia," http://www.qmfound.com/K-9.htm (accessed March 2007).
6. Ibid.
7. Ibid.
8. "Quartermaster War Dog Program," http://www.qmfound.com/K-9.htm (accessed July 2007).
9. Lemish, *War Dogs*, p. 54.
10. Ibid.
11. Born, "Archives."
12. Lemish, *War Dogs*, p. 55.
13. Ibid., p. 53.
14. PBS, "Story 2: War Dog Letter," *History Detectives*, season 7, episode 1, 2009.
15. Lemish, *War Dogs*, p. 54.
16. The list of dogs was taken from the "Veterinary Dispensary, Cat Island Training Project" document in the declassified Cat Island files at the National Archives in Washington, D.C.
17. Lemish, *War Dogs*, p. 55.
18. Stated in a reference memorandum, Subject: Training Dogs for Assault, from WDGS, file WDOCT 353, dated July 16, 1942, to the Commanding General, L.J. McNair, Lt. Gen., U.S.A. Army Ground Forces, taken from the declassified Cat Island files at the National Archives in Washington, D.C.
19. Nisei is an American term from the Japanese language referring to persons whose parents emigrated from Japan.
20. Kat Bergeron, "The War Dogs of Cat Island," *The Sun Herald* (Biloxi, MS), January 11, 2009.
21. Yasuo Takata and Raymond Nosaka, "The Secret Mission of the Third Platoon, Baker Company," *Puka-Puka Parade*, March–April 1980, p. 22.
22. Masayo Duus, *Unlikely Liberators: The Men of the 100th and 442nd* (Honolulu: University of Hawaii Press, 1987), p. 48.
23. Takata and Nosaka, "Secret Mission," p. 22.
24. Ibid.
25. Kat Bergeron, "Japanese-Americans' Loyalty Shined in Island Scheme," *The Sun Herald* (Biloxi, MS), June 18, 1995.
26. Lemish, *War Dogs*, p. 57.
27. Duus, *Unlikely Liberators*, p. 48.
28. Ibid.
29. Kat Bergeron, "War Dogs Trained on Island, Gulfport Mystery Site," *The Sun Herald* (Biloxi, MS), November 9, 2003.
30. Takata and Nosaka, "Secret Mission," p. 23.
31. Ibid.
32. Lemish, *War Dogs*, p. 56.
33. Ibid., p. 57.
34. Takata and Nosaka, "Secret Mission," p. 25.
35. Ibid., p. 24.
36. Duus, *Unlikely Liberators*, p. 49.
37. Lemish, *War Dogs*, p. 57.
38. Ibid.
39. Ibid.
40. Takata and Nosaka, "Secret Mission," p. 25.
41. Lemish, *War Dogs*, p. 58.
42. Ibid., p. 59.

Chapter 20

1. From the journal of Captain Chateau with the d'Iberville expedition.
2. Cecil Johnson, *British West Florida, 1763–1783* (Hamden, CT: Archon Books, 1942), p. 119.
3. Cecil Johnson, *British West Florida, 1763–1783* (New Haven, CT: Yale University Press, 1943), quoted in Dale Rayburn, *Twelve Flags, Triumphs and Tragedies* (Ocean Springs, MS: Greenwell, 1968), p. 153.
4. Nicholas Ladner applied for a grant to Cat Island from the British in 1764. Mr. Somitette's grant was deemed invalid shortly after that in 1767. Spain came into possession of the Coast in May 1781. Ladner was granted Cat Island by the Spanish that same year, therefore, there was no private owner of Cat Island before Ladner.
5. John Walton Caughey, *Bernardo de Gálvez in Louisiana, 1776–1783* (Berkeley: University of California Press, 1934), p. 218.
6. Laville Bremer, "Amichel, a Narrative History of the Gulf Coast," *The Times-Picayune — New Orleans States*, January 2, 1944, magazine section.

7. Pintado Papers, Mobile County Historical Library, Mobile, Alabama, Deed Book 1, p. 17.
8. Commissioner, Report, No. 2, Certificate, No. 5 Land Office, Jackson Court House.
9. Coll'ette King, supervisor, Probate Court Archives, Mobile, Alabama. Letter to the author, May 10, 2001.
10. Ibid.
11. Albert Katz Weinberg, *Manifest Destiny; A Study of Nationalist Expansionism in American History* (Baltimore: John Hopkins Press, 1935), p. 1.
12. Payson J. Treat, *The National Land System, 1785–1820* (New York: E.B. Treat, 1910), pp. 1–14.
13. United States, "An Act for Adjusting the Claims to Lands, and Establishing Land Offices in the District East of the Island of New Orleans," *The Public Statutes at Large of the United States of America* (Boston: Charles C. Little and James Brown, 1848), vol. 4, p. 299.
14. "Land Patents, Understanding How They Work," http://www.teamlaw.org/LandPatents.htm (accessed July 27, 2009).
15. *Surplus Trading Company v. Cook*, 281 U.S. 647; *Western Union Telegraph Co. v. Chiles*, 214 U.S. 274.
16. The word is "requite," which means a receipt showing that part of the land was purchased from Spain.
17. United States, "Chapter CXLVI—An Act to Confirm Certain Claims to Lands in the District of Jackson Courthouse, in the State of Mississippi" (May 28, 1830).
18. The surveyor used the internationally accepted Rectangular Survey System employing meridian lines, base lines, and townships, to indicate the land. For an explanation of the Rectangular Survey System go to Landprints.com, http://www.landprints.com/LpRectangularSurveySystem.htm (accessed April 2007).
19. Recorded on page 576, Jackson Court House Records, Jackson, Mississippi. Recorded Miscellaneous vol. 479, pp. 22 and 23.
20. Heiderhoff, "All about Cat Island." Information also found in Ellis, *Lighthouses*, p. 65.
21. Handwritten deed from Juan de Cuevas to Judah P. Benjamin filed in Hancock County, Mississippi, (Bay St. Louis, Mississippi) Probate Court, March 13, 1837, Deed Book 28, pp. 155 and 156.
22. Terms of the agreement are found in the handwritten deed from Juan de Cuevas to Judah P. Benjamin, March 13, 1837.
23. Eli N. Evans, *Judah P. Benjamin the Jewish Confederate* (New York: Free Press, 1988), p. xi.
24. Pierce Butler, *Judah P. Benjamin* (Philadelphia: G.W. Jacobs, 1907), p. 37.
25. "Judah Benjamin," *Jewish Virtual Library*, http://www.jewishvirtuallibrary.org/jsource/biography/Benjamin.html (accessed June 16, 2005).
26. Evans, *Judah P. Benjamin*, p. 436.
27. Butler, *Judah P. Benjamin*, pp. 417–419.
28. Throughout the history of Cat Island, each of the owners have generally had grand plans, but there is no indication or evidence as to why these four men hired Judah Benjamin to purchase the island from Juan de Cuevas. They never announced their plans for Cat Island.
29. James A. Ramsay family archives, May 5, 2003.
30. Wilton Paul Ledet, *The History of the City of Carrollton* (n.p., 1938), p. 235.
31. Ibid.
32. "New Orleans and Carrollton Railroad," http://www.spiritus-temporis.com/new-orleans-and-carrollton-railroad/notes.html (accessed August 2006).
33. James Amedee Gaudet Collection of Houmas Plantations and William Porcher Miles Materials Inventory.

Series 1. Financial and Legal Papers 1785–1927. University of North Carolina, Library.
34. Houmas House Media Center, 40136 Highway 942, Darrow, LA 70725–2302.
35. "General Sterling Price," Naval History & Heritage Command, http://www.history.navy.mil/danfs/g3/general_sterling_price.htm (accessed February 2004).
36. Paul Yarnall, *NavSource Naval History*, 2003, http://www.navsource.org/ (accessed May 2003).
37. Compiled from Edwin C. Bears, *Historic Structure Report, Fort Pickens, Historical Data Section, 1821–1895, Gulf Islands National Seashore, Florida-Mississippi* (U.S. Department of the Interior, National Park Service, 1983).
38. Ernest F. Dibble, *William H. Chase: Gulf Coast Fort Builder* (Wilmington, DE: Gulf Coast Collection, 1978), pp. 211–214.
39. S. Frederick Starr, *Southern Comfort: The Garden District of New Orleans* (New York: Princeton Architectural Press, 1998), p. 230.
40. "1206 Second Street was built in 1866 for Charles H. Adams by James Freret, for $7,950," *Daily Picayune* (New Orleans), September 1, 1886.
41. United States, *Biographies of the Mayors of New Orleans* (New Orleans: City Hall Archives, 1939), p. 149.
42. The details are described in the Cat Island deed from Juan de Cuevas to Judah Benjamin.
43. *Weekly Herald* (Biloxi, MS), March 9, 1887.
44. "Cat Island Sale—Millaudon to Duggan," *The Daily Herald* (Biloxi, MS), February 12, 1896.
45. Chancery Court, State of Mississippi, County of Harrison, no. 1428. *H. Gibbs Morgan v. J.H. Duggan Jr. et al.* Proceeds of sale made April 1, 1907.
46. Starr, *Southern Comfort*, p. 161.
47. "Louise Dugan Diaries (1868–1879)" (MS, Tulane University), May 4, 1876.
48. Chancery Court, State of Mississippi, County of Harrison, no. 1428. *H. Gibbs Morgan v. J.H. Duggan Jr. et al.* Proceeds of sale made April 1, 1907.
49. City Archives, New Orleans Public Library (available to registered researchers by appointment).
50. Louisiana Division, New Orleans Public Library, *Administrations of the Mayors of New Orleans*, Walter Chew Flower (1850–1900).
51. Ibid.
52. "Louisiana Governors," La-Cemeteries, http://la-cemeteries.com/governors/Parker,%20John%20Milliken/Parker,%20John%20Milliken.shtml (accessed June 2008).
53. Henry E. Chambers, *A History of Louisiana*, vol. 2 (Chicago: American Historical Society, 1925), pp. 4–5.
54. Commissioner's Deed to Henry Gibbes Morgan, December 6, 1897, Harrison County Deed Book 45, p. 188.
55. Walter F. Pratt, *The Supreme Court under Edward Douglass White* (Columbia: University of South Carolina Press, 1999), p. 77.
56. Melvin I. Urofsky, *The Supreme Court Justices: A Biographical Dictionary* (New York: Garland Publishing, 1994), p. 590.
57. John was often written as Jno. in old records.
58. Letter from Jno. M. Moore, the accounting commissioner of the General Land Office, to Stephen Pleasonton, fifth auditor and acting commissioner of the revenue, September 29, 1830.
59. "Favorable Report—Senator McEnery's Bill Quieting the Title. Cat Island in the Gulf of Mexico," *The Daily Herald* (Biloxi, MS), February 26, 1903.
60. Record of Patents: Patent Number 217461. Jackson Court House Records, Jackson, Mississippi.
61. By decree of the Chancery Court of Harrison

County, in no. 1428, *H.G. Morgan v. J. H. Duggan et al.*, October 15, 1906.

62. Chancery Court, State of Mississippi, Harrison County, no. 1428, *E. Gibbs Morgan Vs. J.H. Duggan et al.*, T.A. Wood, chancellor, October 15, 1906.

63. "On Cat Island. Said to Have Been Recently Sold by the Government," *New Orleans Daily Picayune*, September 15, 1907.

64. Stated in a letter, dated March 12, 1908, to the secretary of commerce and labor from Charles W. Russell, acting attorney general.

65. "Suit over Cat Island," *Daily Record-Tribune*, September 4, 1908, p. 1.

66. Commissioner's Deed to Benjamin M. Harrod, Harrison County, Mississippi, Chancery Court, April 1, 1907, Deed Book 82, pp. 45-46.

67. "Chief Engineer Benjamin Morgan Harrod," Chapter 5, Biographies of Important Personages Associated with the New Orleans Drainage Commission and the Sewerage and Water Board of New Orleans, http://www.mvn.usace.army.mil (accessed June 2004).

68. Leonard Victor Huber, Mary Louise Christovich, Peggy McDowell, Betsy Swanson, Edith Elliott Long, Bernard Lemann, and Doyle Gertjejansen, *New Orleans Architecture, Volume III: The Cemeteries* (Gretna, LA: Pelican Pub., 2004), p. 37.

69. Greenwood Cemetery, Fireman's Charitable & Benevolent Association, 5200 Canal Blvd, New Orleans, LA.

70. Theodore Roosevelt, *State of the Union Address Part II* (December 5, 1905).

71. "The Cat Island Proposition, Sport in Dixie," *The Daily Herald* (Biloxi, MS), May 12, 1909.

72. "Sanctuaries for Birds," *The Daily Herald* (Biloxi, MS), March 27, 1909.

73. "Chief Engineer Benjamin Morgan Harrod," Chapter 5, Biographies of Important Personages Associated with the New Orleans Drainage Commission and the Sewerage and Water Board of New Orleans, http://www.mvn.usace.army.mil (accessed June 2004).

74. "Gulfport -Turpentine," *The Daily Herald* (Biloxi, MS), February 21, 1911.

75. Thompson, "Cat Island," p. 13.

76. Ibid.

77. 1930 United States Federal Census — Census Place: Laurel, Jones, Mississippi; Roll: 1151; page 3B; Enumeration District: 8; Image: 744.0.

78. "Deal Is Consumated to Make Cat Island a Popular Resort," *The Daily Herald* (Biloxi, MS), January 19, 1921.

79. "Cat Island to Be Developed," *The Daily Herald* (Biloxi, MS), December 3, 1919.

80. Thompson, "Cat Island," p. 13.

81. "Prospectus for Development," *The Daily Herald* (Biloxi, MS), February 22, 1921.

82. Thompson, "Cat Island," p. 13.

83. Posey, "Cat Island Owner."

84. Zoe Posey, "Cat Island $10 Million Dollar Resort with Causeway to Long Beach to Change Name to Treasure Island," *The Times Picayune* (New Orleans), July 12, 1925.

85. Zoe Posey, "Two Million Dollar Edgewater Gulf Hotel to Be Built. Full Story of It and Markham with Pictures," *The Times Picayune* (New Orleans), July 11, 1925.

86. Thompson, "Cat Island," p. 13.

87. Ibid., p. 20; "Cat Island to Be Foreclosed by George Boddie," *The Mississippi Guide* (Biloxi), September 10, 1930.

88. Ibid.

89. Testimony of Cala Boddie Colbert at the hearing before the subcommittee on National Parks and Public Lands of the Committee on Resources, House of Representatives, One Hundred Sixth Congress, second session, September 30, 1999, p. 59.

90. D.C. Harvill, "Island at a Crossroad," *Coast Magazine*, Summer 2000, pp. 27-30.

91. Ibid.

92. "Cat Island Case to Involve 500 in Litigation," *The Daily-Herald* (Biloxi, MS), March 12, 1959.

93. "Cat Island Case First on Docket," *The Daily-Herald* (Biloxi, MS), February 10, 1968.

94. The author was one of the family representatives who assisted Mrs. Keen and the attorney in organizing family meetings on the Coast.

95. Civil Action no. 2561, United States District Court for the Southern District of Mississippi, Southern Division.

96. A reference from the book *Narrative of the Campaigns of the British Army at Washington and New Orleans under Generals Ross, Pakenham, and Lambert, in the Years 1814 and 1815* by British Lieutenant Robert Gleig, in which he states that Juan de Cuevas could read and write.

97. On March 2, 1905, the Fifty-Eighth Congress of the United States, session 3, chapter 1315 issued "An Act for the Relief of H. Gibbes Morgan and Other Co owners of Cat Island, in the Gulf of Mexico." The purpose of this act was to certify that Juan de Cuevas owned all of Cat Island. It had nothing to do with the ownership of Cat Island by H. Gibbes Morgan as this suit alleged.

98. Civil Action no. 2561, Federal Court, Biloxi, Mississippi, March 11, 1968.

99. Ibid.

100. Social Security Death Index, Number: 427-24-4948; Issue State: Mississippi; Issue Date: Before 1951.

101. Testimony of Cala Boddie Colbert at the hearing before the subcommittee on National Parks and Public Lands of the Committee on Resources, House of Representatives, One Hundred Sixth Congress, second session, September 30, 1999, p. 54.

102. Trust for Public Lands, 116 New Montgomery Street, 4th Floor, San Francisco, CA 94105.

103. H.R. 2541, a bill to adjust the boundaries of the Gulf Islands National Seashore to include Cat Island, MS., 1999.

104. "Half of Cat Island Is Now a Park," *The SunHerald* (Gulfport/Biloxi, MS), March 29, 2002.

105. See the Cat Island map showing the areas purchased by the National Park Service.

106. Deed Book 1577, pp. 246-303, First Judicial District, Harrison County, State of Mississippi (March 22, 2002).

107. Greg Harman, "Family Will Keep Its Half," *The SunHerald* (Gulfport/Biloxi, MS), April 18, 2004.

108. Ibid.

Chapter 21

1. Manuel Flores Muñoz, *Algámitas* (Algámitas, Spain: Technographic, S.L., 2003), pp. 11-15.

2. Mary Fitton, *Málaga: The Biography of a City* (London: Allen and Unwin, 1971), pp. 84-96.

3. Robert Kern, *The Regions of Spain: A Reference Guide to History and Culture*, (Westport, CT: Greenwood Press), pp. 110-115.

4. F.M. Stenton, *Anglo-Saxon England* (Oxford: Clarendon Press, 1947), p. 112.

5. Muñoz, *Algámitas*, p. 26.

6. Ibid., p. 115.

7. Fernando González-Doria and Félix Vaquerizo

Romero, *Diccionario Heráldico y Mobiliario* (San Fernando de Henares, Madrid: Trigo Ediciones, 2000), p. 148.

8. The author met the Cuevas family who are the current owners of the Cuevas house in Algámitas, Spain, on September 11, 2006.

9. Patricia Harris and David Lyon, *Andalucía and the Costa del Sol: The Best of Andalucía's Mediterranean Coastline plus Gibralter, the Vibrant Moorish Cities of Granada, Cordóba and Sevilla, the White Villages of the Interior and the Mountain Villages of the Sierra Nevada* (Guilford, CT: Globe Pequot Press, 2003), p. 94.

10. Ediciones Daly, *Rejas, Balcones y Cercas — Grilles, Balconies & Fences* (Málaga, Spain: Ediciones Daly, 1997), pp. 82–83.

11. Malagueños are the people of Málaga. Some Muslem potters and painters who settled Málaga in the thirteenth century are considered Malagueños.

12. José Amador de los Ríos was primarily a historian and archeologist of art and literature. He was the first to use the term *mudejarismo* to describe a style of architecture in 1859. http://en.wikipedia.org/wiki/Jos%C3%A9_Amador_de_los_R%C3%ADos (accessed April 2002).

13. Alice Wilson Frothingham, *Tile Panels of Spain, 1500–1650* (New York: Hispanic Society of America, 1969), pp. 46–49.

14. George Kubler and Martin Sebastian Soria, *Art and Architecture in Spain and Portugal and Their American Dominions, 1500 to 1800* (Baltimore: Penguin Books, 1959), pp. 99–102.

15. Arthur Byne and Mildred Stapley Byne, *Provincial Houses in Spain* (New York: H. Helburn, 1925), pp. 145–147.

Bibliography

Agay, Denes. *Best Loved Songs of the American People.* Garden City, NY: Doubleday, 1975.

Alexander, Mary Ellen. *Rosalie and Radishes—A History of Long Beach, Mississippi.* Gulfport, MS: Dixie Press, 1980.

Ancelet, Barry Jean. *Cajun Music: Its Origins and Development.* Lafayette, LA: Center for Louisiana Studies, University of Southwestern Louisiana, 1989.

Ancelet, Barry Jean, Jay Dearborn Edwards, and Glen Pitre. *Cajun Country.* Jackson: University Press of Mississippi, 1992.

Andrews, Johnnie, Jr., and William David Higgins. *Spanish Census Reports at Mobile.* Mobile, AL: Bienville Historical Society, 1973.

Asbury, Herbert. *The French Quarter: An Informal History of the New Orleans Underworld.* New York: Alfred A. Knopf, 1936.

———. *The Great Illusion: An Informal History of Prohibition.* New York: Greenwood Press, 1968.

Ash, Russell. *Fantastic Millennium Facts.* New York: DK Publishing, 1999.

Barchers, Suzanne I., and Patricia C. Marden. *Cooking Up U.S. History: Recipes and Research to Share with Children.* 2nd edition. Englewood, CO: Teacher Ideas Press, 1999.

Bellis, Mary. "The History of Steamboats." *http://inventors.about.com/library/inventors/blsteamship.htm* (accessed May 2008).

Benet, William Rose. "Juan de la Cueva de Garoza." *The Reader's Encyclopedia.* New York: Thomas Y. Crowell, 1965.

Blomfield, Sir Reginald. *Sébastien le Prestre de Vauban, 1663–1707.* New York: Barnes & Noble, 1971.

Boeta, José Rodulfo. *Bernardo de Gálvez.* Madrid: Publicaciones Españolas, 1977.

Born, K.M. "Archives of the U.S. Army Quartermaster Museum & Quartermaster Historian, Fort Lee, Virginia." *http://www.qmfound.com/K-9.htm* (accessed March 2007).

Bossu, M. *Travels through That Part of North America Formerly Called Louisiana.* London: Printed for T. Davies, 1771.

Bourne, Edward Gaylord. *Spain in America.* New York: Barnes & Noble, 1962.

Boyd, George Andrew. *Café du Monde: The Original French Market Coffee Stand.* New Orleans: New Orleans, 1977.

Brasseaux, Ryan A., and Kevin S. Fontenot. *Accordions, Fiddles, Two-step & Swing: A Cajun Music Reader.* Lafayette: Center for Louisiana Studies, 2006.

Broadhouse, John. *Facts about Fiddles. Violins, Old and New.* London: W. Reeves, 1879.

Brooks, Phillips V. *Kitchen Utensils: Names, Origins, and Definitions through the Ages.* New York: Palgrave Macmillan, 2004.

Brown, Dee. *Andrew Jackson and the Battle of New Orleans.* New York: G.P. Putnam's Sons, 1972.

Burke, James. *The Day the Universe Changed.* Boston: Little Brown, 1985.

Butler, Pierce. *Judah P. Benjamin.* Philadelphia: G.W. Jacobs & Company, 1907.

Button, H. Warren, and Eugene F. Provenzo. *History of Education and Culture in America.* Englewood Cliffs, NJ: Prentice-Hall, 1983.

Byne, Arthur, and Mildred Stapley Byne. *Provincial Houses in Spain.* New York: H. Helburn, 1925.

Cable, George Washington. *Old Creole Days.* New York: Charles Scribner's Sons, 1883.

Carline, Richard. *Pictures in the Post: The Story of the Picture Postcard and Its Place in the History of Popular Art.* London: Gordon Fraser Gallery, 1971.

Carswell, John. *The South Sea Bubble.* Stanford, CA: Stanford University Press, 1960.

Carter, Hodding, and Anthony Ragusin. *Gulf Coast Country.* New York: Duell, Sloan and Pearce, 1951.

Cassibry, Nap L., II. *Early Settlers and Land Grants at Biloxi.* Gulfport, MS: Cassibry vol. 1, November 1986.

———. *The Ladner Odyssey.* Gulfport, MS: Cassibry, 1987.

Cassirer, Ernst. *The Philosophy of the Enlightenment.* Princeton, NJ: Princeton University Press, 1968.

Caughey, John Walton. *Bernardo de Gálvez in Louisiana, 1776–1783.* Berkeley: University of California Press, 1934.

Chapelle, Howard Irving. *The History of American Sailing Ships.* New York: W.W. Norton & Co., 1935.

Chatterton, E. Keble. *King's Cutters and Smugglers: 1700–1855.* Charleston, SC: BiblioBazaar, 2007.

Chidsey, Donald Barr. *Louisiana Purchase.* New York: Crown Publishers, 1972.

Churchill, R.R., and A.V. Lowe. *The Law of the Sea.* Manchester: Manchester University Press, 1983.

City Archives, New Orleans Public Library (available to registered researchers by appointment).

Cobban, Alfred. *The Eighteenth Century: Europe in the Age of Enlightenment.* New York: McGraw-Hill, 1969.

Coe, Charles H., and Charlton W. Tebeau. *Red Patriots: The Story of the Seminoles.* Bicentennial Floridiana Facsimile Series. Gainesville: University Presses of Florida, 1974.

Coghlan, Ronan. *The Encyclopaedia of Arthurian Legends.* Rockport, MA: Element Books, 1992.

Collin, Rima, and Richard H. Collin. *The New Orleans Cookbook: Creole, Cajun, and Louisiana French Recipes Past and Present.* New York: Knopf, 1975.

Collins, R. *New Orleans Jazz: A Revised History: The Development of American Music from the Origin to the Big Bands.* New York: Vantage Press, 1996.

Connett, Eugene V. *Wildfowling in the Mississippi Flyway.* New York: Van Nostrand, 1949.

Cooke, Lawrence S. *Lighting in America: From Colonial Rushlights to Victorian Chandeliers.* New York: Main Street/Universe Books, 1976.

Cox, Isaac J. *The West Florida Controversy, 1798–1813.* Baltimore: The Johns Hopkins Press, 1918.

Cox, Sam. *I Say Tomayto, You Say Tomahto...* http://www.landscapeimagery.com/tomato.html (accessed August 2004).

Crompton, Samuel Willard, and Michael J. Rhein. *The Ultimate Book of Lighthouses: History, Legend, Lore, Design, Technology, Romance.* San Diego, CA: Thunder Bay Press, 2000.

Daigle, Jules. *Cajun-Self Taught.* Ville Platte, LA: Swallow Publishing, 1992.

Daly, Ediciones. *Rejas, Balcones y Cercas—Grilles, Balconies & Fences.* Málaga, Spain: Ediciones Daly, 1997.

Davis, Edwin Adams. *Louisiana the Pelican State.* Baton Rouge: Louisiana State University Press, 1959.

Davis, William C. *The Pirates Laffite: The Treacherous World of the Corsairs of the Gulf.* Orlando, FL: Harcourt, 2005.

Dawson, Joseph G. *The Louisiana Governors: From Iberville to Edwards.* Baton Rouge: Louisiana State University Press, 1990.

Defoe, Daniel, Charles Johnson, and Manuel Schonhorn. *A General History of the Pyrates.* Columbia: University of South Carolina Press, 1972.

DeHart, Jess, and Melanie DeHart. *Creoles & Cajuns: The Two Faces of French Louisiana.* Folsom, LA: Hamlet House, 1999.

Deiler, J. Hanno. *The Settlement of the German Coast of Louisiana and the Creoles of German Descent.* Baltimore: Genealogical Publishing, 1969.

De la Harpe, Bernard. *The Historical Journal of the Establishment of the French in Louisiana.* Lafayette: University of Southwestern Louisiana, 1971.

De Platt, Lyman. *Hispanic Surnames and Family History.* Baltimore: Genealogical Publishing, 1996.

De Sedella, Antoine. *The Letters of Padre Antonio de Sedella, Cura of the San Luis Cathedral, New Orleans.* New Orleans: Survey of Federal Archives in Louisiana, 1940.

De Unamuno, Miguel. *Tragic Sense of Life.* New York: Dover Publications, 1954.

De Ville, Winston. *Louisiana Colonials.* Mobile, AL: W. De Ville, 1719.

DeVoto, Bernard, ed. *The Journals of Lewis and Clark.* Boston: Houghton Mifflin, 1953.

Dibble, Ernest F. *William H. Chase: Gulf Coast Fort Builder.* Wilmington, DE: Gulf Coast Collection, 1978.

Doughty, Sir Arthur G. *The Acadian Exiles; A Chronicle of the Land of Evangeline.* Toronto: Glasgow, Brook & Co., 1916.

Drago, Harry Sinclair. *The Steamboaters, from the Early Side-wheelers to the Big Packets.* New York: Dodd, Mead, 1967.

Duffy, John. *Epidemics in Colonial America.* Baton Rouge: Louisiana State University Press, 1979.

Du Pratz, Le Page. *Histoire de la Louisiane.* Paris: De Bure, l'aine, 1758.

Duus, Masayo. *Unlikely Liberators: The Men of the 100th and 442nd.* Honolulu: University of Hawaii Press, 1987.

Earle, Alice Morse. *Two Centuries of Costume in America.* New York: Macmillan, 1903.

Eastman Kodak Company. *History of Kodak Cameras.* Rochester, NY: Photographic Products Group, Eastman Kodak, 1987.

Edwards, John. *The Spain of the Catholic Monarchs, 1474–1520.* Malden, MA: Blackwell Publishers, 2000.

Ellis, Dan. *Lighthouses and Islands of the Gulf.* Pass Christian, MS: Ellis, 2000.

_____. "The Mexican Gulf Hotel, a Grand Winter Hotel on Davis Avenue," *Hotels Past.* http://hotels.passchristian.net/mexican_gulf_hotel.htm (accessed June 2007).

_____. *Mississippi Gulf Coast—A Panorama of History and Culture.* Pass Christian, MS: Ellis, 1998.

_____. *Pass Christian Discovered.* Pass Christian, MS: Ellis, 1997.

Ernst Cassirer. *The Philosophy of the Enlightenment.* Princeton, NJ: Princeton University Press, 1968.

Evans, Eli N. *Judah P. Benjamin, the Jewish Confederate.* New York: Free Press, 1988.

Fahey, the Rev. Leo F. *Bay St. Louis, a History of Hancock County's Catholic Institutions.* Bay St. Louis, MS: The Sea Coast Echo, 1942.

Falkowski, William G. *Polka History 101.* Buffalo, NY: Polish Community Center, 1980.

Farmer, Fannie Merritt. *The 1896 Boston Cooking-School Cookbook.* Hardcover, September 1997 (reproduction).

Field, Martha Reinhard Smallwood. *The Story of the Old French Market, New Orleans.* New Orleans: The New Orleans Coffee Co., 1916.

Fitton, Mary. *Málaga: The Biography of a City.* London: Allen and Unwin, 1971.

Flint, Willard. "A History of U.S. Lightships." United States Coast Guard: 1989.

Forbes, Gerald. "The Origin of the Seminole Indians." *Oklahoma Historical Society's Chronicles of Oklahoma* 15, no. 1 (March 1937): 102–108.

Forman, Henry Chandlee. *The Architecture of the Old South: The Medieval Style, 1585–1850.* Cambridge, MA: Harvard University Press, 1948.

François, Raymond E. *Ye Yaille, Chere: Traditional Cajun Dance Music.* Lafayette, LA: Thunderstone Press, 1990.

Franklin, John Hope. *The Emancipation Proclamation.* Garden City, NY: Doubleday, 1963.

Frothingham, Alice Wilson. *Talavera Pottery.* New York: Hispanic Society of America, 1944.

_____. *Tile Panels of Spain, 1500–1650.* New York: Hispanic Society of America, 1969.

Furneaux, Rupert. *The Seven Years War.* London: Hart-Davis MacGibbon, 1973.

Gallego, José Andrés. *Esquilache y el Pan, 1766.* New Orleans: University Press of the South, 1996.

Gaston, Mary Frank. *The Collectors Encyclopedia of Flow Blue China.* Paducah, KY: Collector Books, 1983.

Gayarré, Charles. *History of Louisiana.* New York: W.J. Widdleton, 1867.

Geerligs, H.C. Prinsen, and R.J. Geerligs. *The World Cane Sugar Industry, Past and Present.* Manchester, England: Altrincham, 1912.

George, David. *The Flamenco Guitar; From Its Birth in the Hands of the Guitarrero to Its Ultimate Celebration in the Hands of the Flamenco Guitarist.* Madrid: Society of Spanish Studies, 1969.

Gies, Frances, and Joseph Gies. *Daily Life in Medieval Times: A Vivid, Detailed Account of Birth, Marriage, and Death; Food, Clothing, and Housing; Love and Labor, in the Middle Ages.* New York: Black Dog & Leventhal Publishers, 1999.

Gillis, Norman E. *Biographical and Historical Memoirs of Mississippi.* Chicago: Goodspeed Pub. Co., 1891.

Giordano, Ralph G. *Social Dancing in America: A History and Reference*. Westport, CT: Greenwood Press, 2007.

Gleig, the Rev. G.R. *Campaigns of the British Army at Washington and New Orleans, 1814 and 1815*. London: John Murray, 1821.

Glenn, Richard F. *Juan de la Cueva*. New York: Twayne Publishers, 1973.

González-Doria, Fernando, and Félix Vaquerizo Romero. *Diccionario Heráldico y Nobiliario*. San Fernando de Henares, Madrid: Trigo Ediciones, 2000.

González Sánchez, Vidal. *Archivo Histórico Diocesano de Málaga: Catálogo General* (Historical Archives of the Diocese of Malaga: General Catalogue). Córdoba: Publicaciones Obra Social y Cultrual CajaSur, 1998.

Green, J.H. *Gambling Unmasked! or, The Personal Experience of J.H. Green, the Reformed Gambler; Designed as a Warning to the Young Men of This Country*. Philadelphia: G.B. Zieber & Co., 1847.

Greenwell, Dale. *Twelve Flags: Triumphs and Tragedies*. Ocean Springs, MS: Greenwell, 1968.

Grove, George, and Stanley Sadie. *The New Grove Dictionary of Music and Musicians*. London: Macmillan Publishers, 1980.

Gruber, Alain Charles. *Silverware*. New York: Rizzoli, 1982.

Gutierrez, C. Paige. *The Mississippi Coast and Its People—A History for Students*. Book 8: Marine Discovery Series, 1987. Produced by C. Paige Gutierrez and the Department of Wildlife Conservation, Bureau of Marine Resources.

Haddon, Alfred Cort. *The Study of Man*. New York: G.P. Putnam's Sons, 1898.

Hamilton, Peter J. *The Founding of Mobile, 1702–1718, Studies in the History of the First Capital of the Province of Louisiana*. Mobile, AL: Colonial Mobile Book Shop, 1946.

Harper, Charise Mericle. *Imaginative Inventions: The Who, What, Where, When, and Why of Roller Skates, Potato Chips, Marbles, and Pie and More!* Boston: Little Brown, 2001.

Harris, Patricia, and David Lyon. *Andalucía and the Costa del Sol: The Best of Andalucía's Mediterranean Coastline plus Gibralter, the Vibrant Moorish Cities of Granada, Cordóba and Sevilla, the White Villages of the Interior and the Montain Villages of the Sierra Nevada*. Guilford, CT: Globe Pequot Press, 2003.

Harvey, John Hooper. *The Cathedrals of Spain*. London: Batsford, 1957.

Hasse, Ronald W. *Classic Cracker: Florida's Wood-frame Vernacular Architecture*. China: Pineapple Press, 1992.

Hattendorf, John B. *England in the War of the Spanish Succession: A Study of the English View and Conduct of Grand Strategy, 1702–1712*. Modern European History. New York: Garland Pub., 1987.

Hauck, Philomena. *Bienville: Father of Louisiana*. Lafayette: Center for Louisiana Studies, University of Southwestern Louisiana, 1998.

Haupt, Shirley. *Beacons in the Night: Lighthouses of the Gulf*. Lake Charles, LA: Port of Lake Charles, 1999.

Heaney, Jane Frances. *A Century of Pioneering: A History of the Ursuline Nuns in New Orleans, 1727–1827*. New Orleans: Ursuline Sisters of New Orleans, Louisiana, 1993.

Heart Pine Reserve, Specialists in Antique Heart Pine. "America's Love of Wood," http://heartpinereserve.com/heritage_pg.html (accessed June 2007).

Hebbert, F.J. *Soldier of France: Sébastien le Prestre de Vauban, 1633–1707*. New York: P. Lang, 1990.

Hebert, Tim. *Acadian-Cajun Genealogy & History*, http://www.acadian-cajun.com/gencaj18.htm (accessed August 1999).

Hechtlinger, Adelaide. *American Quilts, Quilting, and Patchwork: The Complete Book of History, Technique & Design*. New York: Galahad Books, 1974.

Herman, Michael. *Folk Dances for All*. New York: Barnes & Noble, 1947.

Herr, Richard. *An Historical Essay on Modern Spain*. Berkeley: University of California Press, 1971.

Hickey, Donald R. *The War of 1812: A Forgotten Conflict*. Urbana: University of Illinois Press, 1989.

Hickman, Nollie W. *Mississippi Harvest: Lumbering in the Longleaf Pine Belt, 1840–1915*. Jackson: University Press of Mississippi, 2009.

Howe, Tony. "Growth of the Lumber Industry, (1840–1930)," *Mississippi History Now* (an online publication of the Mississippi Historical Society), http://mshistory.k12.ms.us/articles/171/growth-of-the-lumber-industry-1840-to-1930 (accessed May 2003).

Huber, Leonard Victor, Mary Louise Christovich, Peggy McDowell, Betsy Swanson, Edith Elliott Long, Bernard Lemann, and Doyle Gertjejansen. *New Orleans Architecture, Volume III: The Cemeteries*. Gretna, LA: Pelican Pub. Co., 2004.

Hughes, Glenn. *Longleaf Pine in Mississippi*. Publication 2201, Extension Service of Mississippi State University, Cooperating with U.S. Department of Agriculture. Published in Furtherance of Acts of Congress, May 8 and June 30, 1914.

Hull, Anthony H. *Charles III and the Revival of Spain*. Washington, D.C.: University Press of America, 1980.

Husley, Val. *Biloxi: 300 Years*. Virginia Beach, VA: Donning Company/Publishers, 1998.

Jablow, Valerie. "The Object at Hand." *Smithsonian* 31, no. 8 (November 2000).

Johnson, Cecil. *British West Florida, 1763–1783*. New Haven, CT: Yale University Press, 1943.

Kalman, Bobbie. *Early Health and Medicine. The Early Settler Life Series*. New York: Crabtree Publishing Company, 1991.

Kaufman, William Irving, and Mary Ursula Cooper. *The Art of Creole Cookery*. Garden City, NY: Doubleday, 1962.

Keen, George. *Andalucia*. Lincolnwood, IL: Passport Books, 1993.

Kennedy, Hugh. *Muslim Spain and Portugal: A Political History of al-Andalus*. New York: Longman, 1996.

Kern, Robert. *The Regions of Spain: A Reference Guide to History and Culture*. Westport, CT: Greenwood Press, 1995.

Kelly, Denis. *Creole and Cajun Cooking*. Vancouver: Raincoast Books, 1993.

Kimmerle, Beth. *Candy: The Sweet History*. Portland, OR: Collectors Press, 2003.

Klein, Julius. *The Mesta: A Study in Spanish Economic History, 1273–1836*. Cambridge, MA: Harvard University Press, 1920.

Kniffen, Fred. *Folk Housing: Key to Diffusion*. Baton Rouge, LA: Association of American Geographers, 1965.

Koker, Hubert L. "Spanish Governor Bernardo de Gálvez Salvaged the Gulf Coast for the Future United States." *Military History*, 1993.

Krythe, Maymie Richardson. *All about American Holidays*. New York: Harper and Row, 1962.

Kubler, George, and Martin Sebastian Soria. *Art and Architecture in Spain and Portugal and Their American Dominions, 1500 to 1800*. Baltimore: Penguin Books, 1959.

Ladnier, Randall. *Jean Baptiste and Henriette*. Sarasota, FL: Ladnier, 1995.

Lafitte, Jean. *The Journal of Jean Laffite: The Privateer-Patriot's Own Story*. New York: Vantage Press, 1958.

———. *The Memoirs of Jean Laffite from Le Journal de Jean Laffite*. Translated by Gene Marshall. Philadelphia: Xlibris, 1999.

Latour, Arsène Lacarrière. *Historical Memoir of the War in West Florida and Louisiana in 1814–1815*. Philadelphia: John Conrad, 1816.

Laws, Bill. *Traditional Houses of Rural Spain*. New York: Abbeville Press, 1995.

Le Bois, Ruby. *Cajun: The Authentic Taste of Spicy Louisiana Cooking*. London: Southwater, 2004.

Ledet, Wilton Paul. *The History of the City of Carrollton*. n.p., 1938.

Lehner, Ernst, and Johanna Lehner. *Folklore and Odysseys of Food and Medicinal Plants*. New York: Tudor Publishing, 1962.

Lemish, Michael G. *War Dogs: A History of Loyalty and Heroism*. Washington, D.C.: Brassey's, 1999.

Lewis, Meriwether, William Clark, and Bernard Augustine De Voto. *The Journals of Lewis and Clark*. Boston: Houghton Mifflin, 1953.

Lewy, Guenter. "Were American Indians the Victims of Genocide?" *George Mason University's History News Network*, http://hnn.us/articles/7302.html (accessed January 2005).

Lhamon, W.T. *Jump Jim Crow: Lost Plays, Lyrics, and Street Prose of the First Atlantic Popular Culture*. Cambridge, MA: Harvard University Press, 2003.

Looney, Ben Earl. *Cajun Country*. Lafayette: University of Southwestern Louisiana Press, 1974.

Lossky, Andrew. *The Nature of Political Power According to Louis XIV*. New York: Doubleday & Company, 1967.

LSUAgCenter, *A Brief History of Crawfish Farming in Louisiana*, http://www.lsuagcenter.com/en/our_offices/research_stations/Aquaculture/Features/extension/Classroom_Resources/History+of+Crawfish+Aquaculture+in+Louisiana.htm (accessed March 2009).

Manuel, Frank Edward. *The Enlightenment*. Englewood Cliffs, NJ: Prentice-Hall, 1965.

Martin, François-Xavier. *The History of Louisiana from the Earliest Period*. New Orleans: J.A. Gresham, 1882.

Martin, Malachi. *The Jesuits: The Society of Jesus and the Betrayal of the Roman Catholic Church*. New York: Linden Press, Simon & Schuster, 1987.

Mason, I.L. *A World Dictionary of Livestock Breeds, Types, and Varieties*. Wallingford, Oxon, UK: CAB International, 1996.

Mayer, Robert G. *Embalming: History, Theory & Practice*. New York: McGraw-Hill, 2000.

McCormack, John. *One Million Mercenaries: Swiss Soldiers in the Armies of the World*. London: L. Cooper, 1993.

McDermott, John Francis. *The Spanish in the Mississippi Valley, 1762–1804*. Urbana: University of Illinois Press, 1974.

McLemore, R.A. *A History of Mississippi*. Jackson: University and College Press of Mississippi, 1973.

McWilliams, Richebourg Gaillard. *Fleur de Lys and Calumet Being the Pénicaut Narrative of French Adventure in Louisiana*. Baton Rouge: Louisiana State University Press, 1953.

Melville, David. *An Expose of Facts, Respectfully Submitted to the Government and Citizens of the United States, Relating to the Conduct of Winslow Lewis, of Boston Superintendent for Lighting the United States' Light Houses, an Accredited Agent of the Treasury Department: Addressed to the Hon. the Secretary of the Treasury*. Providence, RI: Miller & Hutchens, 1819.

Millar, John Fitzhugh. *Country Dances of Colonial America*. Williamsburg, VA: Thirteen Colonies Press, 1990.

Millspaugh, Charles F. *American Medicinal Plants: An Illustrated and Descriptive Guide to Plants Indigenous to and Naturalized in the United States Which Are Used in Medicine*. New York: Dover Publications, 1974.

Morison, Samuel Eliot. *Harrison Gray Otis, 1765–1848: The Urbane Federalist*, 1913, rev. ed. (2 vols. in 1). Boston: Houghton Mifflin, 1969.

Morrison, B.L. *Louisiana's Funeral Customs, Graves & Graveyards*. Gretna, LA: Gulf South Press, 1983.

Morton, Robert A. "Historical Changes in the Mississippi-Alabama Barrier-Island Chain and the Roles of Extreme Storms, Sea Level, and Human Activities," *Journal of Coastal Research* 24, no. 6 (2008): 1587–1600.

Mulroy, Kevin. *Freedom on the Border: The Seminole Maroons in Florida, the Indian Territory, Coahuila, and Texas*. Lubbock: Texas Tech University Press, 2003.

Muñoz, Manuel Flores. *Algámitas*. Algámitas, Spain: Technographic, S.L., 2003.

Murphy, Antoin. *John Law: Economic Theorist and Policymaker*. Oxford: Clarendon Press, 1997.

Naylon, John. *Andalusia*. London: Oxford University Press, 1975.

Newton, Tom. "K-9 History: The Dogs of War!" *A Special Presentation from Hahn's 50th AP K-9, West Germany*, http://community-2.webtv.net/Hahn-50thAP-K9/K9History/ (accessed May 2000).

Nicholson, Susan Brown. *The Encyclopedia of Antique Postcards*. Radnor, PA: Wallace-Homestead, 1994.

Noble, John, Susan Forsyth, and Des Hannigan. *Andalucía*. London: Planet Publications, 2003.

Noel, Charles C. "Madrid: City of the Enlightenment." *History Today* 45 (October 1995).

O'Neill, Charles E., and Marcel Giraud. "A History of French Louisiana: An Essay Review of a History of French Louisiana. Volume One. The Reign of Louis XIV, 1698–1715." Lafayette: Louisiana Historical Association, Summer 1975.

Outland, Robert B. *Tapping the Pines: The Naval Stores Industry in the American South*. Baton Rouge: Louisiana State University Press, 2004.

Pallen, Condé Benoist, John Joseph Wynne, Charles F. Wemyss Brown, Blanche M. Kelly, and Andrew A. MacErlean. *The New Catholic Dictionary. A Complete Work of Reference on Every Subject ... of the Church*. London, 1929.

Payne, William H. *An Introduction to the Game of Draughts. Containing Fifty Select Games, Together with Many Critical Situations for Drawn Games, Won Games, and Fine Strokes. The Whole Designed for the Instruction of Young Players*. London: Payne, 1756.

Perry, Catherine. *A History of Playing Cards and a Bibliography of Cards and Gaming*. New York: Dover Publications, 1966.

Petrie, Sir Charles. *King Charles III of Spain; An Enlightened Despot*. New York: J. Day, 1971.

Phelps, Albert. *Louisiana*. New York: Houghton, Mifflin, 1905.

Picard, Marc. *The Origins and Development of French-Canadian Family Names*. Louvain: International Centre of Onomastics, 2003.

Pickett, Albert James. *History of Alabama, Chapter XVI, Horrible Death of Beaudrot and the Swiss Soldiers*. Charleston: Walker and James, 1851.

Pilgrim, David. "Who Was Jim Crow." Museum of Racist Memorabilia. Big Rapids, MI: Ferris State University, 2000, http://www.ferris.edu/jimcrow/who.htm (accessed May 2001).

Pinal, Francisco Aguilar. *Introduccion al Siglo XVIII.* Madrid: Juncar, 1991.
Pitts, J.R.S. *Life and Confession of the Noted Outlaw, James Copeland.* Jackson: University Press of Mississippi, 1970.
Plauche, Leda H. *Story of the Praline.* New Orleans: Green Orchid, 1900.
Pollack, Peter. *The Picture History of Photography.* New York: Harry N. Abrams, 1969.
Proulx, Gilles. *Between France and New France: Life Aboard the Tall Sailing Ships.* Toronto: Dundurn Press Limited, 1984.
Quave, Pierre. *Pierre Quave Store Journal (1857–1862).* Biloxi, MS: Archives of the Biloxi Public Library.
Quintana, Bertha B., and Lois Gray Floyd. *!Qué Gitano! Gypsies of Southern Spain.* New York: Holt, Rinehart and Winston, 1971.
Ramsay, Jack C., Jr. *Jean Laffite, Prince of Pirates.* Austin, TX: Eakin Press, 1996.
Rea, Robert Right. *Pensacola under the British, 1763–1781.* Pensacola, FL: Fiesta of Five Flags, 1974.
Read, Jan. *The Moors in Spain and Portugal.* Totowa, NJ: Rowman and Littlefield, 1975.
Reeser, Eduard. *The History of the Waltz.* Stockholm: Continental Book Co., 1947.
Reidmer, F.C. *Scuppernong and Other Muscadine Grapes: Origin and Importance.* West Raleigh: North Carolina Agricultural Experiment Station of the College of Agriculture and Mechanic Arts, 1909.
Richman, Irving Berdine, and Herbert Eugene Bolton. *The Spanish Conquerors: A Chronicle of the Dawn of Empire Overseas.* New Haven, CT: Yale University Press, 1919.
Romans, Bernard. *A Concise Natural History of East and West Florida.* New Orleans: Pelican Publishing, 1961. Originally published in 1775.
Rowland, Dunbar. *Encyclopedia of Mississippi History.* Vol 1. Madison, WS: Brant, 1907.
Rushton, William Faulkner. *The Cajuns: From Acadia to Louisiana.* New York: Farrar Straus Giroux, 1979.
Santos, Richard G. *Origin of Spanish Names: Cómo te Llamos y por que te Llamas Asi.* San Antonio, TX: R.G. Santos, 1981.
Shephard, Sue. *Pickled, Potted, and Canned: How the Art and Science of Food Preserving Changed the World.* New York: Simon & Schuster, 2000.
Sherrow, Victoria. *Encyclopedia of Hair: A Cultural History.* Westport, CT: Greenwood Press, 2006.
Shoumatoff, Alex. *The Mountain of Names: A History of the Human Family.* New York: Simon and Schuster, 1985.
Simanek, Donald. "Physic Lecture Demonstrations," http://www.lhup.edu/~dsimanek/scenario/demos.htm (accessed June 2007).
Simmons, Amelia. *American Cookery.* Hartford, CT: Hudson & Goodwin, 1796.
Skinner, John. *Chicken Breeds and Varieties.* Madison: University of Wisconsin, 1978.
Smith, Elsdon C. *American Surnames.* Philadelphia: Chilton Book Co., 1969.
Sordo, Enrique. *Moorish Spain: Cordoba, Seville, Granada.* New York: Crown Publishers, 1963.
South Coast Corporation. *White Gold: The Story of Sugar.* New Orleans: South Coast Corp., 1936.
Starr, S. Frederick. *Southern Comfort: The Garden District of New Orleans.* New York: Princeton Architectural Press, 1998.
Stuart, William, and Kary Cadmus Davis. *The Potato; Its Culture, Uses, History and Classification.* Philadelphia: J.B. Lippincott, 1937.
Stubbs, William Carter. *Sugar Cane; A Treatise on the History, Botany & Agriculture of Sugar Cane.* New Orleans: State Bureau of Agriculture & Immigration, 1897.
Sullivan, Charles L. *Hurricanes of the Mississippi Gulf Coast: Three Centuries of Destruction.* Perkinston: Mississippi Gulf Coast Community College Foundation, 2009.
_____. *The Mississippi Gulf Coast: Portrait of a People.* Northridge, CA: Windsor Publications, 1985.
Sullivan, Charles L., and Murella Hebert Powell. *The Mississippi Gulf Coast—Portrait of a People.* Sun Valley, CA: American Historical Press, 1999.
Swell, Barbara. *Log Cabin Cooking.* Asheville, NC: Native Ground Music, 1996.
Swetman, Glen Lyle, and Glen Robert Swetman. *Biloxi, a Banker's Daybook.* Baltimore: Gateway Press, 1994.
Takata, Yasuo, and Raymond Nosaka. "The Secret Mission of the Third Platoon, Baker Company." *Puka-Puka Parade,* March–April 1980.
Thompson, James West. *Beauvoir.* Bolling Green, KY: Rivendell Publications, 1984.
Thompson, Ray M. "Cat Island." *Down South,* July–August 1961.
_____. "Isle of Caprice, the Coast's Little Island That Isn't There." *Down South,* May–June 1962.
Thurston, H., and A. Shipman. "The Rosary." *The Catholic Encyclopedia.* New York: Robert Appleton Company, 1912 (retrieved June 2010 from New Advent: http://www.newadvent.org/cathen/13184b.htm).
Thurston, Robert H. *Robert Fulton—His Life and Its Results.* New York: Dodd, Mead, and Company Publishers, 1891.
Tiziani, Julius J. *Origin of Names and Treasured Facts.* Bessemer, MI: Gogebic Range Community Resources workshop, 1960.
Totton, Robin. *Song of the Outcasts: An Introduction to Flamenco.* Portland, OR: Amadeus Press, 2003.
Toynbee, Arnold. *The Industrial Revolution.* Boston: Beacon Press, 1956.
Treat, Payson J. *The National Land System, 1785–1820.* New York: E.B. Treat, 1910.
Ukers, Williams H. *The Romance of Coffee; An Outline History of Coffee and Coffee-drinking through a Thousand Years.* New York: Tea and Coffee Trade Journal, 1948.
United States. "An Act for Adjusting the Claims to Lands, and Establishing Land Offices in the District East of the Island of New Orleans." *The Public Statutes at Large of the United States of America.* Boston: Charles C. Little and James Brown, 1848.
_____. *Biographies of the Mayors of New Orleans.* New Orleans: City Hall Archives, 1939.
United States Agricultural Research Service. Animal Husbandry Research Division. *Breeds of Chickens for Meat and Egg Production.* Washington, D.C.: U.S. Dept. of Agriculture, 1954.
Urofsky, Melvin I. *The Supreme Court Justices: A Biographical Dictionary.* New York: Garland Publishing, 1994.
Van Demark, Harry. "Pirates of the Gulf." *Texas Magazine,* May 1910.
Vogel, Claude L. *The Capuchins in French Louisiana (1722–1766).* Washington, D.C.: Catholic University of America, 1928.
Volo, Dorothy Denneen, and James M. Volo. *Daily Life in Civil War America.* Westport, CT: Greenwood Press, 1998.
Waller, Anna M. *Dogs and National Defense.* Washington, D.C.: Dept. of the Army, Office of the Quartermaster General, 1958.
Walton, Guy. *Louis XIV's Versailles.* Chicago: University of Chicago Press, 1986.
Warren, Harris Gaylord. *The Sword Was Their Passport; A*

History of American Filibustering in the Mexican Revolution. Baton Rouge: Louisiana State University, 1943.

Warwick, Edward. *Early American Dress: The Colonial and Revolutionary Periods.* New York: B. Blom, 1965.

Watson, Bruce. "Science Makes a Better Lighthouse Lens." *Smithsonian* 30, no. 5 (August 1999): 30. Reproduced in Biography Resource Center. Farmington Hills, MI: Thomson Gale, 2005.

Weinberg, Albert Katz. *Manifest Destiny; A Study of Nationalist Expansionism in American History.* Baltimore: John Hopkins Press, 1935.

Welker, Glen. "Oceola, (Black Drink)." *Indigenous Peoples' Literature,* http://www.indigenouspeople.net/osceola.htm (accessed April 1999).

———. "Tuskegee Literature." *Indigenous Peoples' Literature,* http://www.indigenouspeople.net/tuskegee.htm (accessed April 1999).

Westerveld, Bab, Joost Eiffers, and Michael Schuyt. *Cat's Cradles and Other String Figures.* New York: Penguin Books, 1979.

Whatley, Randall P., and Harry Jannise. *Conversational Cajun French I.* Gretna, LA: Pelican Publishing Company, 1978.

Wilbur, C. Keith. *Revolutionary Medicine: 1700–1800.* Chester, CT: Globe Pequot Press, 1980.

Williams, Ian. *Rum: A Social and Sociable History of the Real Spirit of 1776.* New York: Nation Books, 2005.

Wilson, Samuel. *Colonial Fortifications and Military Architecture in the Mississippi Valley.* Urbana: University of Illinois Press, 1965.

Wood, Minter. *Life in New Orleans in the Spanish Period.* New Orleans: Louisiana Historical Society, 1939.

Woods, Benjamin. *The Boston Tea Party.* New York: Oxford University Press, 1964.

Index

Numbers in ***bold italics*** indicate pages with photographs.

abatis 14
Abiaka 81, 82
Abita Springs, Louisiana 153
Acadia 61; Acadiens 61, 62, 87
"An Act for the Relief of H. Gibbes Morgan and Other Co-owners of Cat Island in the Gulf of Mexico" 147
Adair, Cala Susan 154
Adair, Carleton L. 154
Adair, Charles Nathan 154
Adair, Elizabeth Boddie 154
Adair, Joseph Adams 154
Adam, Bidwell 125
Adam, E.J. 125
Adam, E.J., Sr. 125
adosado 158
Africa 61, 64, 87
Alabama 76, 79–81, 84, 143
Alabama (tribe) 80
Alabama and Florida Railroad Company 144
Alaska 124
Alcalá de los Gazules 34
Algameca 157
Algámitas, Spain 33, 101, 102, 104, 156–158, ***159***
Alibamons 19
Alicante 160
alicatado 159
Allons Danser, Colinda 87
Almería ***159***, 160
American black duck 124
American Hotel 75
American Kennel Club 129
American Revolution 139
American Society of Civil Engineers 149
Andalucía 34, 36, 85, 102, 157, ***158, 159***, 161; cattle 85; White Villages of Andalucía 158, ***160***
Andrews, George 113
Anglo-American culture 87
Anglo-Saxons 157
Antebellum Plantation Homes 143
Apperson, Colonel J. W. "Jack" 5, 6
Arabs 157

Aragón ***158***, 160
Arctic polar region 124
Areka 80
Arkansas 79
Arm and Hammer baking soda 65
Army: Corps of Engineers 111; Ground Forces 131, 135, 136; Operations Division 130; War College 131
Arthur, Chester A. 100
Asbury, Herbert 24
Ashley, Lillian 150
Asi-yahola 81
Atlantic Ocean 16, 35, 124
Audubon Association 149
Augeida, P. 113
Aury, Louis-Michel 25, 26, 29
azulejos 160

Back Bay 76, 78
Bahamas 121
Baker, John 44
Baltimore 14
Barataria 25, 26, 37, 39, ***40***
Barataria Bay 23, 26, 27, ***40***
bar-built islands 4, 5, 7
barrier islands 1, 5, 12, 106, 115, 126, 146, 156
Baton Rouge 36, 111, 153
Battle of New Orleans 26, 29, 33, 41, 42, 45, 48, 49, 97–100, 141
Baudin, Mr. 19
Baudrau, Jean Baptiste, II 17, ***18***, 19–20
Baudrau, Magdelaine 17
Baukens, Lazarus 108
Bautista, Isavel 33
Bay of St. Louis 4, 8, 30, 44, 59, 61, 73, 75, 76, 78, 86, 91, 111, 122, 145
Bay St. Louis Gazette 30
Bay St. Louis Hotel 75
Bayonne 23
Bayou Barnard 118
Bayou St. John 22, ***40***, 111
Bayou View subdivision 134
Bazille, Joseph François 19

Beacons in the Night: Lighthouses of the Gulf 107
Beau Rivage Casino 5
Beauvoir 76, 98
Bell, Alexander Graham 45
Belle-Isle, Mr. de 19
Béluche, René 24, 26, 29
Benjamin, Judah Philip 142, 143, 145, 147, 153
Bermuda grass 42
Bermudas 75
Bienville, Jean Baptiste Le Moyne de 8, 10, 15, 61, 64
Bilbo, Jim and Wash 31
Billouart, Louis, chevalier de Kerlerec 15–17, 19, 20
Bills, Captain C. 113
Biloxi ***5***, 8, 9–12, ***40***, 50, 59–61, 75, 91, 93, 104, 112, 113, 128, 132; cemetery ***91, 92, 93, 94, 95***; lighthouse 76
Biloxi House 75
Bishop, Henry Rowley 87
Bishop Chanché *see* Chanché, Father John Mary Joseph
Black Seminoles 81
Blackbeard 22
Board of Trade 146
Boddie, Claudia 151
Boddie, George 117, 125, 151, 154
Boddie, George Robert 150–152, 154
Boddie, Marie 150
Boddie, Nathan 114, 119, 150, 152–154, 156
Boddie, Nathan Van 116, 118, 119, 150, 152–154
Boddie, Patrick Pierce 154
Boddie, Sallie Adams 119, 127, 150, 152
Boddie, Sandra Pierce 154
Boddie, Sarah Ann 154
Boddie family 119, 150, 154–156
bootlegging 121, 122, 123
Borries, Felix 113
Borries, Theodore 113
Bossu, Jean Bernard 19

Boston, Massachusetts 75, 149
Boston Harbor 66
Bourbon Street 24
bousillage 55
Brest 23
British 15, 26, 29, 33, 36, 37, 39, 42, 48, 51, 59, 80, 81, 99, 101, 139, 157; armada 38, 48; fleet 39; government 59; Marines 37; Navy 28, 115; pen tradition 51; ships 37
British-American conflict 36
British-Protestant 61
Brittany 61
Brothers of the Sacred Heart 76
Brown, James 76
Buena Vista Hotel 5
Buffington, Sarah Boddie 119, 150, 152–154
bull roarer 74
Burgundy Wars 16
Buteaux, Rev. Stanislaus 73, 76, 91

caballeros 101
Cable Bridge 122
La Cadie 61
Cadiens 61
Cadiz *159*; port of *35*
café au lait 67
Café du Monde 78
Caillavet, Arbeau 5
cajeu 60
Cajun 24, 61; culture 62; food 64; language 62, 100; music 87; two-step 88
Cake, Dr. Ed 4
California 135, 151
calinda 87
calotte 90
Camelot 157
Cameron, Archie 50, 148
Camp McCoy 132, 133
Camp Rimini at Helena, Montana 130
Camp Shelby 136
The Campaigns of the British Army at Washington and New Orleans 45
Campillos, Spain 157, *159*
Campomanes, Pedro Rodriguez de 103
Canada 15, 124; Canadians 9
cane syrup 66
Canton, Georgia 154
Capone, Alphonse Gabriel, "Al" 121; Capone's boats 123
Capuchins 34; monk 105
Carco, Jean Baptiste 59
Caribbean Islands 85
caringa 87
Caro, José 139
Carrollton 143; railroad 143
Cartagena, Colombia 22, 23; flag 22, 25
Carter, Hodding 98
Casa Flores 121, *122*
Casino Hotel Company, Inc. 151, 152
Casteel, H.H. 151
Cat Island lawsuit 153
Cat Island Development Company 118, 150, 151

Cat Island lighthouse *2, 108, 109*, 111–114, *113*, 142
Catalina Island 151
Catholicism 46, 47, 73, 80; Catholic Church 73, 91, 103; Counter-Reformation 34; Mission Church 73; school 78
Catlin, George 82
Cat's Cradle 73
caveau *94*
Ceasar, Harry I. 129
Celeste 48
central flyway 124
Cervantes 23
Champ *132*
Chancery Court of Harrison County 148
Chanché, Father John Mary Joseph 73
Chandeleur Islands 2, 5, *40*, 112, 123
Chapeau, Captain 8
Charles Adams' house 144
Chase, William H. 143, 144
Chattahoochee River 19
Chattanooga 144
chaudière 67
Chef Menteur 30, 144
Cheniere Caminada 23
Cherokee 79, 80, 82
Chicago 121
Chicasaw 39, 59, 79–81
chickee huts 82, *83*
Chicora 113
chicory 67
Chighnizola 24, 29
"The Chimneys" *52*, 59, 76, 86
chinked 55
chippers 117
chitlins 65
chitterlings 65
Choctaw Indians 16, 39, 59, 64, 79–81
Chotard, Bernard 126
chouc-poulon 86
Christianity 47, 79; Christ 94; Christians 46
Christian's Pass 22
Christiansted, St. Croix, Virgin Islands 142
Christmas 74
Church of England 73
cimarron 80
Cincinnati, Ohio 144
circular saw 118
La Citadelle 14
cities of the dead 93
Civil War 4, 58, 68, 70, 75, 76, 90, 108, 112, 132, 144, 146, 147, 149
Claiborne, William C.C. 25, 28
"Clari" 88
Clarice, J. 113
Clarisse, Tom 113
Clark, Gage 126
Clower, Joseph 59
The Coast Beacon 125
Coast Guard 121, 123, 132, 133
Coast Guard Lighthouse 156
Coates, Lt. Col. Robert B. Coates 132

Colbert, Cala Boddie 154
Colbert, Sanders Whitworth 154
Collector of Customs of the Port of New Orleans 147
Colmer, U.S. Representative William 153
Colonel Jack *see* Apperson, Colonel J. W. "Jack"
Columbus, Christopher 66
Combs, Adeline 117
commissioner of the revenue 106
Company of the West 11
Confederate: forces 76; Navy 144; soldier 147
Confederate States Light House Bureau 109, 112
Congo Square 87
contra dance 88
Coosa Indians 80
Coosa River 80
Copeland, James 30, 31, *32*, 120, 123
Coppinger, Polly 81
Cordoba, Spain 157, *159*
Costa del Sol 33, 157
Coto Doñana 34, 35
Cotton Exchange *see* New Orleans Cotton Exchange
cottonade 69, 70
Couidot, Lewis 59
Council of War 19
Coushatta 80
Coweta 19, 80
Cracker style 51; houses 52
Craps 74
crawfish 65
Creek Confederacy *see* Creek Indians
Creek Indians 59, 79–82; Creek federation 79–81
Creole 24, 50, 51; architecture 50; Criolles 61; people 61, 64, 90
the Creole 61
Criolles *see* Creole
Crump, Nannie Mayes 98, 99
Cuba 26, 75, 120
Cuevas, Bridget 38, 98
Cuevas, Catherine Garriga *ix*, 29, 30
Cuevas, Concepcion *161*
Cuevas, Don Pedro de 101–103, 158
Cuevas, Don Pedro Martin Lopez 33, 35, 101, 102
Cuevas, Euphrosine 86
Cuevas, Francisca *161*
Cuevas, Francois 48
Cuevas, Helene 38, 48
Cuevas, Henriette Pauline 46, 47
Cuevas, James 61, 85–88, 98, 103–105
Cuevas, Jean 99
Cuevas, John Joseph 48
Cuevas, Juan de 17, 23, 31–38, 41–43, 45–49, 59, 61, 62, 68, 70, 73, 76, 78, 84, 85, 89, 90, 92, *93*, 95–101, 102, 104, 107, 109, 110, 118, 127, 137, 139–142, 145–149, 153–155, 157, 158, 162
Cuevas, Marie Anastasia 91

Cuevas, Pauline 31
Cuevas, Pierre "Perrique" 78, 104, 153
Cuevas, Ramon 4, 30, 31, 61, 85, 96, 105, 106, 109–112, 142, 145
Cuevas, William 118
Cuevas family 13, 30–32, 34, 35, 37, 44–46, 48, 50, 53, 55, 64, 66, 73, 78–80, 84–6, 89, 95, 98, 102, 103, 115, 120, 125, 141, 143, 145, 146, 148, 153, 154, 156–158; beef 37; children 61, 66, 100, 142; era 49, 73, 75, 76, 78, 96, 99, 105, 112, 124; family in Spain 104, *160*, *161*, 162; garden 65; grant 139; heirs 153; home *2*, *4*, 22, 34, 45, 47, 49, 50, *51*, 53, 54, 69, 71, 86, 89, 91, 99, 106, 113, 118, 127, 140, 155, 156, 157, 161; land in Spain 102, *160*, *161*; vault *92*, *93*, *94*
Cuevas Lumber Company 118
Cup and Saucer 74
curé of St. Louis Cathedral 104, 105
Cusseta 19, 80
customs collector in New Orleans 107
Czech Republic 88

The Daily Herald 98, 106, 151
The Daily Picayune 146
Dallas, Mississippi 152
Dameron, George B. 59
Dauphin Island 1, 10, 11, 17, *40*
Davis, Bette 144
Davis, Jefferson 142
Davis Bayou 121
Daytona Beach 121
Deer Island *40*, 138
Dejean, P.J. 113
Delamare, J.C. 113
Delaware River 61
Del Castle 121, *122*
DeLisle 118
Depression 127
Descartes 102
Detroit Publishing Company 50
Dia de los Tres Reyes 74
Diaz 62
D'Iberville 76; *see also* Reno, Remy
Diderot 102
Digest of the Reported Decisions of the Superior Courts in the Territory of Orleans and State of Louisiana 142
Dog Key *5*, 6
dog trot houses *52*, 53
dogs: donated *131*; training on Cat Island *133*, *134*
Dogs for Defense 129, 130
Don (title) 102
Don Quixote 23
Down South Magazine 98
drinking water 4
Dugan, Mister Thomas Smithfield 146
Duggan, Edith 145
Duggan, F.F. 145
Duggan, Isabel 145
Duggan, J.H. 145
Duggan, J.H., Jr. 145

Duggan, John 113
Duggan, Lillian 145
Duggan, Louise 145, 146
Duggan, Miriam 145
Duggan, P.R. 145
Duggan, T.J. 145, 147
Duggan family 145–148
Duret, Diequir 59
Duroux, Captain 16–19, 21
Dutch 51
Dutcher, William 149

Earlanger, Arlene 129
East and West Florida 138
East Coast crime syndicate 121
East Feliciana Parish 146
Eastern Bohemia 88
Eastman's Business School 146
Eaton, Barney 125
Edgewater Hotel 152
Edinburgh Magazine 45
Edison, Thomas 45
828th Signal Pigeon Replacement Company 136
1846 hurricane 111
1876 Centennial Exposition in Philadelphia 144
El Peñón (The Rock) 157
England: colonies 81; English people 8, 10, 16, 22, 34, 61, 96, 138–140; language 96; privateers 16
enlightened monarchs 103
Enlightenment 102
Epiphany 74
Escatawpa (river) 118
esparto mat *160*
Eubanks, Jerry 156
Europe 10, 11, 34, 55; Europeans 22, 80
Everglades 81, 84
Everitt, Enoch 75
Expulsion of 1755 62

factors 116
"Father of the Coast Boom" 152
Fatio, Felipé 26
Fayard, Joseph 113
Fayard, Louis 91, 92
FBI 136
Ferris, Jacob 42–44, 48, 100
Fifth Auditor and Acting Commissioner of the Revenue 110
filé powder 64
filibusters 9
Fireman's Charitable & Benevolent Association 149
first Isthmian Canal Commission (1904) 149
First Seminole War (1817–1818) 81
Fisher, Carl 152
Fitch, John 61
Five Civilized Tribes 79
flatboats 60
Flemish 51
Florida 31, 35, 54, 57, 75, 80, 81, 84, 104, 121, 156
Floridas 139
flow blue 68
Flower, Adele McCall 145, 146

Flower, Marian 145, 146
Flower, Walter Chew 146
flyways 124
Foote, George M. 151
forbidden dance 88
Ford Magazine 98
Forest and Stream 149
Fort Barancas 156
Fort Hudson 146
fort in Pensacola 104
Fort Louis 10
Fort Massachusetts 132
Fort Maurepas 9, 10–*14*
Fort McHenry 14
Fort Moultrie 82
Fort Petite Coquilles 37
Fort Pickens State Park 156
Fort Pike 30
Fort Pillow, Tennessee 144
Fort Redoubt 156
Fort Robinson, Nebraska 129
Fort St. Miguel 35
Fort San Carlos 156
Fort Ticonderoga 14
Fort Toulouse 19
forts at Rigolets, Chef Menteur, Bienvenue and the Bayou Dupre 144
fraises 14
France 4, 7–13, 15–17, 19, 20, 22, 23, 36, 59, 61, 62, 75, 87, 129, 138, 139; crown 138; French people 34, 51; government 138; language 96; Navy 15, 26; post in Mobile 17; rule 73; settlers 56, 88, 138 ; smugglers 26; soldiers 12, 16
Franciscans 34
Franco-Dutch War 8, 11
Frank's Island lighthouse 108
French-Catholic: Acadians 61; culture 61
French Crown 138
French Louisiana 23
French Quarter 21, 51, 92, 105
French Revolution 11, 70
French wheel *20*
Freret, James Peter 143, 145, 147
Freret, William 144, 145, 147
Freret Cotton Press Company 144
Fresnel, Augustin 108
Fresnel lens 112
Front Royal, Virginia 129, 130
full dovetail notch *55*
Fulmer, James 117
Fulton, Robert 61

Gaither, Colonel Ridgely 135
Galloway, C.O. 116, 150
Galloway, J.B. 150
Galloway, J.F. 116, 150
Galveston 25, 26, 29; pirates 25
Galvez, Bernardo de 29, 35, 36, 59, 139
Galvez-town *see* Galveston
Gambi, Vincent 24, 29
Game and Fish Commission 4
Garden District of New Orleans 146

Garden of Eden 11
Garoza, Juan de la Cueva de *103*
Garriga, Caismir "Coco" *xii*
Garriga family 120
Gayarré, Charles Etienne 11
Gem City of the Mississippi Gulf Coast 75; *see also* Biloxi
General Sterling Price 144
George II 62
George, James Z. 150
Georgia 19, 31, 80–82
Gerard, Father Antoine Paul 73
Germany 61; German people 129
Giles, Ella A. 2
Giron, Diego de 102
glacis 14
glass marbles 74
Gleig, Lt. George Robert 45–47, 49
Gleig's book 48
God 47
goélette 60
golden age of postcards 50
Goldsby, Nellie 121
Good Scotch Point *2*, 31, 123
Goose Point 1, *2*, 37, 86, 124, 155
Goose Point Tarpon Club *2*, 124–128, *127*, 152
Granada, Spain 34, 157, *159*
Grand Isle 23, 112
Grand Terre 23–29
Graveline 17; *see also* Baudrau, Jean Baptiste, II
Great Britain 41, 138, 142; *see also* England
Great Sand Hill 1, *2*, *3*, 4, 13, 54
Great Southern Hotel 144, 151
Greeks 129
Green Oaks Hotel 75
Greenbergs 47
Greenland 124
Greenwood Cemetery 149
Gregorian calendar 74
Gualdalquivir 35
Guadeloupe Hidalgo Treaty 139
Guardia, Pierre 86
Guidry, Oran "Doc" 87
Guinea 87
Gulf and Ship Island Railroad 125
Gulf Coast 4, 8, 11, 13, 31, 32, 48, 50, 55, 59–62, 64, 72, 75, 76, 78, 88, 94, 98, 99, 105, 106, 109, 112, 118, 128, 133, 138, 142, 146, 149, 156, 157; *see also* Mississippi Gulf Coast
Gulf Coast Country 98
Gulf Coast Research Laboratory 4
Gulf Islands National Seashore 4, 155, 156
Gulf of Cádiz 34
Gulf of Mexico 16, 18, 22–26, 29, 33, 37, 39, 42, 44, 49, 54, 56, 65, 79, 82, 97, 107, 109, 114, 121, 123–126, 132, 134, 138
Gulfport 50, 114, 118, 120, 124, 144, 150–152; airport 134; port 116, 118
gumbo 64
Le Grand Derangement 62

Hagalmi 157
half-dovetail notch *55*
Hancock, John 75
Hancock County 75, 116
Hand Catch 74
Handsboro 118
Harriet 113
Harrison, William Henry 75
Harrison County 73, 75, 116
Harrod, Major Benjamin Morgan 98, 115, 116, 148–150, 153
Harvard 149
Harvey, B. 113
Harvey, James 31
Hatchet, Rebecca 150
Hattiesburg 136, 144
Haupt, Shirley 107
Hawaii 132–134
Hazzard 74
heart pine 54, 118
heartwood (lumber) 54, 118
Hebrews 157
Heiderhoff, Frank 13, 14, 29
Hercules 6
Hero of Cat Island 33, 45, 98, 100, 141
"The Hero of Cat Island" (article) 99
Herren, R.C. 151
Hewes, Finley S. 148
hidalgo 101, 102, 158
hidalguia 101
higo de alguno 101
"His Majesty's Honorary Preacher" 34
"historian of Louisiana" 11; *see also* Gayarré, Charles Etienne
Hitchitee 80
Hite, Gordon 121
Hogan, Martin 44
Hoithle Waule 80
Holleman, Bud 113
Holmes County, Mississippi 150
Holy Office in New Orleans 104
"Home, Sweet Home" 87, 88
Horn, A. 113
Horn Island 4, 5, *40*, 111, 156; lighthouse 154
Houmas Plantation house 143
Houn, John 75
Houston, Texas 8
une huche 67
Huet, Marie Henriette 18
Hunt, W. H. "Skeet" 5
Hurricane Camille 26, 154
Hurricane Katrina 92, 112, 154
Hush, Hush, Sweet Charlotte 144

Illinois Central Railroad 142
Indian Removal Act 79, 81, 82
Indiana 121
Indians 16, 17, 19, 39, 82
Industrial Revolution 58
Inquisition 105
Irish: culture 87
ishi semoli 80
"The Island of Barataria" 23
Isle de Dauphin 46
Isle of Capri 6

Isle of Caprice 5, *6*, 7, 126, 128
Italy 61

Jackson, General Andrew 28, 29, 39, 41, 43, 48, 75, 81, 98, 100
Jackson, Mississippi 150
Jackson Avenue 75
Jackson County 31, 73, 75, 116
Jackson Square 78
Jacobs, Mr. Leon R. 121
Jacob's Ladder 74
jambalaya 66
James Copeland Gang 30, 32
Jamestown 115
Japan 129; Japanese people 130, 134; Japanese-Americans 131, 133–135
Jefferson and Lake Pontchartrain Railroad 143
Jefferson Parrish 143
Jensen Brothers Construction Company 121
jeture de laine 69
"Jim Crow" 87
Job, Herbert K. 149
John Law's Mississippi Company 11, 15
Johnny Crapaud 74
Jones, Lieutenant Thomas Catesby 37, 38, 48
Jourdan River 73, 91, 122
Jovellanos, Gaspar Melchor de 103

K-9 Program 129
Keen, Mrs. Jack William 153
Keesler Air Force Base 132
Kentucky 81
Keogh, Joseph F. 153
Kerlerec *see* Billouart, Louis, chevalier de Kerlerec
Kidd, Captain 22
Kiln, Mississippi 73, 91, 120
Kimball, Hunter 4
King Arthur 157
King Charles III 33–37, 101, 103
King Louis XV 17
Kirby, Ephraim 59
Klucer 59
Know Your Coast 99
Know Your State 99
Kohn, Samuel 143
Koran 159
Krebs, Theresa 59

Labatt, Joseph 59
Labbé, Father Guillame 73
Ladner, Claude 59
Ladner, Marianne 59
Ladner, Marie Helene 17, 36–39, 46–48, 65, 66, 68, 90, 91, *93*, 95, 105, 115, 145
Ladner, Maturin 47
Ladner, Nicholas Christian 17, 36, 52, 59, 137–139
Ladner family 36, 47, 142; home 37, *52*, 53
Lafitte, Jean 21–30, *24*, 32, 37, 39, 41, 100, 101, 105, 120, 123
Lafitte, Pierre 23, 25
Lafitte brothers 24, 27, 29

Index

Lafitte/Sedella plan 25
LaFontaine, Ann Maria Francoise 59
Lake Borgne 22, 28, 30, 37–39, **40**, 44, 45, 48, 106
Lake Okeechobee 81
Lake Pontchartrain 10, 30, 38, **40**, 44, 79, 106, 112, 143
Lameuse Road 60
Lamont, Daniel 114
land patent 140
LaRochelle, France 8
Las Alpujarras 34
Laurel, Mississippi 118
The Laurent Millaudon 144
Law, John 11
LeBlanc, Leroy "Happy Fats" 87
Le Brun, Charles 11
Lee, Frederick E. 121
Lee, Georgette Faures 121
Legion of Merit 136
letters of marque 22
Lewis, Capt. Joseph 113
Lewis, Winslow 108, 109
Lewis lens 108, 109
Lighthouse Board 111
lightships 107
Lincoln, President Abraham 74, 90
Lindsey, John 118
Lindsey Log Wagon 118, **119**
linsey-woolsey 69, 70
Lister, Mr. and Mrs. Borjn 26
Little Bay 116
Livingston, Edward 61, 108
Livingston, Robert 61
Long Beach 1, 52, 53, 59, 152
longleaf pine 115, 117–119
Lott, Senator Trent 153
Louis XIV 8, 10, 11, 13
Louisiana 5, 8, 10–13, 16, 23, 24, 31, 57, 59–62, 66, 67, 72, 75, 76, 85, 87, 88, 90, 93, 94, 105, 108, 112, 113, 123, 138, 139, 151
Louisiana University 146
La Louisiane 8
Louisville 61
Louvre 11
Lovell, Major James 132
Lully, Jean-Baptiste 11
Lundy, W.B. 118
Lynchburg Springs 76

Madame Langlois 64
Madison, President James 29, 75
Madison County 76
Madrid 64, 103, **158**
Magnolia Hotel 75
"Maid of Milan" 88
Maine 61
Major Kimmel 131
Málaga, Spain 34, 35, 157, **159**
Málagueños 159
Mal-Lara, Juan de 102
Malone, R.L. 125
Mandeville, Bernard Xavier Philippe de Marigny de 74
Manhattan 139
Manifest Destiny 139
Mardi Gras 74
Mareno, Francisco Ildefonse 34

Markham Hotel 152
marmite 68
maroons 80, 81
Marquis du Chatel, Antoine Crozat 10, 11
Marquis of Esquilache 103
Marseilles 23
Martinique 87
Martin's wharf 30
Mason jars 122
Massachusetts 144
Maurepas, Jean-Fréderic Phélypeaux de 9
Mays and Longstreet (law firm) 148
McArthur, Jim and Jack 31
McCarty sugar plantation 143
McCaughan, John J. 75
McCoy, Capt. William S. 121, 122
McEnery, Senator Samuel Douglas 147
McKinley, President William 114
McLauren, Governor James 75, 151
McRae, Colin 75
Mead, Cowles 44
Medina Sidona 34
Mediterranean 159
Memphis 144
Mercier, Tony 126
Merlin 157
Messr. Morgan & Co. 110
Metairie Cemetery 146
Mexican-American War 111
Mexican Gulf Hotel 126
Mexico 26, 139
Meynier, A.J. 113
Miami Beach 152
Michel (smuggler) 34
Middle Bay 32
Middle Spit 1
Middleton, F.A. 151
Milan 103
Millaudon, Benjamin Laurent 143
Mirer, José 59
Miró, Estéban Rodriguez 59, 92, 104, 105
Mississippi 9, 31, **40**, 44, 75, 76, 81, 90, 99–101, 112, 118, 120, 138, 151, 153, 156; flyway 124
Mississippi City 75
Mississippi Company *see* John Law's Mississippi Company
Mississippi Conservation Commission 4
Mississippi Diocese of Natchez 73, 91
Mississippi Gulf Coast 7, 12, 45, 50, 54, 67, 75, 97, 98, 111, 120, 151, 152, 154
Mississippi Power Company 125
Mississippi River 8, 9, 10, 21, 39, **40**, 60, 78, 79, 81, 111, 124, 138
Mississippi Sound 7, 10, 26, 37, 72, 106, 114, 123
Mistick Krewe of Comus 74
Mobeny, Charles J. 112
Mobile 10, 18, 19, 28, 31, 37, **40**, 46, 47, 59–61, 72, 73, 75, 106, 116, 120, 139, 150
Mobile Bay 8, 36, **40**

Mobile River 10
Mohawk Indians 66
Molière 11
Money, Senator Hernando Desoto 117, 150–152
Money, William 150
Montberaut 19
Montgomery, Capt. J.E. 144
moonshine 120, 122
Moore, Jno. M. 147
Moorish-Andalucian cattle 85
Moran, Pegagia 59
Morgan, Henry Gibbes 145, 147–149, 154
Morgan, Sir Henry 22
Morgan, Judge Thomas Gibbes 147
Morgan vs. Duggan 147
Morin, J.B. 47, 59
Morin, Marie Louise 59
Mudéjar style 159
Murrell, James 31
muscadine grapes 65, 66
Muscogee 81
musique a bouche 87
Muskhogean 80
Muslims 159, 161
myrtle wax candles 57

Naples 103
Napoleon 37
Natchez 80
National Association of Audubon Societies 149
National Prohibition Act 120, 123
Native Americans 78, 79, 80, 82, 139; Native American Party 145
Naval Live Oaks Reservation 156
Negro, Dr. Luciano de 102
Negro Point **2**, 31, 123
Nelson, Captain John 113
Nemesis 123
Neville, Judge James H. 125
New Bedford 110
New Brunswick 61
New England 108
New Orleans 2, 5, 10, 12, 15, 16, 19, 21–28, 31, 37–39, **40**, 42, 44, 48, 50, 51, 55, 59–61, 64, 66, 67, 71, 73–76, 79, 87, 91–93, 98, 100, 101, 104, 106, 107, 112, 120, 121, 126, 138, 142–147, 149; port 145
SS *New Orleans* 61
New Orleans and Carrollton Railroad 143
New Orleans Canal and Banking Company 143
New Orleans Cotton Exchange 146
The New Orleans Daily Picayune 98, 148
New Orleans French Market 78
New Orleans Sunday Times 29
New Orleans Times 13
New Spain 26
New World 61
New York 14, 120, 143
Newell, Andrew J. 30
Nez Coupé 24
Nicaise family 120

Nichols, Lieutenant Colonel A.R. 131, 134–136
Nine Year War (1688–1697) 8
Nisei 132, 134, 136
Non-Pareil 6
Normandy 61
North America 108, 124
North Biloxi 78
North Carolina 81
North Point (Cat Island) 84
Northwest Territories Treaty 139
Nova Scotia 61

Ocean Springs 10, 76, 121; Ocean Springs Hotel 75
Ocmulgee 80
Ocmulgee River 80
Ohio 98
O.K. Corral 31
Oklahoma 79, 81, 82, 84
Old Chimneys 40, 86
Old Turpentine Road 2, 116, 118
Olvera, Spain 157, *159*
100th Infantry 132
one pot meals 66
Ortega 62
Osceola 81, *82*, *83*
Osuna, Spain 157, *159*
Our Lady of the Gulf Parish 73

Pace and Morgan (naval stores company) 116, 150
pallisades 14
Panama Canal 149
Panquinet, Marquerite 59
Panza, Sancho 23
Paris 64, 103, 143; Parisians 62
Parker, John Milliken 145, 146
Pascagoula 11, 31
Pascagoula River 59, 118
Pass Christian 1, 59, 73, 86, 107–109, 112, 125, 142, 146; lighthouse *108*; Pass Christian Hotel 75
Patagonia 124
Patterson, Daniel Todd 26
Patton, James 44
Payne, John Howard 88
Pea Island *40*, 44
Peare, Soinsint 59
Pearl, Willie 117
Pearl Harbor 129, 130
Pearl River 31, 39, *40*, 59, 60, 73, 75, 91, 118
pearlash 67
pelle 68
Penalver, Isabel 91
Pénigault, André-Joseph 9
Pennsylvania 98
El Peñón 157
Pensacola 35, 36, *40*, 112, 139, 144
Pensacola Naval Air Station 156
Perdido Key *40*, 156
Perdido River 75
Petit Bois Island 1, 10, *40*, 111, 156
Philip V of Spain 10
Philip, duke of Anjou 10
Picardy 61
Picayune 30
Pickens, James R 116

Picornell, Don Juan Mariano 25
Pierce, Master Sergeant John 135, 136
piragua 60
Pirate House 26, *27*, *28*
pirates 23, 43, 99
Pirate's Cove 120, 123
pirogue 39, 44, 60
pisé 160
Pittsburgh 61
Pleasonton, Stephen 106, *107*, 109, 111
Poitou 61
Polk, President James 111
polka 88
"Pop Goes the Weasel" 87
Pope Gregory XIII 74
Port-au-Prince, Haiti 29
Porter, Father Michael 73
Posey, Zoe 85, 98, 99
postcards 50
potash 67
Powell, William 81
Prestre, William A. 130, 131, 134–136
Prieur, Denis 145
Prince Edward Island 61
privateers 22, 23
Prohibition 119–121, 123
Protestant immigration 105
Provisional Government of the Free Men of the Internal Province of Mexico 25
pueblos blancos 158–*160*

Quartermaster Corps 129, 130
Quartermaster Remount Branch (Division) 130, 131
Quave, Jean 99
Quave, Pierre Simon 76, 78
Quebec 8, 14, 61
Queen Anne style 144
Queen of the West 144
quick breads 67

raccoons 9
Raddebaugh, W.H. 125
Ramsay, Jack C. 23
Ramsay, James 143, 145
"the real McCoy" 122
Reconquista 101
Reece, Nancy Ann Buffington 154
rejas 159
Reno, Remy 13
requette 140
Revolutionary War 36
Rice, Thomas "Daddy" 87
Rigaud, Pierre François, Marquis de Vaudreuil-Cavagnal de 15, 16, 17
Rigolets 28, 37, 38, *40*, 44, 144
Rin Tin Tin 135
Riolly, George 109
Rios, José Amador de la 159
River Defense Fleet 144
Roaring Twenties 119, 126
Rochemore, Vincente de 15
The Rock (mountain) *see* El Peñón
Roderiguez, Tony 113
Roman Empire 14; Romans 129, 159

Romero 62
Ronda, Spain 157, *159*
Roosevelt, President Franklin D. 129, 149
Rosalie 76
Rossever, Mr. 19
Rotten Bayou 86
Round Island 111, 138
Rum Line 121
Rum Row 121
rumrunners 31, 119
Rural Free Delivery system 50
Russell, Chancellor Dan M. 152, 154
Russell, Governor Lee M. 125–127, 152, 153
La Ruta del Toro (Route of the Bull) 34

saddlebag houses *52*
safety matches 64
Sage of Beauvoir 98
Saint Augustine, Florida 83
St. Charles Avenue 143, 145
St. Charles Borromeo Church 144
St. Landry Parish 146
St. Louis Bay *40*
Saint Louis Cathedral 21
Saint Louis Cemetery 92, 105
St. Milo 23
St. Peter's Street Cemetery 92
St. Philips Street 24
St. Stephens Meridian 140, 147
San Carlos, California 130
San Domingo 9
San Francisco 155
San Miguel de Panzacola 36
Santa Fe, New Mexico 130
Santa Rosa Island 36, *40*, 156
sassafras tea 67
Saxon, Lyle 24
schooner 60
Scotch 123
screw-pile construction 112, *113*
scuppernong 65
Second Seminole War 81
Sedella, Father Antonio de 25, 26, 33, 34, *104*, 105, 157
Seige of Vicksburg 149
Seminole staging area 2, 116
Seminoles 79–*83*, 84, 118
Senate and House of Representatives of the State of Mississippi 44
Seven Years' War 15
Sevilla, Spain 102, 157, *159*
Shady Oaks Hotel 75
Shell Oil Company 153
Sherwood, Henry 112
Shieldsboro 44, 61, 73, 75, 111, 112, 145
Ship Island 2, 4, 5, 8, 10, 11, 17, 37, 39, *40*, 41, 48, 132, 156
Sierras 157
Sieur de la Salle, René-Robert Cavelier 8, 138
Sieur d'Iberville, Pierre Le Moyne 8–12, 13
Signal Corps 136
single pen *52*, 53
Slidell, John 143

Slidell, Thomas 142
Smith, Leonard 98
Smith, Lovance 98
Smith, Major General M.L. 149
smugglers 33, 34, 103, 104; route *35*
Smuggler's Cove *2*, 31, 121, 123
Somitette, Mr. 138
South Bayou 29, 123
South Carolina 82, 143
Spain 8, 10, 22, 26, 33–37, 46, 51, 61, 64, 93, 104, 137–139, 159, 160; armada 36; government 154; grant 140; language 96; nobility 101; at Pensacola 17; Spanish people 34, 51, 62, 64, 81
Spanish moss 55
The Spanish Quarter 51
Spit Cove *2*, 123
Stanislaus College 76
stock market crash 127
Stockton, William 116, 150
Strait of Gibraltar 34
Strickland, J.M. 116
The Subaltern 45
Sully, Thomas 144
Supreme Court of the United States 147
Sweden 115; Swedes 51; Swiss mercenaries *2*, 16

Tallapoosa 19
Tallapoosa River 80
Tallassee, Alabama 81
Taquino, Frazine 98, 100
Taylor, President Zachary 145
Tchefuncte River 112
Teagarden, Dr. William 75
Telephone (game) 100
Tennessee 81
Texas 25, 29, 57, 62, 115
Thanksgiving 74
Third Platoon of Company B 132
13th Louisiana Infantry 147
Thomason, Mitchell 150, 151
Thompson, Ray M. 98
Three Kings Day 74
three-mile limit 121

Three Rivers Missions 73, 91
The Times Picayune 96, 98
Tombigbee River 19
toros bravos (fighting bulls) 34
tortue (turtles) 65
toys 73
Trail of Tears 82
Treasure Island 125, 152
Treasury Department 110, 111
A Treatise on the Law of Sale of Personal Property 142
Treaty of Paris 36, 138
Trust for Public Land 154–156
Tuckabatchee 80
Tulane University 146
Tuskegee 80
twelve-mile limit 121
Twenty-first Amendment 123
Tyler, U.S. President John 139
Tyrone, Don Arturo O'Neill de 17

Ubrique 34
Union Forces 144
Union Parish, Louisiana 143
United States 11, 12, 22, 26, 28, 29, 33, 34, 38, 46, 50, 58, 59, 61, 62, 66, 75, 78, 80–82, 88, 106, 108, 118, 120, 129, 137, 143, 155; Armed Forces 129; Army Corps of Engineers 144; census 61; constitution 154; Customs 23; District Court 153; government 25, 41, 79, 92, 98, 139–141, 148, 153, 154; House of Representatives 155; Military Academy 144; National Park Service 4, 154–156; Navy 26, 111; Post Office 50
University of Mississippi 150

Vauban, Marshal Sébastien Le Prestre de 13, 14
Ventura 112
Versailles 11
Vicksburg 144
Vidou, François 17, 19
Vieux Carré 105
Virginia 115

Virginia reel 88
"Vive Jean Baptiste Baudrau" 21
Volant, Mr. 20
Voltaire 102

Wages, Gale H. 31
Wages Clan 31
waltz 88
War Assets Administration 114
War Department 114
War Dog Reception and Training Center *2*, 129
War of 1812 25, 37, 45, 81, 88, 99, 101, 144
War of Spanish Succession 10, 11
War of the League of Augsburg 11
Washington, President George 106
Washington, D.C. 28, 29, 129–131, 139, 150, 153
Washington, Louisiana 146
Waule 80
Waveland, Mississippi 26
wax myrtle 57
West Florida 139
Westchester, New York 23
whirligig 74
White, Edward Douglass 147
Whittman, Frank 125, 126
Wilkinson, Sidney A. 112
Wirovich, Mike 113
Wisconsin 132, 136
Wisconsin State Journal 2
Wolf River 73, 91, 122
World War I 98, 129
World War II 128, 137

Yale 142
"Yankee Doodle" 87
You, Captain Dominique 24, 26, 29
Younghans Novelty Store 50
Younghans, Edward J. 50
Yucatan 29

Zimpel, Charles F. 143

www.ingramcontent.com/pod-product-compliance
Ingram Content Group UK Ltd.
Pitfield, Milton Keynes, MK11 3LW, UK
UKHW050524150426
5217IPUK00026B/1792